TIME FOR MEANING
Crafting Literate Lives in Middle and High School

RANDY BOMER

HEINEMANN
Portsmouth, NH

Heinemann

A division of Reed Elsevier Inc.

361 Hanover Street

Portsmouth NH 03801-3912

Offices and agents throughout the world

Every effort has been made to contact the copyright holders for permission to reprint borrowed material where necessary. We regret any oversights that may have occurred and would be pleased to rectify them in future printings of this work.

Figure 6.1 adapted by permission of the Estate of James Britton: *Language and Learning,* Second Edition (Boynton/Cook Publishers, a subsidiary of Reed Elsevier Inc., Portsmouth, NH, 1993).

"A Burial, Green" from *The Night Won't Save Anyone* by Marcia Southwick. Copyright © 1980. Reprinted by permission of The University of Georgia Press.

Library of Congress Cataloging-in-Publication Data

Bomer, Randy.

    Time for meaning : crafting literate lives in middle and high

school / Randy Bomer.

        p. cm.

    Includes bibliographical references (p. 225).

    ISBN 0-435-08849-1

    1. Language arts (Secondary)—United States. 2. Reading

(Secondary)—United States. 3. English language—Composition and

exercises—Study and teaching (Secondary)—United States.

    I. Title.

    LB1631.B73 1995

    428'.0071'2—dc20   95-12089

                                             CIP

Editors: *Dawn Boyer and Alan Huisman*

Production: *Melissa L. Inglis*

Interior and cover design: *Jenny Jensen Greenleaf*

07 06 05   VP   15 16

Printed in the United States of America on acid-free paper

For Jake and Sammi,
who every day give me my most precious memories
and my most fervent hopes

CONTENTS

PREFACE

Time for Meaning is the outgrowth of the past eight years in my life as an educator. Some of those years were spent teaching in my own classroom, and some of them were spent as a consultant, working beside other teachers of all grade levels. Consequently, some of the chapters in the book are tightly written from within my consciousness as a classroom teacher, while others open to include the students and the practices of people I've admired.

I've tried to be specific and persuasive but do not mean to be prescriptive. This book is a snapshot of my current thinking, a report on work that has seemed helpful to many teachers I've talked with over the past few years. I think of it as an aid for teachers' own decision making and not as a recipe book. After all, by the time anyone reads it, I'll almost certainly have changed my mind about some of it.

Many readers may be working in schools that have begun restructuring, especially their schedules and curricula. This book may seem to contradict some of those changes, especially ones in which the craft of literacy has become servile to content knowledge in other disciplines, such as social studies. I hope this book will challenge us to make sure that our efforts at school reform are really aimed at what is best for students' growth in literacy rather than only for scheduling convenience. Compromising the value of literary knowing is a high price to pay for an extra half hour, so before I argue for more time, I want to make sure we're clear about what to do with the time we have now. Wiser ways of thinking about time are available, and they are part of the theme of this book. Readers who are working in recently restructured settings may be able to imagine yet newer revisions to their already bold work.

A word about the structure of the book: before and after each long chapter is a short essay, a meditation on time. I believe all the practical tips in the world amount to no meaningful improvements in our teaching if our thinking about time is still situated in the traditional ways of doing school. The little essays, which I called "time pieces" when I was writing them, are meant to provide the needed wide-angle view.

ACKNOWLEDGMENTS

The longer a project takes to complete, the more debts of gratitude it accrues along the way. I've been blessed as I've written this book with what must be one of the most supportive and challenging communities in the history of American education, the teachers, administrators, and teachers of teachers I've met through the Teachers College Writing Project. My days of work are filled with silent and spoken thank-yous to those brilliant and committed educators. For now, I want to thank a few people who have been particularly helpful in the writing of this book, people whose generosity glows in every page, people without whom no one should ever try to write a book.

I began my educational career as a student of Lucy Calkins, and her thinking, her values, her energy, and her way of learning have provided the foundation for my own. She believed I had something to offer way before it was really so and nudged me into situations where I was in over my head, forcing me to grow. Once she went so far as to suggest I write a book, and these pages spring directly from her encouragement, faith, and daily support. Now our collaboration at the Teachers College Writing Project is closer and more powerful than any I have known before, and I look forward to many years of working together.

Katherine Bearden lovingly read every page of the book before I would have trusted anyone else. Many chapters never found their center until after hours of talk with her, and her ideas about revision were always absolutely right. More than that, she never flagged in her encouragement that there was something here worth saying; she chased away the horrors of writing. Without her I probably never would have finished.

At critical points, I sought and got the helpful advice and enthusiastic encouragement of other friends. Kate Montgomery, Isoke Nia, Brenda Wallace, and Katie Wood added their cheerful wisdom to several chapters as well as to the overall shape of the book. In addition to being wise colleagues, Priscilla Moody, Kathy Collins, and Susan Pliner covered my butt at the Writing Project office and probably did me more favors than I even know about. Kathy Collins was also a great help in preparing the final manuscript. Alan Weiner helped me work through intangible internal tangles so that I could become a person who writes books.

My first editor at Heinemann was Dawn Boyer, who brought several years of patient encouragement and later her writerly intelligence to the drafts. Alan Huisman, my second editor, brought to every sentence a careful, rigorous logic the likes of which my writing has never before known. Linda Rief responded to an earlier draft with such kindness that I would happily have written the whole book again just for her. Tom Newkirk generously and accurately commented on the whole book twice, and it is substantially better as a result.

My mother, Joyce Byrd Bomer, my father, Robert H. Bomer, my sister, Vicki Bomer, and my grandfather, George Byrd, have loved me and supported me in everything I've ever done, and in so doing have taught me that the world is a place of great possibility and that the only reasonable use of a life is to make that world a better place.

Rarely in life is it possible to take three giant steps backward and say to people that matter, thank you—not just for this day but for all of it, the whole nine yards. Retirement parties? Oscar speeches? Book acknowledgments! So, to all of you mentioned here: thank you.

TIME FOR MEANING

Forty English/language arts teachers are gathered with me in a classroom. As they have come in, they have been discussing, as we all do so often, the hundreds of different things we are always trying to juggle in our teaching. To get started, I invite them to call out "all the things we either are responsible for or someone wants to make us responsible for." Despite the cacophony, I manage to get a list down on the chalkboard, which soon looks like this:

State tests preps Shakespeare punctuation
novels journalism pleasure- spelling Reading
poetry media studies reading study skills Speech
journals listening Lit. History-
language study critical thinking drama the canon
popular culture creative writing literary terms
history of research paper writing letter writing
English lang. aesthetics reading debate
cooperation integration with College bibliography
   social studies Application word processing
discussion short stories essays
multi-cult. lit. reader response linguistics
feminism film study Grammar < usage
SAT prep vocabulary

As the flood of items slows to a trickle, a pall of hopelessness settles over the room, and rightly so. As long as we define our subject, our teaching, our relationship to our students and jobs, as containing that many bits, we are lost. Our imagined task cannot be done, not in forty minutes a day, not in forty hours a day. Education should be learning to inquire, but secondary schools chopped it into "subjects," which then apparently had to be chopped into "periods." Even that was not enough: what is called English/language arts (and it's telling that there is no clear name for the "subject" I am writing about) was further fragmented into so many shards that each of us is constantly feeling guilty for all the things never "gotten to." This fragmentation of the curriculum in general and the English curriculum in particular reveals a profound disregard for literacy, for inquiry, for students as people with rich and interesting lives and languages, and, most perilous, for time. Our thoughtless neglect and disrespect for time is especially self-defeating.

Most of us usually see time as the problem, the thing of which there is never enough. We say, *if only I had more time,* or, *It's time, time is the problem.* But, as Robert Grudin writes in his wonderful book *Time and the Art of Living,* "time is our medium . . . and saying that someone is destroyed by time is as nonsensical as saying that someone is drowned by air" (p. 20). We need to recognize that time is the given; we cannot get more of it. *More time* is a meaningless idea, when you think about it. How could there be more of time? Time just is. What we are really complaining about is our difficulty in both controlling and choosing what to do with the time we have.

We live in time, we experience everything in time. First one thing happens, and then another thing happens, or they happen at the same time and then something else happens. If our lives are not made of hours and days, then what are they? Time is the only way we know our lives. Annie Dillard writes, "How we spend our days is, of course, how we spend our lives. What we do with this hour, and that one, is what we are doing" (p. 32). Since that is so, this book is about doing with our time what is essential. What we do with time is what we do with our lives. When we are "unable" to spend time on what we most value, it is because we have not found a clarity of purpose. We have lost our maps, lost our rudder, and we drift aimlessly, as if time were not passing, as if this teaching life were not ours to live.

1   *Choosing My Teaching*

I lean against the chalk rail and watch them come in. I know it's a mistake to lean this way. It's not that comfortable, and I have seen too many teachers emerge from this position bearing on their backsides telltale chalk welts, the profession's badge. I make a mental note to dust before turning around, in order to forestall any comments about my butt, and keep watching the kids crash and amble through the doorway.

"Hey, Mr. Bomer. D'you go fishin' this weekend?" Ed asks me this question every Monday and always gets the same exasperating answer from me.

"No, Ed. But I know you did."

It is unfathomable to him that any man would fail to fish on a weekend. To him, it's the whole point. He shakes his head and clicks out of the sides of his mouth. Ray passes him on his way across the room and, without looking, flings a punch to Ed's tricep. Ed chases Ray across the room, planning to retaliate, but decides instead to lie about the fish he caught on Saturday. He mentions Bob Montero, the biology teacher, and I guess that he's been talking fishing with Bob last period, no doubt getting a richer response than he received from me, his nonfishing English teacher. Ed will use this fishing material not only as his topic in his writers notebook today but also to thread together the disconnected beads of his day, his dozens of engagements with both kids and adults, making a unified strand for himself in a way the school system has failed to devise.

A clump of four girls comes in, whispering about someone they have just left in the hall. This is how they come in every day. They are fifteen, after all, and life is full of secrets. Their entrance is so familiar that I almost think I know what is going on, and I have to concentrate a bit more, remember that I do not. I don't know who they were with in the hall, don't know the history behind that hallway relationship, don't know what each girl means to the others, don't know anything really about the lives they trail as they come in here. Over and over again, I make the teacher's mistake of assuming that time begins the moment my students cross the threshold of my room. But if my class is to tell the truth about literacy, I have to guard against that mistake and keep in mind that each student's whole life outside this room is what he or she will use to make meaning.

I glance over to the windowsill where this class's writers notebooks wait in the sun to be returned to their owners. Having looked them over yesterday, I know a tiny fraction of what is going on in these kids' lives, enough to provide my imagination a window on their worlds. If I look at one student at a time and think hard, I can almost imagine flashes of her weekend, her evenings at home, her breakfast and bus ride, her three-minute chats with friends in the hallway, the four or five classrooms she's already been in today, the dramas and schemes about which she rightly cares the most. If I think hard, I can almost force myself out of school time and into lifetimes.

I'm not the parent of any of these kids, and I'm not trying to know them as if I were. I have a job to do, and that job focuses on their literacy, their reading and writing. But I have choices about how I will do my work with them, and I can either embrace their lifetimes, their values, histories, and concerns, or ignore them. I try to base my choices on what I think is the most moral thing to do and what best gets the job done. I believe more and more that attending to the whole lives of my students, through literacy, is the better way into both criteria.

This morning, driving to school, I passed Jerry waiting for the bus. It is only late October, but he looked cold up there on the ridge in the wind, clutching his coat in front of him, his hands not surprisingly unencumbered by books. I thought about his missing front tooth. Jerry is fourteen, not seven; he shouldn't be losing teeth. But last week, he walked in with a big gap in the front of his mouth and was evasive about how it got there. I interpreted. From his notebook and from conversations with him, I know that his family has more or less rented him to a farmer. He works, beginning long before I am awake and often late into the night, and his family gets the money. He sleeps in an upstairs room in the house on the farm, a room in which plastic covers the gaping holes where windows should be, especially in an upstate New York winter. I have reported his abuse to the principal, who has reported it to the county department of social services. We have done our bit as agents of the state, done what we legally can. Still, I can't get him out of my mind. The tiny shards I know of his fractured and bruised experience overwhelm me with questions about what I'm doing as a teacher. He carries a heavy cargo through this door every day at 1:24. Is what I'm doing with him useful or even relevant to his precious and fragile life?

And he is only one of over a hundred students I see every day, every one of whom arrives with baggage that cannot be stowed. Right now, this classroom, this forty minutes, is a nexus of thirty-one converging roads. Each one of the people here has come from a different part of the building, a different lunch, a different life. Leaning here against the chalk rail, I try to read them, try to interpret whether there is any unity in the nexus, whether there's some one thing they are all prepared to hear in a minilesson, whether there's some special need I can answer for "the class." I have a half-dozen possibilities in mind, and I try to sniff out whether one of them best matches the group. But this attention to their individual differences leaves me dizzy. Possibilities clamor for first place. Since a different road leads into and out of this room for each person in it, one map won't serve everyone equally well. To make matters still more complex, that includes me. I bring to these moments and this space all that I have lived through so far, all that I know, and the role literacy plays in my own life.

This is a town of eleven hundred, and I moved here two years ago from New York City, where there were more than twice that many people on my block. That fact alone makes me something of an oddity here, an inscrutable and unapproachable alien to most of my colleagues, my students, and my students' parents. I lived in New York because I was an actor, and when I grew weary of being on the road, away from my family, only marginally a part of the community I lived in, I decided to become a teacher. I thought at the time that teaching was much the same thing as being an actor. Teaching English, I thought then, would give me five audiences a day in front of whom to perform Shakespeare, a captive crowd for whom I could embody my readings, strut and fret my brilliant interpretations of literature. But as I worked with Lucy Calkins at Teachers College, I came to believe that teaching was both more and less than performing at the front of the room. I remember, too, even when I was already in the Teachers College program, spinning elaborate curriculum designs based on my interests, courses for high school students on The History of Western Philosophy, Asian Literatures, Literary Theory, The American Experience. Looking now at Ed, Jerry, Shannon, I want to laugh out loud at those plans and at the image of me standing up here reciting Shakespeare. We are all lucky I changed my mind, though I'm still not completely innocent of the desire to indulge my own literary passions center stage.

Masha saunters in, lugging an armful of books, including two novels and two books of nonfiction. I envy her reading life. I was never like that and still am not. I've never been the kind of person who is constantly reading; I mess around too much, talk to friends too much, watch too much TV. I read a lot, but there are also lots of books I put down and almost forget about for a month, then put back on the shelves, never finished. Sometimes a few months go by when I'm not reading any book in particular, not engaged in any reading project, when I'm just reading around, a few magazine articles, bits and pieces of books. It would be odd for me to say I love to eat, and similarly odd to say I love to read: it's just something I do, a part of life. I take it for granted that I'm a reader, as I do that I'm an eater. Each experience of reading, however, matters deeply to me, affects me powerfully, makes me feel my own life more intensely, changes the way I process my world. What matters to me is not that I constantly devour books but that I fairly often have intense reading experiences. The way I live my literate life resonates in my mind today, as I get ready to speak to this class, as do hundreds of school reading experiences I did not choose and that were not helpful to my growth.

Ed, Ray, Masha, Jerry, and I—each one of us encounters the others with his or her own vision of the world in mind. And this moment, while the kids move into the room and I prepare my mind and mouth to teach them, is infinitely complex. If any of us are going to learn anything today, we are going to construct that learning ourselves. We can only take what we make. And we'll build that learning out of the scraps and fragments of life we already have. In this moment, 1:24 P.M. on October 26, each of us carries thousands of other moments from the past, as well as hopes for the moments of the future. It's the connection between the present moment and all those other times that gives meaning to this instant of our coming together and what makes it so intricate. This thing we'd like to think of as a single "English class" is actually a different experience for each of the people here; I can't hope fully to control the curriculum in this untamed border zone where all our separate pasts butt against one another. My own history and my plans for the future, the past of each kid and his hopes for his life to come, the collective history of this community and its agendas, the history of the subject of English and the direction it is currently pursuing, the very history of America and a host of possible visions of its future—all these time lines collide at the present instant, this initiation of a teaching move, and at every moment like it in my work. Each of these histories and futures is voiced in my head at the same time, and amid the cacophony, I must choose my action for this time, again.

Each of us in this room, including me, carries a school history as well as a personal history. We come in here with expectations about how school goes, about how English class goes, formed by years of experience, and these expectations have been more rigorously taught to us than anything written explicitly into the curriculum. The hidden curriculum is always, *This is how this subject goes, this is what it is.* The kids know what English is supposed to be, and I'm even more enculturated into those assumptions than they are. Even though I was their age and in their grade in school about two decades earlier and two thousand miles away, there is a remarkable sameness to our automatic assumptions, built from our school experiences, about what English is "supposed" to be. Of course, things would go most peacefully and smoothly if we just conformed to those shared expectations, if we did what we all know we are "supposed" to do.

We are supposed to have vocabulary lists and grammar books, reading assignments and quizzes. We are all supposed to believe that English, like other subjects in school, consists of certain piles of stuff that need to be dumped into students' heads. Words—vocabulary—are supposed to be the basic units of content. Everybody knows that memorized lists of words and their dictionary meanings are part of language study. Groups of words—phrases, clauses, and sentences—are supposed to be arranged in the proper relationships. English class is supposed to get the rules of grammar into kids' heads.

The next-most-fundamental pieces of knowledge all kids "should" acquire deal with the proper structure of paragraphs and then the architecture of essays. Essays, we all know, are to be written in response to someone else's questions (mine or some publisher's). And what are those questions supposed to be about? The very best, most-high-flown part of the English curriculum, the literary canon, the great (or at least good) works of literature that everyone "should" read. The English department is also, we all suppose, responsible for imparting to students some or all of the following: test-taking tips, study skills, research procedures, SAT prep, the proper form for the business letter, media awareness.

How did English get this way? How did the time of day where students give their concentrated attention to literacy become so similar in classrooms from New York City to Eureka? It's hard for a fish to become aware of water, for humans to become aware of time, and for English teachers to become aware of the socially constructed nature of their profession. But it might help us in our imagining what's best for these kids filing in the door if we examine whether what we've all been "supposing" about the subject we've gathered for at 1:24 is necessarily so. Often, as we live within our work, the subject of English seems, like mountains, to have been made by God. But it wasn't. There is a particular story behind how our conception of literacy education became what it is, and unless we know that story, and remind ourselves of it often, we are helpless to choose whether or not we want to replay it with every move of our teaching lives.

As I stand here getting ready to teach today, it's hard to imagine that there was a time, not so long ago, when there was no such animal as an English teacher. But the truth is, this line of work is little more than a century old. For most of history, most people didn't go to secondary school and the few who did took Latin. It was only as the general population began to stay in school longer and schools therefore had to become useful to a growing diversity of students that the study of English (as opposed to classical languages) was thought to be at all useful. The reason for this job, since the birth of its kind, could be seen as a project for democratizing language in school, making opportunity in school and society available to more and more-different types of students.

But in spite of this initial impulse to empower the language use of an increasingly diverse population, the definition of the subject was quickly co-opted by people far-removed from those diverse kids. In 1894, a group of American colleges published the Uniform Lists, a list of literary works on which applicants would be tested, thereby accomplishing two things. First, they determined that the attention of high school English teachers and students would be dominated by a canon of texts. Second, they determined what those texts would be, for everyone. English teachers of that day, who were mainly in the job of preparing young white men for college, allowed the list to become the curriculum. Already the authority for determining how adults and kids in English class would spend their time was removed from the teacher and the students in actual classrooms. Moreover, the initiating mandate was to prepare people for an exam, with neither writing nor reading treated as important in itself. Obedience to the authority of the exam was the real curriculum.

These competing pressures, to open the classroom to diversity and to standardize knowledge in accordance with someone else's agenda, still clash in my mind today. Every time I plan what I will do with students, I hear voices that have echoed since the Uniform Lists, more recently including people like E. D. Hirsch, saying that I ought to teach kids a received culture, one that they have not helped make but that nonetheless is dominant. But I also hear strong voices in my mind saying that uniform lists of any kind are irrelevant to the lives of the students I'm looking at right now. These latter voices are the more persuasive to me, especially in moments like this one, when I'm taking time to really see my students and reflect on who they are.

As a matter of fact, way back in 1911, teachers who, like me today, were persuaded that the differences among their diverse students should be valued over any uniform requirements gave rise to the National Council of Teachers of English (NCTE). A group of teachers in New York City became fed up with trying to teach the works on the Uniform Lists to the immigrant kids crowded into their classrooms, so they made themselves into a support group for resisting the status quo and called it NCTE. (Almost immediately, this organization formed in opposition to college professors' bossing other teachers around was taken over by college professors. Go figure.) In 1913, NCTE published a sixteen-page list of books, which, though it was still a list, at least encouraged wider reading than the Uniform Lists. By 1916, so many people were favoring wider reading over the canon that the colleges had to administer two examinations: one that still covered the Uniform Lists, and another for students whose program had stressed wider reading.

The founding of NCTE was only imaginable as part of the larger movement of progressive education. Over and over, the voices of progressive forebears are the most convincing ones I hear when I'm deliberately choosing my teaching. John Dewey, for example, whose brilliance astounds me every time I read him, wrote as early as 1895 that the curriculum cannot come from anyone's list but rather must spring from students' direct personal experiences. He also believed that schools ought to be a place where society tries to become more democratic by establishing classroom environments reflecting a more just and egalitarian world. Clearly these values were more consonant with the original impulse favoring the language people actually speak over dead academic languages than with the authoritarian impulse behind the Uniform Lists.

Lest we think we are the first people ever to try to teach English in a progressive way and the first to fight the battles teaching sometimes involves, it is helpful to recall the literacy educators who earlier in the century attempted to apply Dewey's philosophies. Progressivism for them meant a shift away from academic content or lists of books and toward the needs and experiences of the students. William Heard Kilpatrick, for example, proposed that the "typical unit of a worthy life" is "the purposeful act," the project, and so schools ought to make projects the typical unit of student learning. According to Kilpatrick's "project method," students should engage with a series of projects, which would allow them, "by guided induction," to make their "own formulations. Then they are [theirs] to use" (in Applebee, p. 108). A few years later, the amazing Hilda Taba, anticipating by almost a half-century some of the interdisciplinary work of recent educators, developed a program that stressed student work on collaborative projects under some one "great idea" or overarching principle, which could encompass a wide range of difference in individual life experiences. She tried to get students involved in common, general topics such as "community" or "inclusion and segregation," and under that safe umbrella, to take on critical social problems such as race relations. (Remember, this is in the thirties and forties. The Supreme Court didn't desegregate the schools until 1954, so Taba's work was daring and important.) In 1938, Louise Rosenblatt published the first book about reader response, *Literature as Exploration,* in which she rejected the notion that literature should be "taught" for its own sake, as content, and argued that literature was uniquely useful in the exploration of one's own nature, through one's intellectual and emotional response to a work. The attention, then, was not on the content of English but on people reading. The book made a big splash for a year or so, and then most everyone forgot about it until about forty years later. These and a few other progressive thinkers believed that literature (they didn't do so well by writing) could help people think about their lives and, in fact, live them better. Such attempts early in the century ought to embolden us against those who ridicule our late progressivism as hippieish, newfangled, or trendy. We belong to a tradition that is at least as much a part of the foundation of American schooling as models that stress student memorization of received facts. The echoes of this tradition allow me to imagine teaching and literacy in some way other than the way I was taught. I believe that's good news for my students, since they have so far been taught in exactly the way I was.

The definition of literacy that makes sense to me is the one that seems to fit the students walking into my classroom right now. When Ed or Jerry writes, he is not just conveying meaning into the world or expressing thoughts he's already formed, but rather he's constructing meaning where it previously did not exist, on the page and between the pages, both when his pen is moving and when it is still. He is literate because of his use of language in the construction of meaning from his own lived life. Using writing to interrogate his life, he crafts sense. Similarly, when he reads, he brings meaning to the text; meaning is not written magically from the text onto the blank slate of his mind. No matter how well the words on the page are crafted, no matter how well respected the work, no matter how long ago it was written, the text is not doing the meaning—Ed or Jerry is, by bringing his life knowledge to the piece. He uses his memory to make meaning because memory is, at any given moment, all he has of his lived experience. When we connect something new in the environment to something old in our minds, we say, *That's meaningful;* that is, it has to do with our life.

So each moment I teach, I have to hold on to the value that literacy is the deliberate use of language to compose meaning, even though that definition is dissonant with the ordinary way the word is used in American public discourse, media, business, and schools. I want my literacy classroom to be a community engaged in making meaning, individually and collectively, from lived experience. I have to concentrate hard to keep from reverting to the teacherly self-concept of curator or gatekeeper of supposed content and to create a different teacherly identity concerned primarily with students' ability to make meaning from their present and past lives. This involves a huge shift from what Stephen North has called the "mythic communal self-image" of English practitioners: "the weary but dedicated teacher, bi-focals on end of nose, cup of tea at hand, bent over piles of student themes long into the night, scrawling marginalia, coding corrections to some key on the inside cover of a handbook, marking in a meticulous script grades into the tiny boxed columns of the green, vinyl-covered gradebook—always in red" (p. 29). That's what I had in mind when I became a teacher and what I have to revise constantly. Each day, I have to reinvent the discipline—*and myself in the discipline*—to be less concerned with what the students are supposed to *get* and more concerned with what the students can *make* with the materials they already have.

However, the progressive values that are so persuasive to me have in no way permeated the culture in which I live. If those were the only voices going, then teaching would be a much easier job for me and this moment against the chalk rail reflecting on what to do today would be less problematic. Everyone would be as progressive as I consider myself to be, and that would be that. But neither my administration nor the kids and their parents have much experience, if any, at thinking about learning in the way I try to. Just this morning, I have had a parent conference; as a result, voices other than those of progressivism are more definite in my mind than usual. The parent with whom I spoke worried, as they all do, that even though her daughter is more enthusiastic about reading and writing than she's ever been before, there still may be some less-fun material that the girl *isn't* getting and that is the *real* stuff of English, the stuff the mother had when *she* was in school. What accounts for these remarkably persistent assumptions? Naturally, the early appearance of the Uniform Lists contributed, but there are still-larger themes that permeate our culture, and, if you'll excuse the quasi-Woodward-and-Bernstein pose, these themes derive their power from institutions as powerful as the Pentagon.

During World War I, the U.S. Army, since it was fighting in more distant places than it ever had before, had to rely on written orders to an unprecedented extent. Consequently, the army needed to know whether soldiers could read those orders or not. They devised a test of reading comprehension and tested all recruits with the same exam, something never done before, and determined soldiers' assignments on the basis of those scores. School administrators were impressed.

The army's ease and clarity in slotting people into categories appealed to a strand of thought in education that was actually a branch of progressivism in the early days of the century and that continues to this day, the application of business and industry principles of "scientific management" to schools. In the sloppy thinking characteristic of American business, *science* is the same thing as *efficiency*. (In business, language doesn't have to make sense, it just has to make money.) Partly because schools were having to accommodate much larger groups of kids (and therefore larger staffs, physical plants, and budgets), superintendents became more like factory managers than instructional leaders, and they began obsessing on the concerns of factory managers: efficiency and cost/benefit analyses. If a school was to be efficient, it would, of course, have to do away with nonessentials. This threw English teachers into a frenzy: we have always had an inferiority complex about defining ourselves as possessing a fixed and necessary body of knowledge, especially if it has to be useful. As Wilbur Hatfield wrote in *English Journal* in 1922,

"Unless it can be made clear, even to the practical mind," that English is worth all the time and money it uses up, it "will surely be replaced by subjects more obviously useful" (in Applebee, p. 85).

Since the front office had to be able to tell that the expenditures for a particular class or program produced a sufficient yield, they needed a bottom line. But this was *hard:* how do you count the pieces of smartness somebody gets from the transmission of information? Enter Thorndike, the test man, who wrote:

> Whatever exists at all exists in some amount. . . . Education is concerned with changes in human beings; a change is a difference between two conditions; each of these conditions is known to us only by the products measured by it—things made, words spoken, acts performed, and the like. . . . To measure a product well means so to define its amount that competent persons will know how large it is, with some precision, and that this knowledge may be recorded and used. . . . We have faith that whatever people now measure crudely by mere descriptive words . . . can be measured more precisely and conveniently if ingenuity and ardor are set at the task. . . . This is obviously the same general creed as that of the physicist, or chemist, or physiologist. (In Cremin, p. 185)

Done. The superintendents had their bottom line, and words that sounded like *science* to prove it. Of course, English teachers knew—anyone who'd ever read a book knew—that the new type of test was thoroughly inappropriate to the learning of writing and literature. But the system required a measurable product, like so many mousetraps, or else the subject could not escape the superintendent's scalpel of Efficiency. And besides, everyone said the new tests were fairer because they were more "objective," they were more reliable because you could grade them accurately even if you were tired or drunk, and they were so efficient (easy). So what if the subject, because it had to be tested, came to be defined by its more obvious, superficial, and trivial parts?

English classrooms sank more deeply than ever into an entrenched sameness. See if this sounds familiar. The most frequently taught titles in 1924 were *Macbeth, Julius Caesar, A Tale of Two Cities, Silas Marner,* "The Rime of the Ancient Mariner," *Idylls of the King, The House of Seven Gables,* and *Ivanhoe.* All but *Idylls of the King* were on the Uniform Lists before 1900, *some of them placed there when they were still contemporary literature.*

Dora V. Smith reported, in her 1933 study of English classrooms, that by far the most common activity was an intensive whole-group reading of a single text, with (in the case of novels) students reading to page X for homework and writing out sentences in response to teacher-written questions, which they recited when called upon. (*Harold, what did you put for number seven? . . . Anyone have anything different? Anybody? Anybody?*) From there, the class would proceed with what teachers called discussion but what was really mostly recitation, the teacher asking a question and calling on one student at a time to answer. Smith's study included mostly schools in New York State, which then, as now, had a liberal state syllabus in

English; however, then, as now, most teachers reported that available textbooks, not the state syllabus, determined what their students did in class. Smith cited other handicaps to more-daring practices: paucity of book supply; local insistence on more-formal elements of instruction; teachers' lack of philosophy or reflection; lack of knowledge of alternative materials (such as books or poems); and fear that state and college exams would differ in emphasis from the state syllabus. Smith stated, "No impression remains more vivid after conference with hundreds of teachers throughout the country than the fear under which they labor because of the requirements (real or imagined) of the institution higher up" (p. 74).

It is as true now as it was then, at all grade levels, in every part of the country. The kindergarten teacher "prepares" kids for first grade, the first-grade teacher "prepares" them for second, the fourth- or fifth-grade teacher gets them ready for the demands of middle school, the eighth-grade teacher terrifies them with what the high school will demand of them, and the whole point of secondary English is that effulgent first semester of college—which prepares them for the rest of college. Everyone teaches for somebody else. "They" require it. There has always been a "they." And "they" have always been, whether or not they have truly existed, a reason to remain professionally stagnant, an excuse for staying the same, the same as our neighbor in the next classroom or in the next state, the same as we always were.

In 1957, the Soviet Union launched Sputnik, and the Cold War took over everything. There was money involved. Congress passed laws giving math and science lots of money so that we could compete with the evil empire, and English teachers wanted some cash too. It suddenly became more important than ever before to define English as a particular body of content, preferably one indispensable to national security. At the Basic Issues conferences in 1958 and 1959, English was finally deliberately defined as a body of specific knowledge—specific works and technical terms for literary analysis, the sequence of which was determined by the logic of the subject matter—in the charge of English teachers to preserve and transmit. The true experts on this content, however, were college professors—of English, not education. The curriculum these experts devised could be national, since it would be definitive and since regional or individual differences would be irrelevant. The whole plan could be sequential from kindergarten through graduate school, with secondary English consisting of the "mastery of certain blocks of knowledge." The continued pressure from superintendents to arrive at a measurable bottom line made such a curriculum peculiarly tenacious in schools.

It helped that there was at the time a way of thinking about literature that gave a right answer. New Criticism had emerged earlier in the century from the modernism of Pound and Eliot. Old-fashioned criticism, with its judgmental equivalence of moral goodness to aesthetic beauty, just didn't make sense when applied to modern poets or writers like Faulkner or Dos Passos. The New Critics, such as John Crowe Ransom, I. A. Richards, William Empson, Cleanth Brooks, and Yvor Winters, wanted to separate the actual text on the page of a work of literature from everything else—the author or culture that generated it, the reader or her culture, or any reference to anything like real life. The text, they believed, should be considered in a sort of hermetically sealed but perfectly transparent jar. The reader's tools, wielded like scalpels, were the terms that identified literary forms or devices. If one was skillful enough with these tools and if one remained purely concentrated on the words of the text, the work would—*voila!*—yield something very close to a scientifically certifiable meaning. Rosenblatt, of course, had already responded to this, but the New Critics had then been outsiders in the public schools; now they had something timely to offer, a positivistic body of content for an increasingly academic view of English.

I remember the scowl on the face of a math teacher in the faculty room of a school where I taught, as I explained, in answer to his query, how I teach writing. When I'd finished my brief description, he said, "That sounds like that happy hippie peace-and-love liberal shit from the sixties. The pendulum's just swinging right back, and I've been around long enough to see it go back and forth a few times." Then he got up and walked out. He may have been teaching in the sixties, but that didn't mean his clichéd interpretation of this century in education was accurate: the sixties, in the teaching of English, was the most reactionary period in our history.

When James Squire and Roger Applebee visited hundreds of classrooms between 1963 and 1966, what they found was "fully in accord with the academic model for English instruction, with its glorification of the college classroom and lack of interest in most aspects of progressive methodology." Fifty-two percent of class time was devoted to studying literature, with the balance of the time split between learning grammar and writing essays about literature. Recitation and lecture predominated, with Socratic questioning accounting for 23 percent of class time. They found no evidence of group work at all. Teaching techniques in the nonacademic tracks were even less varied, possibly because these classes were often taught by the least adequate teachers in the department, with more time spent on worksheets and seat work.

This study from 1966 reported practices not significantly different from today's standard procedures in the teaching of English. Even more alarming, Arthur Applebee's 1989 study of classroom practices in English yielded results not unlike Dora Smith's of fifty-six years earlier. Literature as such, mostly whole-class study of book-length works by dead white guys, still takes roughly half of the time of English class. Of the most commonly taught books, only *Silas Marner* has fallen from the 1966 list. Very few major works selected have women or minority authors, even in nonacademic classes where college admissions are less an issue, even in urban schools, even in schools where minorities are the majority. Teachers report that they spend around 30 percent of their class time on writing, but by that they mean, 75 or 80 percent of the time, expository writing about literature not much different from that on the Uniform Lists. That brings the chunk of time spent on the study of canonical, teacher-selected whole-class book-length works to around three quarters of the typical English course currently offered in American high schools, not much different from the 1966 proportion. Students spend another 15 percent of their time on grammar, vocabulary, spelling, and other received particles of meaning. Pedagogy still consists almost exclusively of teacher-centered recitation/discussion that leads to an interpretation the teacher received from someone in a university somewhere, with almost no group work or individualized instruction. There is a little attention to readers' responses to literature, but only as a motivation toward the "real work" of the *real* interpretation of the text that would make the New Critics proud.

That things are worse in the classes some call "nonacademic" reveals the extent to which teachers, despite the ease with which they blame colleges for the way the subject is structured, persist in seeing the discipline of English as a pile of stuff the kids are supposed to get. For the kids who don't love school, we just make it more boring. In nonacademic classes, students do more seat work, worksheets, précis, more grammar and skills, and much, much less writing. The teachers express even less concern about pleasure in reading, relationship of literature to life, the development of one's own response, critical thinking, or respect for diverse opinions. In spite of the difference in the way these kids are taught compared with their college-bound peers, however, there is no variety in the works of literature they are assigned to read: their literature program is equally built on "the books everybody ought to have read." Because there is no pressure to have everyone in nonacademic classes know the same things for college, we might expect to feel freer there to experiment and expand the definition of English class, but our need to feel like a dispenser of information seems to overwhelm that sense of freedom.

The pressures from the wider culture outside my classroom are so intense that I grip the chalk rail to keep my balance. I focus my eyes more steadily on the kids taking their seats in my room. As far away as some of the historical events I've described may seem, their residual force can still shape my actions in today's class if I allow it. I do have some choice about which forces of history I will move with, but I have to make that choice continually.

Before I moved into this classroom, it had been occupied by two generations of pack-rat teachers. They never threw anything away. The file cabinets, cupboards, and bookshelves were bursting with textbooks, workbooks, dittos, and student work dating back to the thirties. I spent a week carrying boxes of trash to the dumpster, and when I finished, the hallway outside my room, piled with textbooks for the custodians to store or dump, was the joke of the school. I began then to realize, as I do again today, how much my own teaching is full of the thrashing and jerking of the profession's history, how I unknowingly saddle myself again and again with a hundred years of conflicting goals. Any time I kneel beside fourteen-year-old Ed for a writing conference, I see his tenuous grasp of the rules of written English, how his topic is boring, how his thought is glib, how his narrative is nonsequential, how his paragraphing and sentence differentiation are almost nonexistent, how his subjects and verbs often fail to agree, and how so many of his words are misspelled, and I want to start dumping on him all of the things he does not know. Clearly here is an empty vessel it is my responsibility to fill up with my subject, English. Only by an imperfect act of will can I hold my tongue except to say, *Talk to me, Ed. What's this all about?* and listen and begin to nudge him toward posing big questions about his experience.

Every moment in teaching contains the past century of learning to teach English: from the Uniform Lists to the Dartmouth Conference, from General Semantics to the project method. None of the contravening pressures have gone away. While we fill in the bubbles for computerized grade reports, hundreds of voices whisper in our ears: Thorndike's, Dewey's, our mentors', and our own high school English teachers'. We teach in schools still obsessed with efficiency; we still hunger to hear the voices of our students; we still know that literacy is largely an affair of the heart; we still want to seem academically credible to our students and our colleagues in other departments. We will never satisfy all of those pressures, nor should we try to or even want to. Teaching is full of choosing, and so we make up our minds about what is most essential about literacy and then work *only* there.

We have just forty minutes a day, so we have to weave together the separate strands of our subject and get busy on what matters. I believe that means reading and writing whole texts all the time, with primary attention to my students' making meaning of their lives inside and outside the classroom. Those lives and meanings are the subject of the class, and it is by focusing on them that I can bring reading and writing together in my curriculum.

Students' memories are the raw material from which they make meaning. By bringing experience to their reading and writing, they can forge a deeper and more precise understanding of themselves and their social and natural world and then take that deeper understanding with them, away from the text and the classroom, to help them live more thoughtful, examined lives. I can't enter the realm of language and meaning and remain somehow value-neutral; my project is to collaborate with my students to make them and me better people in a better world. If that's idealism, well, something has to get me up in the morning and make me aspire to be good at my life's work.

And so I choose again. I dust off my backside and raise my voice a couple of decibels over the din. "All right, let's get started. . . ."

TIME AND POSSIBILITY

Before the sixth century, time was spiritual, sacred, because it was tied to nature. Man-made, routine agendas were almost unknown until the 500s, when the Benedictine monks invented the schedule. St. Benedict said, "Idleness is the enemy of the soul," and to keep the brothers' souls in good stead, the order formalized their activities into hour-long work periods. The concept of the hour was almost unknown in any other corner of medieval society. At a regular, appointed time, the brothers were to pray, eat, bathe, labor, read, reflect, sleep, even "go out for the necessities of Nature." This was very bizarre behavior at that time, and these monks were regarded as time fanatics. Since the brothers had no watches—*the clock hadn't been invented yet*—a bell was rung every hour, to make sure everyone started doing their thing on time. (So that everyone knew what to do when the bell rang, they made a book of hours.)

About fourteen centuries later, factories—and the schools built to supply workers for those factories—also needed to control when groups of people did what. Jeremy Rifkin's account of the Autocrat, a bell-ringing clock manufactured by the Electric Signal Clock Company in 1891, is a telling example. Since it was not obvious why anyone would need or want such a thing, the company published a marketing brochure that explained to principals and factory managers that this device could extend their control beyond the human limitation of being in only one place at a time. It assured, "These signals . . . are the voice of the principal speaking through the standard clock in his office . . . [and] will call 'time' on the teacher who rides hobbies in public school work, who devotes fifty minutes to teaching Geography and ten minutes to Arithmetic. . . . School officials, superintendents and principals will have the satisfaction of knowing that whether they are in the school building or absent from it . . . their schools are running on exact time." Of course, the Autocrat is still around, even if it is now more subtly named.

When we realize that aspects of life that we have always assumed were just *so* are only so because of one particular story, and might have been different,

16

we face a dizzying possibility. What if we were able, just for a day, to overthrow in our own minds the book of hours, the bells, the Autocrats? What might our lives with our students be if they and we were out from under strict authoritative control of appetite, elimination, activity, attention, and passion?

2 Creating Literate Environments in Secondary School Literacy Classrooms

We teach within containers of time and space. If we wipe clean the inside of our containers, all we have is an empty rectangular room and forty minutes. We know well what our forty minutes looks like when measured on a clock; its shape is so imprinted on our minds that we can effortlessly pivot it around the circle, starting an imaginary class period on any minute and knowing where the ending bell will ring. I don't say that's all the time we should have, only that for most of us, that's reality for now. (If anything, it's a generous estimate, since in many high schools, the English class, which most students have to take, is the most frequent target for interruptions to accommodate guidance information, senior class meetings, and anything else that needs to be conveyed to the entire student body.) But since that's all the time we have, let's be extremely conservative about how we fill it. After all, what you put into a container is what makes it seem spacious or crowded. If, for example, we used our classroom for an office, seeing students there one at a time, it would seem absurdly spacious. Instead, many of our classrooms are so packed with large students that they seem absurdly cramped. Similarly with our time: forty minutes is too long for some things, such as a first reading of a short poem, and too short for other things, such as a discussion of a novel combined with a vocabulary lesson and an opportunity to do some writing. So rather than always looking for new and nifty things to unload into our classrooms and our class time, we should guard its emptiness jealously.

We need to be sure that whatever we move into this time, this space, contributes as much as possible to our building an environment that invites the work of literacy, students using print to make meaning of experience. Traditional teaching views students as a blank slate, but process teaching insists that we change what it is we see as blank. The students are far from empty, bringing with them funds of knowledge, memory, and experience that we need to learn to draw upon. They are the real subject matter of the class. What we then take as our blank slates are the environment and the curriculum, and we need to select carefully and conservatively what we will write on them. As I have mentioned before, the other shift we are making is in our attention, from the subject matter of English to the English classroom as a learning environment for students. As John Dewey said, "We never educate directly, but indirectly by means of the environment" (p. 19).

I want my classroom and my teaching to be primarily *receptive* rather than transmissive or gregarious. The default position in my teaching and in the way I engineer this environment is one of listening rather than talking, seeing rather than performing. I'm certainly not going to refrain from teaching, but my approach in teaching is first to invite—or push—the kids to engage with their own literate work and then to teach them new things they need to know while they are working.

And so my priorities, especially early in the year, are to involve each class in a study of who we are as readers and writers and to turn a group of individuals who happen to be in the same room at the same time into a literate community. These are complementary goals, since students' acquaintance with one another with respect to reading and writing is one of the most important building blocks of the collaborative social environment. Even if they have known each other through years of playgrounds and sports, pizza parties and detention hall, they most likely do not know each other as readers and writers, and certainly are not yet *this community* of literate learners. What's more, since the teacher is such an inherently powerful constituent of the classroom community, there can't really be a community in my class unless I am part of it. So, on the first day of school and for at least a couple of weeks after that, rather than my giving out materials, listing rules, or explaining a syllabus, we begin the work of becoming "us" by investigating the raw materials of the course, the lives of the people in this place.

The foundations of a literate environment: the lives of students

Students' lives are full and rich and even in June will be scarcely grazed, so in September it helps to begin by focusing on some particular aspect of those lives. Our work together centers on literacy, so that's where I begin getting to know who these people are. I ask students to author their life history as readers or writers, to tell and write the stories that seem to have made them who they are today with respect to reading or writing. What they remember helps both them and me, as their teacher, to understand their experience of literacy and where it fits into the rest of their lives. Spencer, for example, writes,

> Some reasons I don't read are that when I was in school I was in a play and I only got to say 2 words. and everyone would correct my speach like one day in 4th grade I was reading off a word list one of my words was earthquake and I said "earthquacks" and man did my teacher get mad. She said no its earthquake.
>
> The reasons that I mostly read sports stories is most of the time I know what they are talking about. Because of this I know a lot about sports and I figure if I know a lot about a subject then when I tell someone they can't tell me I'm wrong because I know what I'm saying.

For eighth-grader Spencer, reading puts him in danger of being wrong, of looking dumb, so he does a very smart thing and reads texts for which he feels confident he has the appropriate background knowledge. His stated motivation still reveals his anxiety about the reading act, but this way, even if he doesn't understand what the text says, he already knows the information. His knowledge allows him to scaffold his reading, making it easier, more powerful, and more beneficial to his growth. I need to know this as his teacher, because it allows me to make sure that Spencer calls forward his knowledge about a text's subject before reading, even if the text is not about sports. If I merely give the class a short-answer reading survey instead of spending time elaborating their literate background, I end up with the sliver of information that Spencer enjoys sports books, which is much less useful.

Spencer's classmate Guillerme writes,

> One of my fondest memories of reading is that of when our whole family would gather on a Monday night and read a book called "Uncle Arther's Bedtime Stories." All of us kids would get comfortable on the couch while mom or dad got situated and ready to read. After much arguing or debating as we call it now we'd come up with one we all wanted to hear. We'd all listen like in a trance until someone, and I've been guilty a few times, said "Stop, wait just a second, I'll go real quick." Then off to the toilet they'd run and then they'd be back and ready to hear the rest of the story. These stories we heard always had some sort of meaning to them or moral I guess we'd call it, and we'd always listen hard for it to see if we could notice it and understand what it meant. This I think was the beginning of me really starting to form opinions about pieces.

Later in the year, when Guillerme seems reticent about taking leadership in his reading group, I remind him of how he has been a part of such a comfortable yet intense community of readers in his family. It helps him see the work in class as familiar rather than alien to his experience, and it changes his stance toward his group's work and his role in it. He not only becomes more animated and courageous in discussions, but also helps to solve group problems on at least two occasions by referring to the reading his family did together at home.

Ronald, a senior, writes,

> My life history as a writer is a long and pain staking one because I have dyslexia it is diffacult for me to read at a fast pace all though it is not overly diffiulct for me to read I do run into a few snags now and agean. When I was younger I went to more doctors, specialist to see what the problem was. I had E.A.G. or E.E.G. test done on me I've had more tutors to last two life times or thats how it seems but I read good enough to get along in the real world.
>
> In class when I have to read I will always read a paragraph or two a head so that when I read a loud I won't mess up. It use to piss me off so bad when I would be reading and I would say the wrong word but know what it was but not be able to say it. It was like it was stuck in the back of my throught. I

shouldn't say it like it doesn't happen any more because it does. And people would say the word and I would know what it was and I would say shut up.

It is hard and it will always be.

Katie, sitting next to Ronald, writes,

I mostly remember the awful times through school. English was never a good subject for me. I was never good at writing. I always had a hard time trying to learn how to put adverbs, verbs, pronouns, nouns, adjectives, prepersitional phrases, etc., I never could get the hang of putting sentences together. Now I sometimes wonder if the sentences I write make sense.

Ronald and Katie attest to the despair about meaning in literacy with which many students leave public school, their firm conviction that literacy is nonsense, their belief that they are "just not that type of person," the fatal heartsickness in their reading and writing lives. Especially with mature students, I spend several days of class time letting them critique the damage that has been done to their self-concept as readers and writers. They often argue long and hard about whether I should even be allowed to call them "readers" and "writers." Though I may seem disloyal to the very system that puts a paycheck in my mailbox each month, I try to help them understand that the problem is not inside them, in the way their brain is constructed or their native intelligence, but in the experiences they recall when they write about the pain or confusion they have felt in school. With so few weeks left before they forever choose to exclude themselves from any opportunities that might resurrect the remembered humiliation, I try urgently to disengage their concepts of "reading," "writing," "interpreting," or "meaning" from the nonsense they have been told and shown about those concepts. Neither this book nor any other could ever be so damning an indictment of traditional literacy instruction, or so urgent and inspiring a call to change, as a wad of letters written by a roomful of second-semester seniors in response to the question, What has your life history as a writer been like?

If students already have writers notebooks (see Chapters 3 and 4), they write these memories there, allowing them to emerge gradually over the year. Often, though, I want to start this work before they've had a chance to get their notebooks, so I write a question at the top of a page and photocopy it like a worksheet. Even better, I write the class a letter in which I recount some of my own memories of my early experiences as a reader or writer (usually I treat reading and writing separately at first, since the individual focus aids memory) and then ask them to write me back. Their letters and the conversations in class about them spur new memories for me, so I write them again, and we go back and forth like that a few times over these first couple of weeks. They share some of these stories in small groups, which I insist be reconfigured every time they meet so they have conversations with as many different people as possible. (I usually favor groups that stay together for a long time, but for the purpose of building a classroom community, here in the school year's salad days, I encourage a lot of dating around.)

I ask a few students to share experiences with the class if they represent some common type: the person who was humiliated by the possibly innocent but thoughtless actions of a sibling, a parent, or a teacher and who is consequently inhibited about writing or reading; the person who has fond memories of reading or writing outside of school; the person who feels powerful as a reader or writer because of the encouragement or praise of some significant person; or the person who, mainly because of school experiences, is confused and frustrated about the meaning of literacy. These experiences are so common that several other students will usually respond, *That happened to me, too.* This sharing of autobiographical fragments always touches on aspects of life other than literacy—what their homes are like, what school feels like, important people in their lives—and it naturally leads into the storytelling I often use to help them get started writing (as I describe in the next chapter). This natural telling about our lives not only makes writing easier, but also helps build community, as do the writing and sharing that follow.

I hope it is clear that, to me, these actions in which students share what their lives have taught them about reading and writing are more than icebreakers, glibly carried out to the tune of "Getting to Know You." In choosing what I will tell out of, say, a dozen years of experience with print, I am naming myself, claiming an identity *as a reader or writer.* When you tell me about yourself, I realize that my identity is not the same as someone else's, and thus I learn that I am a *particular* reader or writer. Once I've identified myself as a writer, even if writing still scares me to death, I have located writing not as some school activity that is outside me, but as part of my life, for better or worse, and that gives me the hope of being able to change and grow. As Robert Brooke writes in *Writing and Sense of Self,* "Learning to write really means more than just learning specific content, organizational and grammatical rules, rhetorical concepts, or writing processes—it means coming to attach to the self a set of writers' roles, negotiating an understanding of the self as someone who uses writing for personally and socially important purposes" (p. 140). The same could perhaps be said even more emphatically about reading. I would add that in order to create a social environment that encourages the risks necessary for growth, each learner has to have as part of his identity as a writer a sense of membership in this classroom's community as a writer, a knowledge of "where I stand, how I fit into 'us.'" Consequently, all of this self-exploration has to be experienced as a collaborative, social act, and I, as the teacher, have to talk it up as an important part of this class's shared inquiry.

One of the ways I give official value to this work is by very visibly and vigorously keeping records of what students say and do. As soon as the class rosters are relatively stable, I make a sheet for each class with each student's name on it, leaving a couple of blank spaces for new students, and then photocopy enough for every day of the quarter. At the end of the quarter, I add new names or delete the students who have moved, then photocopy it again. Readers may recognize this as a revision of Nancie Atwell's "status of the class" form. I found her form too crowded to write what I needed to, and I had to use too many other supplemental forms to keep records that were adequate for me. Naturally, every teacher needs to invent his own forms, since note taking is so intimately individual and needs to be tailored to the way the teacher thinks and moves in the classroom. Schools and districts trying to standardize record keeping are therefore making a big mistake and undercutting their own efforts.

At this point in the year, I write down anything that will add to my emerging portrait of each kid as a literate learner: interests and passions, anything he says about his instructional history, areas in which she feels strong or weak, social situations in which he seems comfortable or uncomfortable, an area of expertise that might be a resource for the class, the way she holds her pen, a habit of scratching out mistakes, writing speed, how his concentration on reading varies within a single sitting. As the year progresses and our work focuses more on reading or writing, I use this same space to record both what students say and what I ask them to do, which defines the curriculum continually unfolding for each reader/writer. Of course, I don't get it all down, but what I do have helps me remember later and also provides a baseline from which I can evaluate later growth, in collaboration with the student. This note taking also lets the kids know that I consider this work on getting to know ourselves and one another serious business. Sometimes they are uncomfortable at first when I write as they talk, but I explain why I am doing it, to try to put them more at ease. Eventually, they are flattered by my recording their words—it's a way of valuing what they say—and they pause to let me catch up, even repeating things they think were important to make sure I get it right. My writing therefore adds an immediate quality of reflection to their speech.

If I have six classes, I keep six piles of the forms on a shelf. When a class walks in, I grab one from the appropriate pile and slip it onto my clipboard. The forms have three holes along the left side (already punched in the paper I put in the photocopier), so I can, at the end of each week, install the forms in ring binders, one for each class. That way, if I want to see "the story of Joe" across the semester, I focus my eyes on Joe's strip on the page and just flip through from front to back. My records are not only open to students, but whenever I can, I deliberately go over them in conference, so that the student can understand and augment my evolving interpretation of her as a writer.

Out of all this inquiry into our life histories, habits, and identities as literate learners, we can begin to talk about what our class should be like, attempting to provide more of the helpful kinds of experiences and less of the hurtful or confusing kinds and at least seeming to tailor the classroom's structure to the needs of the particular people inhabiting it. In doing so, I hope to enfranchise the students into my ways of thinking about English class and disarm their traditional, commonsense notions about "what we are supposed to be doing in here." By reflecting on our pasts, we can use the present moment to imagine the conditions of our future growth. We can talk about what reading and writing can mean beyond just getting a good grade to get into college, which will lead to a higher-paying job. (I don't totally discount the economic ambitions of students, especially those who are poor or marginalized, but I do intend for our literacy learning to be something more than rote obedience to please authority.) If our work is going to have a common purpose, if we are going to become a community, such conversations are indispensable.

Transforming a group of individuals into a community

The word *community* may be a problem for some readers, so let me be explicit about what I mean. Obviously, there is no one way to be a community, and in my experience, every class is different and would be even more different with another teacher. I don't have in mind a warm and cozy image of everyone loving everyone else, but my students and I do need to cultivate an awareness of and respect for each other as members of this community. In other words, Max doesn't have to like Ronald as a person, but he does have to behave respectfully to Ronald as a member of this group. It's this respect that promotes an atmosphere of "trust," another possibly overly romanticized word, by which I mean the permission we give each other to take intellectual risks without risking too much embarrassment and social pain. Being able to write something that may turn out to be bad or that may expose some personal vulnerability requires that the people around me also value risk taking. Over the course of the year, a community has to develop a complex network of such shared values. What's most important in my notion of community, though, is a feeling of "us-ness," a recognition that we are a group with certain experiences and values not shared by anyone who is not us. The people outside the door are "others," and they are the ones we are writing for, the audience of evaluators against whom we are checking "our" work. Often, when my efforts to create communities in my classroom fail, it's because the class and I never really congeal into a group by performing for people who are not part of "us." We need to be aware of the others "out there" in order to be able to work for common purposes. (See Chapter 4 for one way my students have published their writing for outside audiences.) Each teacher probably has to evolve her own definition of community, but whatever it is, a group of kids who show up in a third-period class in September are most assuredly *not* one yet. There is work to be done.

Experiences that build a foundation for community

In my past life as a professional actor, I sometimes earned money leading improvisational acting workshops at summer arts camps. I saw how quickly kids who didn't even know each other, who came from different towns and schools, quickly grew close and developed trust. Part of it was the summer, sure, but part of it was the spirit of play and openness engendered by doing improvs. I began doing some of these games and exercises in my classroom, to boost the feeling of being part of a club and to take the sting out of the kids' adolescent self-consciousness. My students have told me that doing such exercises "taught us that what we did was okay. We weren't going to be laughed at by the others because we were all doing the same type of thing. That gave us all a sense of unity." They learned "to get along with others and to trust that they would catch us when we fell."

I track down or make up improvs that I believe will reinforce the qualities I am trying, early in the year, to nurture in my classes: relaxation, concentration, heightened sensory awareness, observation, trust, and group spirit. Since I won't take the time to give complete instructions for the activities, I'll discuss the most common ones, the ones many people will have encountered before, and I'll justify their use in this context. Interested readers may want to consult works by Viola Spolin such as *Improvisations for the Theatre*. Spolin remains the authority on these matters, and though you may well find her theorizing annoying and dated (she wrote in the sixties), she is clear in her descriptions of games and exercises and so is a useful resource.

RELAXATION   Two or three minutes of focused relaxation, giving the kids a chance, for once, to sweep the clutter from their minds, makes sense when you consider the frantic fragmentation of their days. Though theatre students usually do this exercise lying down, that's never been an option in my classrooms, so I have them sit up straight with their feet flat on the floor, properly aligned but relaxed, their heads straight, their eyes closed, and their hands resting palm down on the tops of their thighs.

Once everyone's settled, in my most soothing voice, I call attention to parts of their bodies that might be tense: feet, legs, shoulders, hands, necks. I sometimes use an image of warmth or light or softness filling those muscles. I ask them to take three deep breaths in sync with my instructions: *Take a deep breath, and release.* Then, I sometimes take them on some kind of imaginary journey, saying something like, *You're floating on a cloud, high up where nothing can touch you. You're safe, relaxed, just floating.*

The objective is to get them, even briefly, into something like an alpha state, a mind free of deliberate, controlled thought. (If you're tempted to say they're always there, I'll beat you to it.) I don't do this every day, of course, but even occasionally, it subtly changes the texture of the energy in the classroom.

CONCENTRATION   Other exercises focus on concentration rather like that of two people engaged in a conversation in which each cares very much about what the other is saying, clearly a boon to a writing workshop. The most popular exercise of this sort is the mirror, in which two people act as reflections of each other's movements. If the traditional mirror seems too difficult at first, it may help to do it as a group for a couple of days.

In the group version, one person faces the class and moves hands, arms, head, torso, slowly and smoothly, and the class mirrors those movements, trying to put all of their awareness into the leader's actions, not copying the movements after the fact, but mirroring them as they occur. As students move on to doing this exercise in pairs, getting better with repeated experience, they should eventually try to forget who is the leader and who the follower. This fosters an intimacy not usually found in any kind of classroom.

HEIGHTENED SENSORY AWARENESS   Some exercises open students not only to each other, but also to the world around them, for which adolescents often have so little time. In using these exercises, I'm trying to awaken students to the kind of intense *noticing* that writers like Annie Dillard so often discuss. In the *trust walk,* students, in pairs, one with eyes closed, the other with eyes open, walk around the room or the hall or some area outside, the "sighted" one leading the "blind" one. The task of the one who can see is to treat her partner to a varied and full sensory experience. She helps her partner touch wood, really feeling it as if for the first time, to smell pencil shavings, and to feel the sun's warmth near the windows. The task for the "blind" student is to keep a blank mind and perceive without labeling, which will at first be difficult. When I hear "blind" students announcing objects, as if this were a guessing game ("Desk." "Trash can—I'm not touching that!"), I try to ease them away from this way of thinking: it's just this objectification through naming that keeps us from seeing more primally.

Observation

First cousins to the sensory exercises are those emphasizing observation, their purpose being to bypass the ordinary editing we do of visual data. A good way to begin one of these exercises is to go right into it from a mirror exercise. Students have been paying very close attention to their partners, but there are things they will (naturally) have failed to observe. Partners turn their backs on each other and then try to describe as much as they can about the other's appearance, particularly what the other is wearing. Then each makes three subtle changes in appearance, such as buttoning a top button, unlacing a shoestring, loosening hair. They turn around and try to figure out what has changed.

Sometimes, I also ask them to turn their backs to me and describe what I'm wearing or to recall what their homeroom teacher was wearing or what a parent had on that morning. Students often think I'm saying they ought always to "notice what everyone is wearing," which of course isn't the point at all. I'm only trying to make them more aware of how little detail we habitually note and the concentration that is necessary in recalling it, an awareness that will serve them well in writing.

TRUST   Trust exercises have, for the last twenty years or so, been mainstays of beginning acting classes, but it seems to me they are of even more value in a writing workshop. The simplest is the trust circle, in which a group of probably no more than eight students stands in a circle and supports the one standing in the center, who makes his body stiff and allows himself to fall forward or backward or around in a circle, kept from falling only by the other students. Though there's always much laughter and squealing, this exercise is meaningful, even touching, in that it metaphorically reflects the palpable trust and responsibility that will characterize each day of the writing workshop.

Group spirit

There are, finally, those exercises that get to the heart of the matter, here in the beginning of the year or just before the workshop is launched: exercises that ask students to function as parts of a whole, to see themselves, just for a moment, less as egocentric individuals and more as cogs in a machine. The "machine" aspect of these exercises may be difficult for many adolescents, since it means they must do something silly without being self-conscious. As with most of these exercises, the real payoff comes only with repeated performance, since the first couple of times are disasters.

The task: to build, adding piece by piece, kid by kid, a human machine of interconnected parts. Each student is part of the whole, adding a movement and a sound in rhythm with the rest of the machine's works. This usually works better if I and the kids agree that the machine does or makes something particular, since it will suggest to them specific qualities of sound and movement. I've always had the impression that the metaphor "takes," that students do feel, even in the midst of the complaining and the blushing and the giggling and the eyeball rolling, like parts of the larger whole. But even if it doesn't, the members of the class are bound to feel a lot less silly reading their writing out loud than they did swinging their arms and saying *pssht. . . pop!* Like all of these improvisational exercises, it is at the very least an icebreaker, though it can be much more than that, too.

Building community with shared literature

Literature, of course, provides opportunities to gather together and share an experience and so can contribute to the construction of community. At this point in the year, my purposes in selecting and using texts are to demonstrate that literature can move us personally and to provide the class with a set of shared experiences of being so moved. Therefore, I choose stories, poems, memoirs, and picture books that I hope (though you never know for sure) will make us cry (or almost), make us laugh, or lift us with inspiration. I've chosen stories like Robert Cormier's "Guess What: I Almost Kissed My Father Goodnight," Ouida Sebestyen's "Welcome," and Leslie Norris's "Blackberries"; poems like Mary Oliver's "The Summer Day," Edward Hirsch's "A Photograph Ripped in Half," Daniel Mark Epstein's "Miami," and Terence Winch's "Success Story"; memoirs such as sections of Maya Angelou's *I Know Why the Caged Bird Sings* and Donald Murray's "I Still Wait for the Sheets to Move." Some of the most effective pieces I have ever used early on in the year have been those written by students: my own in previous years, students in friends' classrooms, or sometimes the students quoted in books about teaching by people like Tom Romano, Linda Rief, Nancie Atwell, Lucy Calkins, and James Moffett.

Sometimes I just read these pieces by students or professional authors aloud; other times I photocopy them onto transparencies so we can all look at the text together. It seems to help make the reading feel like a community experience when we gather close and share a common visual focus. I especially like to use picture books, since they intensify the experience by giving everyone a shared piece of art to look at while they hear the story. Some younger adolescents at first feel threatened, thinking I am treating them like children, but once they hear a couple of these powerful picture-book texts, they come to trust my choices, which have included *Always Gramma*, by Vaunda Micheaux Nelson, *Faithful Elephants,* by Yukio Tsuchiya, *Amazing Grace,* by Mary Hoffman, *The True Story of the Three Little Pigs* and *The Stinky Cheese Man and Other Fairly Stupid Tales,* by John Sczieska, *Moe the Dog in Tropical Paradise,* by Diane Stanley, and almost anything by Bird Baylor.

After one of these readings, I do not expect an intense discussion of the piece. I simply ask students how the piece affected them, what it made them think about. Usually, we write for a few minutes before they answer, just to get their minds going. Later, they become more adept at thinking on paper immediately after hearing a story; for now, the purpose of the writing is to help them rehearse their thoughts before speaking, and I tell them so. Since I'm using this literature mainly to invoke students' voices and stories, we owe no allegiance to the text itself. (There will be another time for learning to construct valid interpretations.) If we are very lucky, the talk will drift far from the original text, taking us to a place where we are having real conversations about things that matter to us.

In these first few weeks we are together, we are trying to construct the essential foundation of a literate environment—students' belief that they have things to say about their lives that will be valued here and an expectation of response from others. Students have to become persuaded that they can and should always be formulating and revising a response to what they read and hear, even before it is completed, that they can and should answer back, in writing or vocally, or just to themselves. I don't think these values are idiosyncratic to my classroom; rather, they are reflections of ordinary human thinking processes, upon which I am trying purposefully to construct an environment for my students. The language theorist M. M. Bakhtin writes:

> [T]he utterance [whether written or spoken] is constructed while taking into account possible responsive reactions, for whose sake, in essence, it is actually created. As we know, the role of the *others* for whom the utterance is constructed is extremely great. . . . The role of these others, for whom my thought becomes actual thought for the first time (and thus also for my own self as well) is not that of passive listeners, but of active participants in speech communication. From the very beginning, the speaker expects a response from them, an active responsive understanding. The entire utterance is constructed, as it were, in anticipation of encountering this response. (p. 94)

Active minds, therefore, depend on active communities. To have a good year of learning in a richly literate environment, it is worthwhile to fast-forward our sense of community and our expectation of conversation and face-to-face interactions among equals. Conversation, community, collaboration, provide the bedrock, and now we need to look at the structures we will erect upon that foundation, structures that, unlike these beginning-of-the-year activities, will be predictable enough that it is not necessary for me as the teacher to choreograph, explain, or direct, structures that will channel and sustain students' developing independence as literate learners.

Arranging a classroom to support student work

Let's return to that big, empty rectangle we mentioned at the beginning of this chapter. It is wise to begin with it empty, to avoid the decades of inherited clutter

I described at the end of Chapter 1. What takes up shelf and file space in most of America's English classrooms are textbooks, old dictionaries, and handouts, all of which could be turned to better use through recycling. But if we look at English classrooms as physical environments for people to be together and work with pleasure, to converse, critique, and create, the real problem in most places is less clutter than barrenness. Of course, much school architecture doesn't help, with cinderblock walls glaring fluorescent reflections across a prairie of bland linoleum. But it's more than that, too. The cinder blocks glare because there's nothing on the walls, and when there is, it's up there so long that when it comes down, the shadow of its shape remains. All the lines in the room are perpendicular, because identical books are the only things on any surface. Almost everything in the room, with the possible exception of a few items on the teacher's desk, reflects corporate publishers' vision of a homogeneous, depersonalized world. Gertrude Stein's remark about Oakland comes to mind: once you get there, there isn't any *there* there.

Though there are some practical reasons for ignoring the physical place in which we try to create our learning communities, mostly it is a product of secondary school culture. Whatever the explanation, we ought to consider a change in values when we remember how basic the experience of place is to our feelings and thoughts. Tony Hiss writes in *The Experience of Place:*

> Our ordinary surroundings, built and natural alike, have an immediate and a continuing effect on the way we feel and act, and on our health and intelligence. These places have an impact on our sense of self, our sense of safety, the kind of work we get done, the ways we interact with other people, even our ability to function as citizens in a democracy. In short, the places where we spend our time affect the people we are and can become. . . . Our relationship with the places we know and meet up with—where you are right now; and where you've been earlier today; and wherever you'll be in another few hours—is a close bond, intricate in nature, and not abstract, not remote at all: It's enveloping, almost a continuum with all we are and think. (pp. xi–xii)

To me, this is not just a question of decoration, answerable by throwing up a few posters and bringing in a few plants. I do those things, but I don't think a superficial attention to place addresses the real need. A pleasing sense of place arises in part from spaces organized to be constantly in use by the people who work there. Rooms that are depressing are those that have been neglected, black holes, no-man's-lands, Miss Havisham's rooms. So I plan the classroom arrangement based on, first, the activity I anticipate will be carried out there and, second, the message the arrangement might send to the students. This second criterion instantly dictates that the desks will not be in rows and that the teacher desk will not face the student desks like a pulpit. That much I know; but it doesn't tell me how the room *will* be arranged. The first criterion, arranging for anticipated activity, involves considerably more intricate planning. Allow me to sketch out some of the considerations that come up again and again.

1. What will I need to make this a conveniently supportive learning environment for myself?

The classroom has to support my writing, reading, thinking, and work with students, so I need a place where I feel comfortable doing that work. That is why I have always kept a teacher desk in the room, usually pushed into a corner. I rarely sit there when students are in the room, but it is a place to spread out work and keep necessary things like the clipboard I use for record keeping. If I don't have a predictable place where I discipline myself to lay down the clipboard when I'm not using it, I will never find it when I need it and will never build the habit of taking notes about my students. I also need a place for those records to accumulate; for me that means a cupboard shelf holding a number of binders, one for each of my classes. On my desk, I also keep an "in" tray, where students can put notebooks, drafts, and letters they want me to read, and an "out" tray, where students know they can reclaim these items the next day. This frees me from wasting time collecting and redistributing paper every day. I also need file cabinets or something equivalent in which to store class sets of poems, short stories, nonfiction pieces, essays, memoirs, and so on. When I request these from administrators, I point out the thousands of dollars I am saving the school by never buying an expensive textbook or anthology. In these file cabinets, I also store copies of student work, my students (current and former) and the students of friends. Near my desk, I also keep a shelf full of professional literature, or at least copies of the chapters I think may be helpful as resources during the school day.

2. What will students need access to in the room in order to work independently?

In addition to my "out" and "in" box, there are several other areas in the room designed to make students independent of my footwork. In several spots, I keep file boxes or milk crates for their process folios (manilla folders in which they keep their work in progress). Rather than assigning one box to each class, I have a box for A–G, another for H–M, and so on, in different places around the room, which keeps all thirty from storming one corner as they come in. The kids know where their work is and, once they are into the routine, can get it without my doing anything. Someone in each class is appointed process-folio president and is in charge of making sure the file boxes stay neat and organized instead of becoming deep piles that require major excavation and demolition before delivering up someone's work. Portfolios, the students' collections of their finished work, go in the drawer of another file cabinet. Since these are only rarely needed by an entire class at once, traffic control is less of a concern.[1] Not surprising, I have a shelf of reference

---

1 I do not discuss portfolios fully in this book. Interested readers may want to see the relevant chapters in Linda Rief's *Seeking Diversity*. Other books that might be helpful include *Portfolios: Process and Product*, edited by Pat Belanoff and Marcia Dickson, *Portfolio Portraits*, edited by Donald Graves and Bonnie Sunstein, *Portfolios and Beyond*, by Susan Glazer and Carol Brown, *Portfolio Assessment in the Reading-Writing Classroom*, by Robert Tierney, Mark Carter, and Laura Desai, and *Teaching Without Testing* (a special issue of *English Education*), by Denny Taylor.

books: three or four dictionaries, maybe one thesaurus, a few copies of a few different style handbooks like Strunk & White and Warriner's (Warriner's is not good, really, for looking things up; mostly I keep it here as a symbol for colleagues, parents, and administrators). A classroom library of books the kids admire is absolutely necessary. It is not enough that the school has a decent library. Students need to be able to grab books while they are writing. In addition, if there is any short text we have all shared (for example, if I've used it in a minilesson, as a read-aloud, or as a whole-class reading), I keep about eight copies in a manilla envelope taped to the wall, so that kids can quickly remind themselves how the author accomplished this or that. For the same reason, I have a small area of the room where student work is displayed—not everyone's finished pieces, mind you, but copies of student writing to which, in order to illustrate some point about writing, I have referred in minilessons or which the student has read to the whole class.(A wall— with the possible exception of one in a public bathroom—is not, in our culture, a place where people stand to read long pieces of writing and so is not, in my view, a good vehicle for publication.)

3. What could students have with them here to create personalized writing places?

Every writer I know has a carefully fashioned writing environment. I write these words facing a window with a beautiful view. Beside my computer stand some of the books that are framing my thinking lately, and just looking at their spines while I write excites me and rearranges what I say. I have a coffee cup full of pens, pencils, scissors, tape, glue sticks, so that I can make notes of thoughts irrelevant to what I am writing here at a particular moment. My notebook is always beside me. I also have a microcassette recorder at hand, in case I get mired in detail and can no longer hear my writer's voice. I have pictures of people I love on my desk, and nearby a bulletin board that contains a few inspiring quotes and some cartoons about writing. It seems to me that knowing how to construct an environment where you feel good about writing is a fundamental thing to learn about the writing life, but too rarely do students get that opportunity. Our teaching situation makes it almost impossible even to think this way—almost, but not quite. I once found a big stack of thick, hard-cardboard rectangles and brought it to my classroom. The students made personalized desk blotters by covering them with paper or fabric, pasting on photos, drawings, postcards, quotes, poems they liked. They doodled and graffitied on them, and when they got tired of looking at that, pasted something else on top. I "obtained" a table that was just taking up space in a faculty room, and the blotters lived there, stacked according to class period. In my classroom, the bulletin boards are mostly for students to use to communicate with other students, to recommend books or request recommendations, to solicit information on a topic, to display big pictures they make or find, to rally each other to causes and campaigns. Sometimes, when we are working on memoir or poetry, it helps students to have personal objects with them when they write, and I provide a space in a cupboard where they can store these things. Their day is divided into so many different parts; they can't come from home every day having remembered everything they might need. If they need something for their writing time, it should be in the place where they will write. Some students have favorite writing implements or kinds of paper, and to make sure they can have these when they want them, I give them a drawer in my teacher's desk or some other special place in which to squirrel their treasures away. Some teachers I know have built or scavenged mail boxes reminiscent of the ones common in school front offices, so that they can enfranchise the adolescent compulsion to pass notes as part of the literacy classroom. Finally, there are different social needs for different points in the writing process. There are times when I turn down the volume on my answering machine and other times when I take my writing to school with me. By establishing two or three spots in the classrooms as conference areas, I can give students a chance to talk to each other without having constant talking at their desks. If I hear voices from those spots, I know the talking's legal; if noise is coming from anywhere else, I ask for quiet. If a couple of kids have been "in conference" for fifteen minutes, I can ask them to sit down and get writing again. I also keep several desks on the other side of the room from the conference areas, over which I post a sign that says *Quiet,* for writers who especially don't want to be interrupted right now. These are the ways I can predictably help the writers and readers in my care to construct personal productive spaces for themselves. As the year goes on, the particular lives of these kids in these classes always give me new ideas.

4. How can I create better learning environments if I travel from room to room, with no room to call my own?

Some teachers have no doubt been frustrated with this whole discussion of physical environment because they have no classroom of their own, but have to "float" or "travel" from room to room. While I'm sympathetic that that situation nullifies most of the particular suggestions I have made here, it is still possible to have a literate environment, even in an empty room. My situation as a consultant is no different, traveling as I do from classroom to classroom, with little or no control over the materials I use for teaching or the physical arrangement of the room. So, to these people I offer the following advice: first of all, let your cart be the place for your clipboard, your binder(s) for cumulative records, and your "in" box, as well as a row of ten to twenty novels, poetry anthologies, or books of short stories you know well, from which you can draw examples in conferences with students. Have manilla envelopes there too, with copies of a few pieces of literature you have shared with students. Keep writing folders arranged by class in those plastic holders libraries use for magazines, and only take one or two class's folders with you on a given "trip." If you work with portfolios, keep them in your office or someplace else in the building, like, say, the principal's office, and send students for them when they need them, which is not every day. Designate areas of the room that are conference areas and quiet areas. Rehearse the desk-rearranging waltz again and again early in the year so that, as soon as the bell rings, the students know how to move their desks quickly into the arrangement you prefer. Explain to the kids why it is so important for the room to be arranged that way, and insist that it be right. Never let it slide, even in a shortened period. Sharing a space does not mean the desks have to be in rows during your class. Having worked in all kinds of adverse conditions, I've come to believe that nothing can prevent a good literate community from forming if the teacher maintains a clear vision of what she wants to happen in the classroom and insists that it become reality. Remember, too, that the most important elements of a literate environment are the community of readers/writers I discussed above and the predictable structures in time, which I will below.

The shape of time—predictable structures in the reading-writing workshop

The physical classroom preparations I've outlined provide a context, a helpful support to a reading/writing workshop, but they do not *constitute* the workshop. What makes a workshop a workshop is a set of actions in time that provide students with a scaffolding for their work on literate projects extending for days and weeks. Those structures may include, but are not necessarily limited to, minilessons, work time, writing conferences with both teacher and peers, response groups, and whole-group share. The sole focus in each interaction is on what the students are *doing* in their ongoing work rather than on a detached curriculum, and they are all based on the idea that people can learn *about* language only when they are actually doing something purposeful *with* language. In a workshop classroom, all teaching has to fit into the learner's intention, whether that intention is to use writing to figure out a problem, to read a book that is more difficult than those the student ordinarily reads, or to communicate a grievance to the principal. In order to make decisions about what to teach, then, the teacher has to maintain a frame of mind that listens and watches students, trying to provide the advice or direction that best fits the student's developing intention, that challenges the student to grow but is within the student's present grasp. Just as in establishing community I first receive the students by getting them to reflect publicly about their life history and literate habits and preferences, so the first step in each and every conference and in planning each and every minilesson is to research and develop a theory about where the learners are in their growth and what they are trying to do in their reading or writing. All of my instruction is based on response, all of it informed by research on these students. And it is further guided by my own sense of what good writing or successful reading entails. I try to meet them where they are and push them toward my image of "better." The whole act of teaching, whether an individual student or a whole class, might be represented in the diagram in Figure 2–1, which I have adapted from Short and Burke's *Creating Curriculum*. The decision about what to teach when always springs from two funds of knowledge, an understanding of the student and an image of good writing or successful reading for this experience. These negotiations require that the class structures stay stable across time, so that I can focus on learning rather than giving new directions every day.

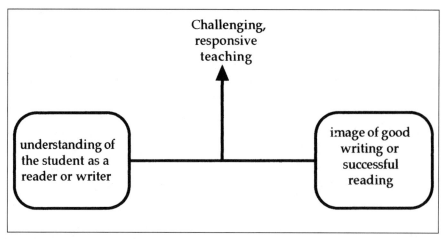

FIG. 2–1: *The act of teaching English/language arts as stemming from two funds of knowledge.*

When I first began using a workshop structure in my classroom, I made it predictable—sometimes. Maybe a couple of times a week, or perhaps for twenty minutes of a period, I would have a "predictable" writing workshop, thinking, I suppose, that the *structure* was predictable, regardless of how erratically I employed that structure. I didn't realize how dysfunctional that unpredictable predictability was until *I* began to write seriously. When my forward progress on a piece was interrupted for a few days by other agendas, I returned to the project disoriented, and it took a couple of days to get on a roll again. Annie Dillard describes this problem in *The Writing Life:*

> A work in progress quickly becomes feral. . . . As the work grows, it gets harder to control; it is a lion growing in strength. You must visit it every day and reassert your mastery over it. If you skip a day, you are, quite rightly, afraid to open the door to its room. You enter its room with bravura, holding a chair at the thing and shouting, "Simba!"

I have even found this to be true in my reading life. When I am reading a novel, regardless of its difficulty, if I skip a few days, it takes much more intellectual energy to pick it up again, and when I do, for the first half hour, I'm flipping pages: *Now where were we? Who is she again?* Because I know it's going to be like that, I avoid even looking at the book lying there on the table, because I'm intimidated by the effort.

A literate life requires fairly high maintenance. For reading or writing to be easy demands momentum, concentration, commitment. I want reading and writing to be as easy as possible for my students—lord knows, even at that, they're hard enough. And to make them easy, I keep the decks clear, the work time predictable. When Rudy knows that every day in my class he's going to be working on his piece of nonfiction, sometimes writing, sometimes reading the texts he has chosen to inform his writing of that piece, he can be thinking toward that time, mentally rehearsing and preparing for the moments he is dug in with his pen actually moving. In fact, if he is writing with commitment and intention every day, he cannot help but be rehearsing it, albeit often unconsciously, the way we drive along rehearsing conversations with our spouse or principal. In this way, the forty minutes of class time radiate outward to affect his life far beyond their relative proportion to the rest of the day.

Because a predictable time to work is so important in a reading/writing life, I jealously, obsessively protect the regularity of workshop structures in my class, wherein we write every day of the week or read every day of the week. I do not take an accommodating view toward interruptions from the guidance office, the senior class, the band, the sports teams, the principal. I don't break up my class period into different agendas, nor do I break up my week that way. Rather, I allow something to come to the foreground for part of the year, and then we work on it every day. With that kind of focus, a forty-minute period, though still not as long as the two hours I would have in a more perfect world, is long enough to do significant work on that one thing every day.

Student work time

Ordinarily, a discussion of workshop structures would begin with the minilesson, since it often comes first in a class period. I want to begin, though, with the part of the workshop that is most important, the only indispensable structure, the time when students are working without being directed by the teacher. By that I don't, of course, mean that students are doing anything they want: they do have to be working on their ongoing literate projects. If it's a chunk of the year when we are working on writing, they are writing in their notebooks, drafting or revising their pieces, or conferring with me or a friend. If reading is on the front burner, they are reading silently, writing in response to what they are reading, or talking with a partner or a group. They do not have a choice about engaging with the structures of the workshop, with the work we are about; they do have choices about exactly how they will spend their time and the precise nature of the projects they work on. This work time is always the bulk of the period. Though its precise length depends on the additional structures that may be appropriate on a given day, its minimum length is around twenty-five minutes; almost never would I make it a smaller chunk. For the class as a whole, this is time to concentrate and dig in (to the extent possible in only twenty-five minutes) without being interrupted.

At the beginning of this "writing time," "reading time," or "group time," I sometimes sit down to read or write alongside the kids. I do this for a couple of reasons. First, it's an important demonstration to them that I value in my own life and learning the things I'm asking them to do. Often, especially when I'm writing, I become aware that several of them are just watching me, wondering whether I'll cross anything out, whether I'll get stuck, or how fast I write. The second reason I begin reading or writing with them is because it seems to help the class settle in to the task at hand. If I begin by circulating and conferring, the tight bubble of concentration I want in the room is sometimes more elusive. I write for only a few minutes (this doesn't do wonders for *my* writing life), and then I begin my work with students.

I carry my clipboard with me, with the appropriate record-keeping form attached, and make a pass around the room. I know of several students with whom I need to confer because my records let me see that I haven't talked with them individually in a while. Usually, I have around six or seven conferences in a period, some a quick touching of bases, some longer and more involved in the details of what the student is working on. That rate ensures that I will get around to most students in a week, if I keep track of whom I need to see and don't allow myself to be pulled in by the students who happen to be the most emotionally needy.

The conference is the cornerstone of my teaching because it is the most individualized and specific and therefore the most accurate work I do. Whether I am working with seventh graders, seniors, graduate students, or veteran educators, I am struck again and again by how important it is to hear what the writer or reader is trying to do and then to offer advice about how to get there. I may have said the same thing to the whole class only days or minutes before, but there's something about hearing it in a conversation in which the learner has gotten a chance to talk first that makes it relevant and useful.

I try to follow a simple structure in my conferences. First, I kneel down beside the student, putting my head lower than hers to facilitate eye contact even if she's looking frequently at the page. This keeps my gaze focused on the person doing the writing or reading rather than on the text. I ask a brilliant question like *What's up?* or *What are you doing right now?* My only objective here is to get the student talking; until I know what she is all about, I don't have much to say. With adolescents, who tend to be more reticent about elaborating than younger kids or adults, I usually have to ask a couple of follow-up questions to get the student to elaborate on some aspect of her work. As she is talking, I may skim the page of the piece of writing or the book, trying to connect what she says to what I see. (Like Nancie Atwell, I do not read student writing in a conference with an adolescent student (or an adult): the pieces are too long. I tell students that if they want a reading, I'll be happy to take their piece home and confer with them tomorrow; they just need to put it in my "in" box at the end of the period.) While I listen, I am developing a hunch, a theory about what is really going on for this kid. There are always several possibilities for the best thing to say; it is hardly ever obvious, and there is no Platonic right conference for this moment. Out of the possibilities, I choose *one,* which I believe is the thing this student most needs to hear right now in her life as a writer.

What I say may take the form of information: *You know something a lot of writers do?* or *When I'm reading, I feel the same way sometimes, and here's what I do.* It may be a direct suggestion: *Why don't you try rearranging it like this?* or *Do you think it might help if you just skipped that part and then tried . . .* When I make a suggestion like that, I try to follow it up by some general principle about reading or writing: *The reason I suggest that is that sometimes readers. . . .* Other times, in fact most often, my suggestion may come very close to an assignment: *Why don't you go back in your notebook and look for places where you. . ., or Go and get the other book you were reading and. . . .* When I set this kind of course for a student, I mean for her to follow it. It's not a casual suggestion; there's something in the doing of it I want the student to learn. So I jot it down in my records, and I return to that student the next day or the next and see how it went. If she didn't do it, we need to talk about how she made that decision and what she did instead. I'm not telling her what to write in her piece or how to arrange it on the page, but I am telling her to try some action along the way, which may or may not end up in the final product. Since the individual conference is my most important mode of instruction, I want to make sure I at least try to make a difference in that student's habits of reading or writing in every conference.

The art of the writing conference has been described in rich detail and anecdote in several places, first by Donald Murray in *A Writer Teaches Writing* (Chapter 8), and later by Lucy Calkins in *The Art of Teaching Writing* (Chapters 13 and 14) and *Living Between the Lines* (Chapter 14) and by Nancie Atwell in *In the Middle* (Chapter 5). In later chapters of this book, there are specific examples of conferences and some discussion of how they change with varying situations.

Besides independent student work and teacher conferences, the other thing I expect to go on during this block of work time is peer conferring, especially when we are writing. If a student wants to bounce a piece off a friend, he can ask her if this is a good time and then go to one of the legal conference areas either to talk about a problem he is having with his piece or to let her read it. In my experience, adolescents almost always respond to each other's writing with, *It's good. I like it.* Maybe, once they have internalized one or two of my values about writing, they might say something like, *Add details and correct the spelling.* At their stage of life, when their main job is to define themselves in relation to peers, it's just too socially dangerous to say anything, even a question, that might be interpreted as criticism. I have tried to work with them on this, but to be honest, I've never been satisfied. A few other teachers tell me I'm wrong, but I can't lie and say I've ever seen one-on-one peer conferring among adolescents to be rigorous inquiry that results in significant revision. That does not mean this time is worthless or wasted, however. It is crucial to have cheerleaders in the lonely business of writing. Often in writing this book, I have given drafts of chapters to friends, hoping they would just say, *It's good. I like it.* Moreover, anytime a student has a peer read what he has written, his sense of audience is strengthened, regardless of whether the feedback is helpful. Sometimes just a vote of confidence is all that's needed to keep a writer writing. The more rigorous collaborative inquiry into writing well, I think, can occur in response groups, which I describe below.

Whole-class structures

Most days, but not all, I begin class with a whole-group meeting. It just seems more friendly, more like what a community should do, even if it is nothing but a short lecture. As I mentioned before, what I talk about in these minilessons is based on what the students are doing. My notes from conferences give me more than enough ideas. I do not have a list of minilessons all scoped and sequenced in my mind or in my teaching notes; I build these talks directly out of my sense of what many of the kids are doing. However, no matter how complex my assessment may be of what these kids need to learn, my motto in minilessons is simplify, simplify, simplify—no, make that just simplify. Both from my own experience as a teacher and from watching others, I have come to believe that the most difficult—and one of the most important—things to remember about minilessons is that they are mini, not maxi. I have to remember to select (just like in a conference) only one of the many possibilities of what I might say. I have tried to ban from my minilesson vocabulary all connectors like *Oh, and by the way, Another thing,* and *Which reminds me.* The bell for the end of class will ring at the same time, regardless of how much time I have or haven't turned over to the students' own work, so I try to make my point in less than ten minutes. Then I shut up.

Sometimes, instead of lecturing, I get the students to do a short exercise together, always based, once again, on what I see them doing. If many of them are reading on a surface level, for plot only, we might do something like look at the first page of a story together and try to formulate questions that explore the possible point of the story. If they are writing memoirs and I think that many of them are treating the settings in their pieces glibly, I might show them an example of a rich exposition of setting from a memoir and then ask them to select one important place they mention and flesh out a description of that place in their notebooks, without stopping, for five minutes. They might share with a neighbor what they discovered from doing the exercise. Like minilessons, these exercises have to be finished in ten minutes, so they can get to work. What I do not do is give them topics (such as *my best friend* or *the best thing about sunsets*), because how would those be built upon their work? I also do not give them gratuitous activities like *Everybody make a web, Everybody do a Venn diagram of your novel,* or *Circle all the prepositions in your piece,* because those seem like school exercises and don't fit with my sense of what most "real" readers and writers do. Any exercise I invite them to do has to be very near the core of their work, something I could imagine wanting to do myself, in the course of an authentic reading/writing life.

When I first started teaching through a writing workshop, I usually tried to have a time at the end of every period when one or two students would read their piece to the class. I did this because, well, because I thought I had to: Calkins, Graves, and Atwell said so. Unfortunately, my students had not read any of those people's books, and they for the most part didn't want to read their heartfelt pieces in front of thirty other fifteen-year-olds. I insisted nevertheless. When no one volunteered, I went down the roll, commanding, *You have to share* something *when it's your turn.* They got mad, and I, ever insightful, realized that I was being just a tad too coercive. I began to think that in spite of all my efforts to build community, it might just be too socially dangerous for many adolescents to risk looking stupid in front of their peers. Besides, the pieces were so long that reading them aloud took up too much of the period, and I wasn't sure, even though I tried to demonstrate conference techniques as follow-up, that the listeners were getting enough out of this. For the writer, it was castor oil, still unpleasant no matter how much I protested it was good for her. For the listeners, listening to mediocre drafts badly read was usually really boring. Guiltily, secretively, I gave up "the share."

After a while, when I would have an interesting conference with a student, when we discussed something I thought might benefit the whole class, I would ask whether in the last few minutes, he would tell the others about what had been going on in his writing, perhaps what the problem had been, and what he and I had figured out as a solution. He might read relevant sections aloud. If we were focusing on reading, he might talk about the book a little bit, but focus on the strategy he had tried for reading or responding. Usually, I would pitch in to help the rest of the class see how this strategy might apply to other situations. After doing this at the end of the period for a time, I realized it was no different, really, from a minilesson, so I began sometimes doing it at the beginning of class. These two whole-class structures, the modified share and the minilesson, are now one for me, and I may decide to do them at the beginning of the period, the end, or, if both are very short (say, five minutes), the whole group comes together at both ends of the workshop.

When my students are working on drafts of writing, twice a week, on the same days each week (Tuesdays and Fridays for example), response groups meet for the last twenty minutes of class. On these days, I do not do a minilesson or anything else at the start of class, but rather get us writing as quickly as possible. For me, response groups are self-selected and permanent for a long chunk of the year. If you and I are in a group together, I can help you much better if I know something about how you have written or read other times, how you have solved similar difficulties in the past. A shared conversation, stretching across time, seems to me to be essential if work in a group is to be truly collaborative and richly inquiring. If groups have social problems—and they always will—they have to be negotiated just as they must in every other area of life. It is also important that these groups, however often they meet, do so with absolute predictability. If my group is going to do me any good, I have to be able to think, mostly unconsciously, toward my response group's meeting, anticipating what my group will say about this section or that strategy.

I instruct the response groups first to set an agenda, to figure out which one or two people will be getting help today. I forbid them to go around the circle, letting each person read her piece, and thereby avoiding conversation altogether. Rather I explain that their work together should be like my writing conferences with them. First, the writer talks about what she is trying to do. Then she might read the draft or a section of the draft. Then the group talks about how they see her doing what she says she is doing, ways she might have gotten off course, and they think together about ways to revise or proceed.

I circulate among the groups, listening in for a while and then usually trying to help them listen better to each other. Usually, they have different ideas, but they act like they are all saying the same thing. I punch up the differences in what they are saying and try to set them to arguing. I am trying to stir up the dissonance that leads to the intellectual negotiation that pushes learners to outgrow themselves, thinking together what they could not have achieved alone.

When students are reading self-chosen books as the focus of our work together, groups meet only once a week. The main purpose of groups at such times is simply sharing, recommending, disrecommending, comparing habits of reading and the problems of finding time. Other types of social arrangements for reading are described in Chapter 5.

A workshop environment exists in a rhythm between blocks of time reserved for independent student work and other times when the whole class or small groups meet together. Whatever I am teaching, whether it's reading independently, reading a shared text, or writing, the class is a workshop. At no time in the year does students' sustained work toward a chosen goal become less important. The projects that carry them through time, rooted in their past experiences and prior knowledge, are always the heart of the work. My job as a teacher is to build an environment that receives their thinking, their living, their work, and that extends what they are able to do as readers and writers.

TIME AND INTENTION

Nothing makes more of a difference in our perceptions of time than who controls it. Even as we talk about being "in control" of time, however, we know it's nonsense. Time cannot be controlled like a car or a television set. Time just *is*. What can be controlled, by ourselves or by others, is our ability or freedom to choose our actions, to formulate our own plans and carry them out. When we say our time is our own, that's what we mean—that we can follow our intentions, perform the actions that most immediately receive our heart's energy.

To live in time successfully, we have to learn to manage our own deliberate being in time. That is, we have to learn to embody in time our best intentions, to do what we mean to be doing, to live on purpose. It takes most of us our entire lives to learn this, and some of us never do. That's partly because until we are adults, people in authority so vigorously control our schedules that we never have a chance to learn to intend our own acts.

If we want to support our students as they craft their literate lives, we have to give up the authority to micromanage their work and instead return that authority to them. The time structures we create for our classrooms can be deliberate and defined but also open enough to respect students' own planning. The deadlines we do impose can be late enough in the writing process that students can still own the tempo of their work. Simply backing off from our control in this way respects the organic time of the work, the rhythms, the tempo, the duration of its phases. Literacy is supported thought, and each person's thought occupies time differently. Consider the following statements by some famous authors:

> I write very little, only for two hours in the morning, and then I stop, even if it's going well—in fact, especially if it's going well. . . .—Jean Anouilh (in Murray, 1990, p. 46)

> I put a piece of paper under my pillow, and when I could not sleep, I wrote in the dark. —Henry David Thoreau (p. 351)

41

[I] write with my watch before me, and . . . require from myself 250 words every quarter of an hour. I have found that the 250 words have been forthcoming as regularly as my watch went. —Anthony Trollope (in Murray, 1990, p. 64)

When my horse is running good, I don't stop to give him sugar. —William Faulkner (in Winokur, p. 81)

Reading these statements and others like them, we quickly conclude that the management of energy and attention in the writing process is an individual matter and is in many ways the central reality of the process. In fact, uniformity and external control are really only useful when a social purpose, such as a publication date, requires it.

A writer has most of all to learn to trust her own mind, to follow the line of thought that most directly extends from where her mind is now. She has purposefully to vary the tempo of her thought as it works with life material, speeding along the easier parts, slowing down at the places she needs to investigate in more detail. Only when she knows that she's on her own track, in hot pursuit of her own truth, can she concentrate well enough, think energetically enough, to experience the surprising flashes of understanding, the epiphanies, the moments of being—the candy that will bring her back to literacy again and again.

3

Writers Notebooks
Tools for Thinking and Living

W hen I moved from New York City to a small town in western New York State, I left behind the friends whom I had always shown my writing, the community whose ongoing conversation helped me feel I had something to say. I knew that since I was in a new teaching position and a new house, in a new area of the country, it wasn't going to be easy to keep writing. So I did two things: I set up a room of my own for writing, and I took on a big project. All my writing before had been poetry and memoir and short nonfiction; this time I decided to write a young adult novel, which I would try to get published. I'd been reading lots of adolescent literature for the past year or so, and I had developed a feeling of "I can do that." I planned to get up extra early every morning, around five, to write, but I sensed it would take more than a short piece, especially one that probably wouldn't get published, to get me out of bed.

The night before I was to launch my new adventure, I left several blank legal pads and my favorite pen on my desk. The alarm went off at five o'clock, and I rose purposefully, took a shower while thinking about my topic—a boy and his father on a hunting trip—dressed, and went into my study. It was cool and gray, and I could hear mourning doves outside: perfect. I wrote "Chapter 1" at the top of the page and waited for the novel to come out.

Nothing.

I stared at the yellow paper and blue-green lines, played with the strip of glue at the top of the pad, snapped the cap on and off my pen.

Nothing. Blank page. Blank mind. Blank in between.

The empty page stared up at me, and beneath it were four hundred more just like it, all of them waiting for me to fill them with—something. It wasn't that I was blocked: there were lots of things I could write about. But this was supposed to be a big project—it might take as much as a couple of months (it took three years to finish and still isn't published)—so I wanted to have lots to say about it, and I didn't. I tried just starting anywhere, but it was forced, and I couldn't tell how the incident fit into the bigger picture of the novel. I needed a new writing strategy. So I went and got a cup of coffee. (That's my most common strategy; it doesn't do any good, but it makes me believe for a minute that the problem has gone away.)

While stirring Equal into my coffee, I thought about the novelists I knew about, ones whose *Paris Review* interviews I'd read, writers I'd studied enough to know something about their process. I knew that some of them, like Henry James, Dostoyevski, Dickens, and Steinbeck had kept notebooks. I'd read parts of these notebooks when I had gone on single author reading binges. I'd seen some of their notebooks in New York Public Library and Columbia University library exhibitions. I also remembered that Beethoven had kept notebooks and that most artists kept sketchbooks. Since I believe that processes that work for great authors will work for anybody (if with lesser results), I wondered if a notebook would help me develop a conception of my novel, a sense of what I wanted to say and what kind of thing I wanted to make of it. The idea appealed to me. It seemed to fill the gap I sensed in my own process. How could I make something like a novel by simply starting at the beginning and writing to the end? It was far too complex, too loose and baggy a monster, to admit of such a clean, linear process: it needed stewing. Besides, Lucy Calkins and my other friends at the Teachers College Writing Project in New York City were exploring writers notebooks in their own writing and as classroom tools, so keeping one would allow me to conduct a separate but parallel experiment.

I went back into my study and rummaged around until I found a composition book with a marbleized cover, placed it on top of my pile of legal pads, wrote "Novel Notes" in the blank provided for "Course Title," opened it, and started writing. It worked: it became a place for thinking through some of the issues on which my novel would obsess: fathers and sons, gender roles, self-definition, patriarchy, and revolution. I read everything I could about fathers and sons and responded to it in the notebook; I gathered lots of memories about time I spent with my father, my grandfather, and other people's fathers; I reflected on events with my own boy that seemed to define us as father and son; I tried on different voices and techniques; I clipped and pasted in articles about gender, especially how men get to be men; I outlined the plot about fifty different ways; I explored different possible points of attack. I wrote for a year in my notebooks (by now there were three), and when I came back to Chapter 1, I wasn't blank anymore. I had a lot more confidence in what I was trying to do. Also, I knew that if something went wrong in the writing or if I hit a snag, I could use the notebook to work it through. It was, during the process of drafting and revision, my workbench.

Drafting and revising—a writing classroom

At the same time I was starting my notebook, my eighth-, tenth-, and twelfth-grade students were beginning their writing workshops. I liked the idea of their getting started writing on the first day of school, which I'd read about in the work of Nancie Atwell and Mary Ellen Giacobbe, so, as I had done for several years, I explained how to brainstorm a list of topics—"just anything that comes to mind, it doesn't have to be a good idea, just an idea, even bad ideas can lead to good ideas"—narrow that list to a few of the more appealing topics, and then choose one and get started. And they tried. Some of them had trouble coming up with any topics. I commiserated. "I know it's hard. It's always hard for me, too." Others found a topic and wrote it, as if a title, at the top of a page: "My Trip to Florida," "How I Learned to Ski," "When I Stuck My Tongue to the Fencepost." And then they stared at the page. I walked around, exhorting them with expressivistic advice: "Don't think, just write. It'll come if you just get started. Let your pen lead your brain." All that true stuff that is so unconvincing when you're starting to write something you believe is going to be judged somewhere down the line. Here, on the first day of school, though I explained that they'd have plenty of time to revise and make it better, they were writing for a reader—me, the teacher—who their prior school experience taught them was likely to be unfriendly.

Somehow, though, mostly because I was the boss and I told them to, they got started. I walked around and conferred with them, hoping to help them see the potential for meaning in their pieces, hoping to get them to reflect on their experiences rather than merely report them, hoping to engage them in some critical thinking and conversation with me and others about the ideas and values they hinted at in their nascent drafts. I wanted to confer in ways that would change the way they looked at the givens in their life, not merely suggest that they add some details or clean up some diction. Sometimes I tried to help them reconceive the piece in terms of what it meant to them, but since their sense of the topic often stopped at "I'm writing it because it happened and you told us to write," I got blank stares. Other times I tried to get them to abandon the topic and start something else. This met more with hostility, since they had already written, they said, for four days on this, and this is what they wanted to write. So I compromised and resorted to eliciting details, trying to help narrow the focus or clarify the sequencing, and then moved on to the next student.

"How's it going, Craig?"

"Fine." (Long pause—"wait time.")

"How's your piece coming?"

"Fine." (Long pause—wait time Craig was still happy to leave unfilled.)

"Tell me about it."

"Oh, it's about this summer. Workin'."

Though I believed that Craig should talk to me about the draft, not that I should just read it, I finally gave up and skimmed the damn thing over his shoulder:

This summer I worked at Pizza Hut. It was a real good experience for me. In this composition I would like to tell you about some.

When I first started out in May the 25, I was in training. The first chore I wanted to do was meet everyone. I had to meet about twenty people. Some of them were real nice and some were not so nice.

The first thing they had me doing was washing dishes. . . .

But after about three months of that they started to train me on how to make pizzas. . . .

When I first started out for the first four weeks I worked five days a week for thirty hours. . . .

One major thing that did happen to the business when I was working their this summer. It was on July fifth the manager of the store moved away. Then we got our new manager his name was Kyle. He is really nice. . . .

There was one special thing that I did like about working their and that is my friends came in a lot. . . .

It was on August the 1st that we found out we could have a softball team. . . .

It was on July the 30 that we found out that we were going to have six people leave us. . . .

The rest of the summer went alright nothing special happen. But since I'm back to school I only work four days a week for twenty hours.

"Craig, one thing I notice is that you've done a pretty good job of dividing your topic into chunks and organizing those." I was groping for something to praise, just to get the conference moving—and I really could tell that organization, of the type he'd been taught writing reports and essays in previous English classes, was a focus of his attention. But it seemed like such a trivial thing to talk about in this writing conference, somehow, especially since the more important problem was that Craig hadn't attempted to ask bigger questions that might lead to an interpretation of his experience, some meaning.

"Why was working at Pizza Hut important? Why did it matter to you?"

"Because I had to have a job."

"Yeah, but since you chose to write about it, it seems like it must have meant something to you." I had now resorted to the creation of meaning by insistence. "I mean, one thing I see is that you seem to focus on all the people you worked with there. Like it wasn't the job so much as being part of the group, having a place in this community of working people. What do you think?"

"Well, yeah. There's the part about meeting the people and the old manager and the new manager and my friends coming in and the baseball team and the people who left and the people who replaced them."

"Yeah. That's what you're mostly talking about here. Not about really doing the job with your hands, but the people you were with."

"Yeah."

"So maybe when you revise this, you could focus more on that, let that be your point, since it seems to be in there anyway. You know, a lot of the time, writers take the facts about something and then say, *Is there some big idea that can make this come together in a meaningful way?* It seems to me that's something you can learn to do, in this piece and in the pieces you write later."

Pretty good conference, I thought. Not great, since I talked way too much, but better than most of the others this period. From that desperate lunge about organization to a pretty smart reading of what Craig was trying to say. He seemed pretty eager to get started, too, when I left. Maybe I'm not such a rotten teacher after all—maybe.

Two days later, Craig's piece was in my "in" box. Recopied. A little neater. No significant revision.

Well, what was he going to do, even assuming he did understand my point? Add the heavy thinking at the end? I, of course, had in mind he might rewrite the whole piece, reconceive it in terms of the theme we'd discussed in conference. But Craig was a senior, tracked nonacademically, writing about a job very like the one he would take after graduation. Why should he break a sweat revising in a way he wasn't sure he knew how to do?

Craig's narrative at least had some potential for a rich meaning. Other kids wrote pieces that were even bleaker. I began to think of Dan and Mark and Brenda as thirteen-year-old Samuel Becketts, able to bring me to my knees in awe at the nothingness of existence. Pubescent postmodern minimalists.

Then, I started thinking about my own notebook and talking to my friends at the Teachers College Writing Project, and I began to wonder whether writers notebooks might be a tool to help my students collect data about their lives and to begin to reach for meaning in advance of writing a draft. I didn't really know what that would mean yet, in a classroom, but my understanding of composition theory, my knowledge of how other writers write, my awareness that people I respected were trying notebooks in classrooms, and my reading of my own life as a writer indicated it might be worth a shot. So, about a month into the year, I set a deadline for all pieces currently in process, a sort of watershed day, after which we would amend the workshop, revise the draft of English class.

While they were finishing their previous pieces, I turned my attention in whole-class minilessons to the idea of the writers notebook. I asked them to choose one and have it with them when they arrived in class on Monday. Taking my cue from Lucy Calkins (Calkins with Harwayne 1990), I explained that, as much as possible, the physical fact of the notebook ought to reflect the personality of the person who writes in it. "You're going to be carrying these notebooks around with you all the time, so if you want it to fit in a purse or backpack, you should consider that. Get something that would make you want to write. If you want a pretty, clothbound journal, get that. For me, those seem almost too nice for my messy thoughts. If you think a spiral notebook fits your thoughts better, that'll be fine. I'm using this marble-covered composition book for mine. I like the way it feels almost but not quite like a bound book. And I like the size of the pages. They're also easy to find in stores. Now—how many of you think you might lose your notebook before you get out of the building the first day you have it? Ed, raise your hand. Yes, you will, don't even try it. Since that would be a disaster—just the most terrible thing that could happen—you need to get a loose-leaf binder— maybe something like this—which will stay in here, and also a "traveling note- book" with detachable three-holed sheets, to go around your life with you. If you don't like that idea, think of another one and talk to me about it. That way, you'll get the portability a real notebook needs and also have the cumulation of all your work here in the classroom rather than strewn about the western New York countryside. Okay, now tell the person sitting beside you what you think you want to get for your notebook." At first, that's all I said. I didn't want to start muddying things with explanations about how to keep the notebook, since they weren't ready for that yet. I tried not to say too much at once.

The next day, I started explaining to them, even though they weren't going to write in the notebook yet, what it was and how it fit into the writing and reading we'd already been doing. "Do any of you take art? You know how a lot of artists carry sketchbooks? They carry them around in case they see something they want to remember and use later in a painting or sculpture or something. If they see a certain interesting face, they sketch it in there. If they see some bones lying on the ground in an interesting pattern, they sketch them, so that they can use that image later. But also, carrying that sketchbook around causes them to see more, to notice things they might otherwise miss. Melissa, you keep one, don't you? Would you bring that in tomorrow so we can talk about how you use it for your thinking and painting?

"In some ways a writers notebook works in the same way. Writers carry them around all the time, to jot things that occur to them, to describe things they see, to copy things they read, to write down funny or interesting or beautiful things they hear people say. They collect things in their notebook, things from their lives. If you've ever written a research paper and you had to keep note cards, you might think of a writers notebook as note cards for your whole life, a place where you can collect research and thinking about you and all that's around you. You see something, and you throw it in there. You overhear a conversation on the bus, and you get it down, word for word, just in case you might use it some day. It's like the box you used to have—maybe some of you still do—that contained your treasures, the things in your life that meant the most."

In the next day's little talk, I went on to explain that a notebook is also a place for thinking, not just recording. Sometimes, even if nothing prompted it, writers just sit down and start writing, start thinking on paper, accepting whatever comes. As William Stafford says, "To get started I will accept anything that occurs to me. Something always occurs, of course, to any of us. We can't keep from thinking. Maybe I have to settle for an immediate impression. . . . If I put down something, that thing will help the next thing come, and I'm off. If I let the process go on, things will occur to me that were not at all in my mind when I started. These things, odd or trivial as they may be, are somehow connected. And if I let them string out, surprising things will happen . . . I am headlong to discover" (p. 18). I explained to my students that when they write in their notebooks, they won't always know what they are going to say before they say it, and that's a good thing— it's just the sort of thinking/writing that belongs in a notebook.

I read to them from Peter Elbow's *Writing With Power,* William Stafford's *Learning the Australian Crawl* and *You Must Revise Your Life,* Donald Murray's *Write to Learn* and *Expecting the Unexpected,* Toby Fulwiler's *The Journal Book,* and Natalie Goldberg's *Writing Down the Bones.* Goldberg writes:

Our bodies are garbage heaps: we collect experience, and from the decomposition of the thrown-out eggshells, spinach leaves, coffee grinds, and old steak bones of our minds come nitrogen, heat and very fertile soil. Out of this fertile soil bloom our poems and stories. But this does not come all at once. It takes time. Continue to turn over the organic details of your life until some of them fall through the garbage of discursive thoughts to the solid ground of black soil. Rake over your shallow thinking and turn it over. If we continue to work with this raw matter, it will draw us deeper and deeper into ourselves. . . . (p. 14)

During the next couple of days, I tried to show them the difference between a writers notebook, a journal, and a diary. To some extent, I pushed the difference, since it's really a matter of semantics. It seemed to me, though, that if they had written in journals before, it had probably involved mostly summarizing present goings-on in their lives. The word *diary* seemed even more to imply the recording of this day's events. This was precisely the type of writing-what-you-already-know I wanted to avoid in the notebooks, so I hoped that the semantic delineation would help. Moreover, it seemed that journals and diaries are ends in themselves—you write in your journal in order to have written in your journal and in order to benefit from that thinking. But writers notebook—or Murray's term, *daybook*—seemed to imply a place to collect *toward* pieces of writing, which was the point. The notebooks were to serve as launchpads and workbenches for larger projects, which would be written for particular purposes and audiences. I explained this to the kids, a little at a time, but I realized that changing their thinking about writing was going to take a lot more than a new word for materials.

Helping students get started with notebooks

When the day came to launch into notebooks, the kids, with a couple of predictable exceptions (Ed said he'd bought one but already lost it), walked into class with the squeaky new notebooks they had chosen: it smelled almost like another first day of school, only sweatier. I suddenly realized, looking at all that paper stacked in front of them, that if it was hard for them to feel they had something to say with a single sheet of paper in front of them, it would be even harder with a hundred pages of empty notebook staring them in the face. They needed strategies for getting started, especially since notebook writing involved beginning anew (though not necessarily finding a new topic) a lot more often than writing one long-term piece did. I knew one important way to let kids rehearse for writing was to get them talking. Shelley Harwayne at Teachers College had told me about some storytelling she'd done with kids, so I decided to try something similar. I thought of a cluster of memories from my childhood, ones I thought most of the kids could relate to, so I could jump-start the talking.

"Did you ever sit around with a friend," I began, "and you start telling some story, and about halfway through you see your friend's eyes light up because your story has just reminded him of a story. And then he waits until you're done so he can tell his story. And then his story reminds you of a story, and you try to hold on to it while you listen to him so you don't forget the story you want to tell. It seems to me that conversations between friends, if you're just hanging out and talking, tend to go like that, sort of swapping stories. And pretty soon you have this line of about thirteen stories just waiting their turn to come out, like skydivers in their plane. I want to see if we can get some of that going in here today."

Everyone looked around nervously, self-consciously.

"Don't worry, I'm going to go first, and you just see if my story reminds you of anything, and we'll go from there. I'm not even sure mine is a story, really—more like just a memory. When I was little, we lived next door to this vacant lot, and that's where we used to play. It was our baseball diamond and our football field and our combat zone for playing war. It was also the site of all our forts, and we built lots of them. Some of them weren't really forts but clubhouses or something else, but we were always making places in that lot. Once, someone had mowed the field, and all of this tall grass was lying around like hay.

"So my friend Jeff said, 'This grass is so long, we could build a clubhouse out of it.' I immediately got a picture in my head of the first little pig's straw house, but since I didn't know of any wolves in the area, it sounded okay. We started piling the grass into long mounds, about a foot high in the shape of different hallways and rooms.

"'Hey, Jeff,' I called out, 'These walls are too short. They have to be taller so we can put a roof on.'

"Jeff called back, 'We'll worry about that later.' So we built all these halls and rooms for different purposes: one for parties, one for games, one for comic books. After we had finished, we sat in one room for a few minutes—and then went on to something else. We never went back to it to play and we never fixed the walls. I guess the point was just to make up the place."

I went on to tell about another slapdash fort we made from the scrap lumber we found at a construction site, and I finished with the story of our last and most ambitious idea for a clubhouse.

"We decided we wanted to make a set of tunnels and caves, kind of like they had on *Batman*. [I was talking about the television show; they were thinking about the movie.] I really believed this could work, and it was going to be sooo coooool. So we went and got my dad's shovel from the garage and started digging. Now this is San Antonio in the summer, so it's about 105 degrees out and we're digging in this dry, rocky, chalky dirt we have there. We probably worked for a couple of hours on it, our faces all red. Only that vision of the Batcave kept me going.

"My mom came out and frowned when we told her what we were doing. She said, 'You can't go into tunnels underground. The earth will fall in on you.'

"We hit her with Batman, which seemed to put her in her place. Anyway, she needn't have worried, since our hole was only about two feet wide and eight inches deep, and we were getting very sweaty. Besides, we didn't have a good track record with forts."

I stopped there, and looked around the room.

"So—does that make any of you think of a story from your own life?"

Several kids shifted in their seats, looking down at their desktops. Sarah and Jean rolled their eyes at each other across the room. An adolescent silence fell over the group. I forced myself to keep smiling, though I was getting nervous. This was not how Shelley said it went with fourth graders. But I was not about to start talking again, just because they were thinking and not speaking. It might cure my own silence, but it would do nothing to fill their silence, which was what we were here to do. So I started counting to myself, to keep busy, singing the *Jeopardy* song, silently reciting poetry.

"Are we supposed to be thinking of a fort story?"

"No. I don't know. Anything. Whatever comes to mind is fine."

Finally, some brave someone said, "I've got one," and began humbly to tell a story from her life.

A couple of other kids sketched out stories to the whole group, but very little energy was flowing behind the talk. I decided that the big group was inhibiting them: there was too much for adolescents to lose if they looked stupid in front of such a crowd. So I said, "Okay, now that we've got some stories going in your head, get into small groups and tell each other stories. Just let the stories you hear remind you of your own."

They seemed to explode into their small groups. Within seconds they were in seven groups of about four each, with one person in each group animatedly telling a story. I should have remembered from the beginning that secondary students do better in small groups than in whole-group work, especially when there's a social risk, a risk of being embarrassed.

I walked around and listened, occasionally joining in when someone's story reminded me of something. "Now that you've had some time to talk through some memories, you probably have several stories sort of lined up in your head, waiting to be told. That's good; it's a feeling of being full of your own life, and that's probably an important feeling for writers to have. Let's get writing in our notebooks now. You can write a story you've already told, or something you haven't said yet, or maybe something else is on your mind. Write fast, and let whatever you think take shape on the page. You just had a chance to talk, so I don't want any more talking; this is silent writing time. Any questions? Okay, I'm going to write too, so don't bother me." I sat down and started writing in my notebook and didn't look up for several minutes. When I did, no one was staring at a blank page, and no one was whining about having nothing to say.

Adding variety to writers notebooks

It went so well in all my classes that I got a little worried. They loved this memory writing, which was good, but I hoped they didn't get the idea that's all you do in a notebook, which would be bad. I wanted them to know that lots of kinds of thought, not just memory, can go into a notebook. I realized there were many ways I could have launched the notebooks and any one of them would probably have defined for the kids what notebooks were. They had been in school long enough to know that you don't diverge from the teacher's instructions. Most of them had only the year before been using notebooks to keep vocabulary lists. They were not used to thinking they were supposed to invent new things to put in there. I decided that over the next couple of weeks my main purpose would be to introduce them to the array of possibilities in writing to think.

I taught them about freewriting first, by simply naming it and defining it: "You write as much as you can as fast as you can for a certain amount of time, say ten minutes, without allowing yourself to stop. The pen just keeps moving, even when you don't feel like it or don't know what to say." Then I demonstrated on the chalkboard, truly without allowing myself to plan what I was going to say. When I got to the bottom of the board, I kept free-associating orally for a few minutes, so they'd get the idea of following a train of thought. Then, without further instructions or explanations, I said, "All right; you try it. Ready, set, go" and they were off. Many produced more text in that eight minutes than they ever had in their lives. I walked around and exhorted those who wanted to quit. Later, I would freewrite along with them, but now, while it was new and a little scary, I needed to stay on nudge patrol. "Keep writing, don't stop. *You can't be done.*" Afterward, I had them talk to each other about how it felt and about what surprised them. The whole thing took about fifteen minutes, after which we started our regular daily writing in notebooks. How to get started and what to write about was now their problem to solve, either going on with something they'd written about in freewriting or shifting to something else. I conferred with individual kids, asking them and myself how their understanding of writing as a mode of thought and of notebooks as a tool was evolving.

In the time that otherwise would have been used for a minilesson, I had them freewrite like this several times in the first few weeks of working in notebooks, and they learned that, to write, you don't always have to come up with a topic first. Then, when I was conferring during the rest of the period, while they were writing what and how they chose to in their notebooks, if a student was hung up on the blank page, I could say, Well, all right, look at the clock, start freewriting, and don't stop until the big hand is on the eight. I'll be back around then to see how it went for you. My purpose in teaching freewriting was to give them a useful strategy for notebook writing, so I expected them to use it when it might help.

Since the kids were writing in notebooks and not for readers, minilessons on qualities of good writing, revision strategies, or editing would have been inappropriate. They needed to learn the kinds of thinking on paper that might fill a notebook, so that's what I tried to teach in the first few minutes of every class. But rather than just talking about it, I often devised exercises that would give them tactile experiences of different ways of writing to think. When I wanted them to know that the slowed-down muscular thinking that writing is could help them see the world more vividly, I asked them to write for a long time about some single object. First I demonstrated orally with an eraser from the chalk rail, then I sent them outside to find a brick or a tile or a shoe, to see it with fresh eyes as if they didn't know what it was, and to describe how it really looked. They liked being able to go outside, and when they came back in, they played a guessing game, reading only the description and having others try to identify the object. Another time, I sent them out into the hallways of the school to spy and eavesdrop and record what they saw and heard.

Though these exercises were more directive than I would be when the students were writing for readers, I explained that such activities are not ends in themselves but strategies for getting past the blank page or out of the rut of diary-type entries. I didn't give exercises that involved a particular topic or that seemed gratuitous or merely clever. I just wanted to help them develop some writerly habits of living, such as a wide-awake way of seeing, a curiosity about the lives being lived all around, and an awareness of hundreds of life stories worth telling. The activities only filled the first fifteen minutes or so of the period; the rest of the time they wrote in their notebooks in whatever way they wanted. I certainly didn't want the notebooks to become like workbooks with very long blanks, where they primarily followed my agenda; however, freeing the hand and the eye and the mind paradoxically involves training them to be free. Just cutting loose all bonds and shouting "Write wild, write free, write with ease!" may send some writers scurrying for safety in boredom and actually end up being more inhibiting. They need to know that we have in mind for them to *do* something, to use strategies of thinking and writing and to outgrow those strategies by inventing new ones. As Maxine Greene points out, freedom doesn't always mean freedom from; it might mean freedom to. Adolescents probably have to *learn* to play in English class, to improvise, to open their awareness to what is inside them and what is outside them. I catalogued some of the different types of entries I had seen them make so far and posted the list (see Figure 3–1) on the wall, just for a few days, to encourage more variety in their notebooks. It may not be obvious what some of the items mean, since the list came out of the dialogue and language of one particular classroom. Naturally, each classroom has to find its own list of possibilities for writers notebooks and then must continually outgrow that list, not be limited to it.

The kids had only been writing in their notebooks for a week or so when I began encouraging them to read the whole notebook (or chunks of it) frequently. One day, I began class by saying I wanted everyone to begin writing by reading their notebooks and pausing to write new thoughts in dialogue with themselves in the white space or on facing pages. Many writers found they had not left space for this kind of layered writing, so I encouraged them to learn that new habit. When they had finished writing back to themselves, most students started new entries by revisiting topics they had broached in earlier entries. As time went on, rereading became my most frequent suggestion for a getting-started strategy. This recursive thinking process seems to me central to the whole idea of writers notebooks, in addition to laying the foundation for the larger projects that writers will build from their notebooks later on. (See the next chapter.)

- memories
- reflections—self-definition
- noticings in the world—observations
- wonderings—questions
- speculation about meaning of events
- reading response
- snippets of language
- clippings
- pictures
- images that stick in the mind
- lists
- experiments with really long and really short sentences
- ideas for stories—kernels
- family stories
- dreams
- descriptions
- experiments with genre or style
- wanderings from freewrite—free association
- revision of thinking
- information
- quotations
- interviews
- sensory impressions
- copied text
- caught poetry and found poetry
- decision making
- overheard conversations
- imagined dialogue
- conversing with oneself
- plans
- celebration of victories
- reflections of writing pieces
- personal descriptions/profiles
- writing again about something from an old entry

FIG. 3–1:   *Some possible types of notebook entries.*

Boosting students' use of notebooks outside class

I had asked the kids to carry the notebooks around with them all day and to write frequently at home and in other places they happened to be: on the bus, waiting at the dentist's office, in study hall. I fantasized that these notebooks would become so overwhelmingly important to them that they would want to write in them continually, plotting a map of their life's thoughts. I was not quite astonished when it didn't work out that way. They usually liked writing in the notebooks in class, but it just didn't seem to cross their mind outside class. The fact is, they had plenty of homework they had to do for other classes, and since they didn't have to do English, most of them didn't. Though I didn't relish packing their lives with one more adult's agenda, I could see that the notebooks were losing their walking-around-life-with-eyes-wide-open sketchbook quality or rather that they'd never achieved it. So, in spite of my reservations, I assigned it for homework: five entries a week, two of which had to be at least a page long and should take at least half an hour to write. There was only the standard moaning and groaning, to my surprise. I hadn't figured out yet when I was going to collect them, so I told the kids it was going to be a surprise spot-check. The old mystification-of-power trip.

A couple of days later, I interviewed several kids throughout the day about how it felt to have the notebook for homework. First, they made the obligatory sourpuss face. I said, "What? Is it just another homework assignment, like you have your algebra, your biology, your history, and your writers notebook?"

Lawrence said, "Well, not really. I do my notebook last, so if I really get into something, I can keep going longer if I want. I don't know how long it's going to take. The other things, I have to do like numbers one through ten or whatever.

And something else, when I'm on the way home, my brother drives so we don't talk. I just look out the window, and now I've started looking to see if there's something I can write about in my notebook."

Bingo. Lawrence was seeing his world differently because he was keeping a notebook, and that was the point. Carrying his notebook helped him pay more attention to himself and his environment, to value the fine fibre of his own experience, to see ordinary days as veins of meaning ripe for mining. It was an achievement, this caring; and it did not happen just because I hoped it would. Building my expectations into predictable classroom ways of working helped most of my students find a more literate life.

Early on, the entries they made at home revealed their writers notebooks to be baskets for collecting whatever thinking or noticing they did while living their lives. A John Lennon song says, "Life is what happens to you when you're busy making other plans," and writing became something like that for my students, something they did while they were thinking about something else.

Carly wrote, "I am going to write down different sounds I here. Furnace running, cars going by, people talking, radios, water running, toilet flushing, clock ticking, dog barking, people tapping there feet, whistling, turning of book pages, old houses creeking, hammering, chewing of gum, people yawning. These are a few different sounds that I here when I was at a slumber party at my friends house."

Marey wrote, "I am looking at the clouds settling in the valley. To me it looks like the end of the world, where the other part of the world starts on the other side. The trees are wet, it rained but every morning rain or not the clouds settle in the valley. In one place on our bus ride the clouds hover just above us. Clouds are strange. They have their own mystery for us to wonder about."

John put the following rambling stream of thought in his notebook while he was watching television:

I'm watching this tv show called Tour of Duty. It is about Vietnam. It goes through the war with this one group of soldiers. It shows how cruel and messy the war was. I don't watch it for all the violence and blood. I'm watching because it shows the war through the eyes of the soldiers not the government's eyes. There's alot of killing. But killing is wierd to me. To animals it's a part of life, a way of survival. But to people it is bad. For animals it is a way of population control. Disease is too. But people fight them every step of the way. It was meant to be a perfect balance. Maybe that's why the world is going to hell. Are we screwed up or is life screwed up. Something must be wrong or else everything would be perfect. Why do people have to be so nosy. Everything that comes along we have to figure out and conqure. Thus causing invension, putting ourselves on a pedastle. Do we really have to be superior. They persicuted Hitler for trying to create the so-called "perfect race." But isn't that what we are trying to do as people. Putting ourselves above all else. Putting ourselves before the perfect balance. Screw evolution. Let's get back to the way it was supposed to be. Putting ourselves on the same level as all else. Trying to solve the problems we created. How stupid can anything be. Why make all of these problems that make life so hard. Are we that board with life that we have to make problems to solve. Or don't we know the point of solving a problem is so there isn't a problem anymore. Why don't we get down to the whole point of life which is survival. Get back to real life which is the unwritten part of Life, liberty, and pursuit of happiness. We have to be showered with luxuries. But the only real luxury there *is* is survival. We messed the world up past the point of fixing. So we might as well end the world and hope and pray that the next people don't screw up like we did when we upset the perfect balance.

Once the kids got rolling on writing throughout their lives, they and I could better see the patterns in their day-to-day thinking. Two of Wendy's entries, which appeared on consecutive days, illustrate what it is like to be fourteen better than five textbooks on adolescent development:

12/17   I think I've made up my decision about the world. I think it depends on the way you make the world. If you hate and despise the world and everybody in it, you're going to have a very hard life. I think I'm going to try to like most people.

12/18   Today we had no school, but I was sort of disappointed because it seems whenever there's no school because of snow or ice, my hair looks good and I have the perfect outfit. It never fails.

Improving the quality of notebook entries

Now that they were getting into the habit of writing in a notebook, we could work on getting better at making thoughtful entries that would be potentially useful in their writing lives. I kept talking about thoughtful writing and sharing examples of it from students' work, from my own writing, and from published work. I also made several structural decisions calculated to instill an air of thoughtfulness into the room.

First, I decided to have them respond to literature in their notebook rather than in a separate "reading journal." I have never kept separate journals for reading and life, and I can't imagine Virginia Woolf pausing after reading a poem to ask herself, *Now should this go in my reading journal or my writers notebook?* If we were trying to build literate lives, then my students' reading should feed the thinking in their notebook, which would feed the writing, which should change their lives, which should affect what they bring to their reading, and so on. Since I was at this point in the year not trying to monitor their reading or not-reading of book-length works, there wasn't even a management reason to have them report to me in the form of a reading log. So they didn't; instead, they used pieces of literature, like pieces of life, as points of departure for thinking. Often, we would read a short story together, or an editorial, a news article, a poem, even another student's notebook entry, and I asked them to freewrite from the gut in response. Some of their best, most interesting, most thoughtful notebook entries came in response to literature. After all, they were getting a boost up from some good writers.

Still some kids struggled, writing every day what happened in soccer practice, until I finally realized I was asking them to write something they'd never read. With any type of writing, kids need a schema for what they're trying to make, which can only be built through reading experience. Trouble was, I couldn't just pick up an anthology of writers notebooks at the bookstore, and even if I could, it would now have been published for readers and therefore no longer be the expressive writing (writing for the writer) I wanted them to do. Truly to appreciate a writers notebook, moreover, they would have to be able to discuss it with the writer. It dawned on me that the most important source for their knowledge about keeping a notebook might be me—my own notebook. I started talking to them about how I kept my notebook, when I wrote in it, how it felt to sit down with it, the variety of entry types I had found, and how it was useful in my writing. I read to them from my notebook and made overheads of entries from it, and when I came across a new insight there about writing or myself as a writer, I photocopied the entry—doodles and cross-outs and all—and handed it out as part of a minilesson. I tried not to let my sharing of some of my notebook affect the authenticity of what I wrote there, but eventually it did; there were things in my life I couldn't open up to thirteen-year-olds. I ended up keeping a notebook at school, which I wrote in with my classes, and leaving my notebooks for my novel and other writing at home. It was a necessary compromise.

In writing conferences, the pressure was off me and the kids to "fix up" everything they wrote, and that allowed us to talk about content. What is important about this, to you? How can you think about it in a way to make it meaningful? Can you press at it a bit to make it more significant than you first realized it to be? What other events or issues in your life are connected to this one? Have you ever read anything that might make you think differently about this? In these conferences, I felt myself trying to teach the habit of reaching for meaning from even the smallest, most ordinary moments of life, and in so doing, I was reaching further than I ever had before in literacy education.

Other conferences focused on ways keeping a notebook was changing the writer's life. I don't mean huge emotional upheavals where the kid fell to the ground, shouting *I see the light!* but rather tiny adjustments made necessary by the requirements of constantly writing in response to life. Guillerme had taken to staring out the window of the bus on the way to school, allowing the passing landscape to filter through his eyes and into his notebook with entries about different kinds of fences, the leaves changing colors, and how free everyone outside this bus seemed. Problems with peers often sent Spencer to his notebook. Whenever he felt people were looking down on him, he would argue, privately, to himself, his own superiority, flexing his intellectual muscles in the mirror.

I often reflected that writing in notebooks, simple and unassuming as it was, allowed my students to plant writing more deeply into the bedrock of their experience than the almost constant writing for an audience they had done before. For example, Marlee wrote the entry shown in Figure 3–2, and Candice wrote:

Today on the farm we finished off a field of corn that we picked. I've always liked to help unload a wagon of shelled corn. I climb up in and keep pushing the corn out at the bottom where my brother is and [he] keeps the corn from falling on the ground. Today on this nice fall day I stood on all the corn and looked around at the farm, house, woods, and the world in general and I realized how lucky I was. I really can't picture my life without the farm. Everything would be so different. I would hate to live like all my friends. Such an awful life. People act like I'm held back from activities and my social life because of the farm. If that's what it would take to keep the farm in the family and to keep it as it is, I would sacrifice anything, and I mean it. Farm life is so wonderful, I love it dearly. I really don't [know] how I'd survive if I didn't have my cows and my "homey farm" kind of attitude surrounding me.

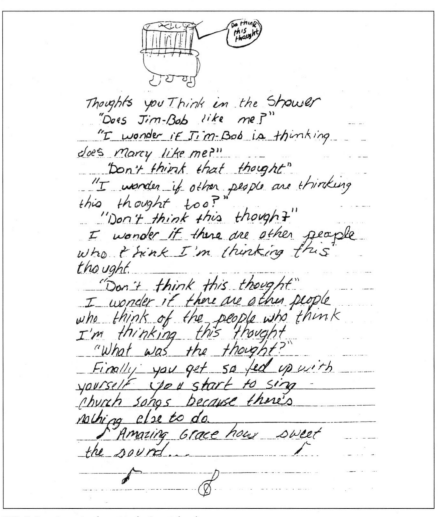

FIG. 3 2: *An entry from Marlee's notebook.*

But of course the farms in this country are dropping like flies, and there's not many of my kind left. I'm not sure how long our own farm will exist even though we are out of debt. If people only knew what we are going through. But nobody knows or cares. It's damn sad!!

These and earlier examples in this chapter are some of the good entries, but they are, of course, only part of the story. I've not included many bad notebook entries, because they make bad reading. I can't honestly pretend, however, that all the notebooks were great or that my life as a teacher was an unbroken string of inspiring successes. In fact, at the beginning, many of the notebooks seemed atrocious when I judged them against my high expectations, and I was depressed and discouraged and again convinced I was the worst teacher in the world. Eventually, like every other teacher of literacy, I had to learn to accept the kids' approximations toward a literate behavior, in this case the keeping of writers notebooks, just as kindergarten teachers rejoice in their little kids' breakthroughs toward using the alphabet to represent the sounds they hear in their words. That's not to say I just left kids the way they were: I expected growth and demanded it. But I began by asking, What is the writer's current apprehension (or misapprehension) of notebooks, writing to think, and purposes for writing? Then I tried to name that for the writer, by saying something like, You seem to understand X about writing in your notebook. And then I tried to extend the writer's range of possible work in thinking. The teaching always began with accepting and responding to what the writer had accomplished rather than expressing anxiety over what she hadn't.

I stumbled around with the question of what to do with share time. Once or twice, I asked for volunteers to read from their notebooks, and they all looked at me as if I'd asked them to undress. A couple of times, I invited particular kids to read especially successful entries from their notebooks aloud, and they did, and I think the class learned something from it. But later, when it was time to try to make publishable projects from the work in notebooks, they didn't use those great entries. Why should they? They'd already published them. Eventually I came to see the end of the period as a time for talking about what we as writers were trying and learning in our notebooks rather than as a time for reading our writing aloud. About twice a week, we had these conversations as a whole class, so that I could talk to everyone at once. Two other periods each week, every Tuesday and Thursday, response groups met for the last fifteen minutes of class. On these days, I did either an especially short minilesson or none at all. Whether in small or whole groups, I began these times by throwing out a question:

- Did anyone try a new type of notebook entry today?

- Choose a sentence you think you wrote well and read it aloud. Then tell why you think it's good writing.

- How did you get started today, and how does that strategy differ from what you have done before?

- Did anyone have a hard time keeping on writing today? What did you do about it?

- What kinds of words appear in your writing when you start moving from "this happened" reporting into more reflective thinking?

Keeping our share time focused on writerly conversations like these, rather than reading aloud what we wrote today, both preserved the kids' need for some privacy and also helped us continually view writing as a process of thinking and decision making.

Evaluating writers notebooks

One day, in about the eighth week of school, one of those ominous memos from the principal appeared in my box, requesting to see me during my prep period that day. So far that year, I hadn't had any trouble with administrators (and it was early November already!), but somehow I could smell it coming. He was in his nice-guy, we're-all-in-this-together mode when I walked in. A parent had called and demanded to know why there was no weekly quiz grade for my class. She made her son plot his grades on a graph hung inside his closet door, and with no daily or weekly worksheets coming home for English, there was a conspicuous absence of one red line. I explained to the principal about the notebooks and the reader-response work and how they were all leading toward major literary projects. I read to him from a couple of great notebooks I "just happened" to have brought along. Still, he asked, couldn't I just give a short quiz every Friday?

On what?

Vocabulary or spelling or something.

No. I said if he wanted periodic grades, I would give them. But they would have to be meaningful within the classes' purposes. I would not lie to my students about the nature of literacy.

That's how I came to develop a way of grading the notebooks, queasy as I was about it.

I stomped back to my room, stopping by friends' rooms to gripe on the way. I got a cup of coffee. For a few minutes I paced. Then I walked up to the pile of notebooks I had collected the day before. I flipped through them and found I could pretty easily evaluate them, in a coarse way: this one's great, that one's crap, that one's okay, this one's got nothing in it. I realized that I could, since I had to, pretty easily grade them. A for the great ones, B for the okay ones, C for the barely so-so ones, D for the ones that showed little effort or no improvement, and F if the kid hadn't done anything. I asked myself how I knew which was which, to try to uncover the criteria by which I was evaluating. First, I thought, the notebook needed a bunch of entries, at least a long one or several short ones for each class, plus five (two of which had to be longer) for homework. So volume was one criterion. However, plenty of kids had enough entries, but they were monotonous, always about who broke up with whom or some other summary of the day's activities, which indicated they were using schemas from diary writing rather than understanding the collecting that can go into writers notebooks. The best notebooks had different entries about lots of different topics and also in lots of the different "notebook genres" I described above. So variety was another criterion. But a notebook could have hundreds of entries with plenty of variety and remain so superficial that the student seems not to be thinking at all, but rather cranking out entries on automatic pilot. This particularly tended to be true in honors classes, where the kids learn with great facility to fill in the blanks in the required way, but none of it ever means anything to them. So thoughtfulness was another criterion. These criteria—volume, variety, and thoughtfulness—didn't seem vague or subjective to me. The first two seemed, in fact, objective, and the third—well, it seemed to me that as a literacy professional I should be able to recognize and describe thoughtfulness.

I set up a class rotation, so that I was collecting every kid's notebook once every two weeks. I never wrote in them—these were writers notebooks, not dialogue journals—and I only permitted myself one- or two-word comments on a sticky note, along with the letter grade. The purpose of the grading was not to instruct but to answer the school system's requirements. I wanted the kids to learn from my teaching and their work, not my grading, so I never felt guilty about a lack of teacher response. I had seen too many colleagues burn out trying to write back to a hundred and fifty journals only to end up abandoning them as classroom tools; what was important to me was for the kids to continue to do good work in the notebooks. My response would have to come in conferences.

New thinking about the qualities of good writing

Creating a routine for reviewing every student's notebook helped me get to know the notebooks better. By evaluating them more clearly in my own mind, I developed some benchmarks for what was important in student notebooks. I saw that in the best ones, kids learned to move from generic reporting of "this is a true story" toward entries that might later prove helpful in writing a piece for a reader. A writers notebook, as I mentioned before, is different from a journal, in that its purpose is to serve the writer as he moves toward a more invested, reader-based writing project. As the day approached when we would be using the notebooks for just that, I started looking for collections of entries and habits of thought that were likely to pay off in student writing.

I began to see that even short fragmentary entries that included very specific information, often in the form of concrete description or precise dialogue, were probably going to be more useful than summary reportage of whole incidents. Like quotes and facts in a journalist's notebook, the most specific entries (regardless of the ultimate genre) would provide the writer with hard data for her piece, which would make the reader's experience more precise and particular.

Another helpful habit I saw was the reflex between particulars and generalities. Different writers of any age start with different kinds of thought: some begin with experiential specifics, others with more general meanings or categories. As I read kids' notebooks, I began to see that the usual school markers of intelligence had nothing to do with these patterns of thinking, since many of the students the system had identified as thinking at a low level often began notebook entries with abstractions or generalities. For either type of writer, however, the job is to move toward the other. If you begin with specifics, you have to enlarge your thinking toward meaning; if you begin with generalities, you have to go after the facts. I began to name for students what I saw them doing, encouraging them to go ahead and begin with whatever was most comfortable for them and to realize that some of their writing work would involve this move between "little" and "big." (Quickly enough, this metaphor became a sexual joke, so I had to change to "facts" and "ideas.") Though my concern was helping students equip themselves for writing well for an audience, the ability to move between the particular and the general is essential for any thoughtful endeavor: it is the move from a single experiment to a scientific principle; it is the move from mathematical concepts to problem solving, from the textual givens of a piece of literature interpretation, from getting treated badly by a girlfriend to beliefs about love and relationships; it is the move between practice and theory in teaching.

Something else I saw in the notebooks, which I encouraged as helpful for developing pieces of writing, was playful experimentation with language in which the writer was game to goof around on the page. Usually this sense of play resulted in the most literary, most aesthetically interesting notebook entries I saw. What's more, these entries were more daringly inventive than anything I'd seen kids try in their more inhibited writing for audiences. I hoped kids like Guillerme, who played with form in an admirably controlled way, even when simply relating a incident from the day, would be able to keep their frolicsome spirit alive when they began work on projects:

"Lousy luck! I can't believe I'm just sitting here letting you eat that in front of me!"

"Ha! Ha!" came a snicker.

Well it's my sister's birthday and I'm sitting here watching her eat lobster in front of me . . .

"May I please just have a little piece?" I tried again.

"Geez, let me get a taste first. Okay?"

"Happy Birthday Laura, you're lucky it is or I'd just walk over there and grab a piece of that lobster."

"Chill out," I found my outer body saying to my inner body. "It's her birthday give her a break."

"Wait till my birthday I'll show her. I'll get a lobster twice that size to eat in front of her."

"Robbie, would you like a bite."

"Sure."

Always before, I had tried to help students fit their natural thoughtfulness, wonder, and curiosity into their initially flat reportage pieces, which, though it was possible for a few students, just did not work for everyone. Many students, most likely because of their learned expectations about school, have trouble retrieving their most reflective self while they feel an audience looking over their shoulder. The notebook gave them a way to bring the writing to the site of their thinking, rather than forcing them to summon up their thoughtfulness in the service of a written performance in school. It was becoming clearer than ever to me how intelligent and interesting my students were in their daily intellectual lives.

Whenever I mentioned Donny to Kelly, his resource room teacher, she rolled her eyes and shook her head. She loved him and wanted to help him, was more devoted to him, probably than anyone else in his life. (Easy to love, when you weren't trying to force him to do schoolwork, Donny was personable, funny, and tiny. For some reason his doctors hadn't been able to correct, he didn't grow; he was fourteen but looked seven.) Lovable or not, he was exasperating in school, especially to Kelly, rarely sitting still long enough to complete assignments for most classes. Because she was saddled with the responsibility of seeing that he got his homework done, she was usually struggling with him. But when he finally started writing in his notebook, it became one of the few things he would work on at home. He would come to Kelly first thing each morning with some new gem, which she in turn would send him to show me. We were both proud of the intelligence and sensitivity that came so clearly to the surface in his short entries, and once again we knew that Donny had been prevented from shining in school all these years mainly because school was not built with him in mind. Here are a few of his entries:

1/3

Today was a boring day. I attempted to build a snow fort after school but the snow wasn't wet enough to pack. I threw snowballs at my dog for awile (which he likes to catch in his mouth) until my gloves got wet and my fingers got numb.

1/4

This morning I woke to the sound of soft music and the smell of pancakes. I had not had pancakes for along time so it took me a few minutes to figure out what it was. I immeditly hopped out of bed and got dressed. I went into the kitchen and saw my dad finishing off the last of the pancakes. I ended up eating cornflakes.

1/19

Last night I stayed outside real late. It was unusually warm and the almost full moon kept the whole place light. I studied the moon and wondered how it would be to go there. then I had an urge to become an astronaut.

As I saw these good things happening in the kids' notebooks, I praised them and asked the kids to talk about them to their classmates. I kept saying that these kinds of notebook entries, detailed ones, playful ones, thoughtful ones, would help when they started making things people would read. But as I said it, I could see those were just words to them. My students were just having fun in the notebooks; they had no sense of what I meant by using this stuff to make projects for publication. And, when it came right down to it, I wasn't that sure I could envision it either; it was still just an idea I had heard from Lucy Calkins. It was time to get beyond the notebooks, to push my students and myself to go public. After all, there was much work I wanted to do with them on the craft of writing for readers, the conventions of different genres of writing, and the conventions of sentences, punctuation, and words. As long as they were only writing for themselves, I knew that kind of talk was pointless.

I started warning them that we were going to be adding projects to our writing work soon, and I started figuring out how I was going to help them do that.

TIME AND WRITING

We live our lives, but we don't live with them, any more than the banks of a river live with particular molecules of water. Time goes by, time passes, time flies, all is flux. I am at a party, talking with friends; I am at work and can only remember fragments of the party's good time. I meet my students and they are a sea of alien faces whose names I can never hope to learn. Then I know them all well, I think, and we are part of one another's lives. Then they are gone, and I again don't know them or their names. Then I see one of them at a store, his hairline receding, his children in tow. The constant motion is dizzying. I'm all for experience, but it goes through me like beer.

Like all bodily experiences, sound is fleeting, lost with the gust of air it rides upon. Talk, language in the air, goes through us and vanishes. It changes us, but the conversation is vanishing even as it occurs. And so—human beings came up with writing as a way to make language stick around, outlast its own moment. When I write in my notebook, I send a memo to my future self, and in so doing, as Robert Grudin puts it, I expand my being in time. It is the only way I have of stemming the flow, damming the river, planting a permanent post. Experience, even the experience of writing, is still just as frustratingly fleeting, but I've made something stick. I've invested in the future and the closest I can come to traveling back in time is later returning physically to the page upon which I wrote. Then, thinking along with my past self, I can reinvest in the future by writing more. Stephen Spender, discussing how he rereads his notebook, wrote that when he comes across an entry about past experience, it "is not exactly a memory. It is more like one prong upon which a whole calendar of similar experiences happening throughout years, collect" (p. 121). Once my thought becomes concrete text, it stands still. I can look at that page over and over, thinking further while old thoughts remain before my eyes as prompts. Because literacy is stable, I can use my past as a place to stand while I reach for something new.

The rate of speed in the act of writing, moreover, is very slow compared with thinking or even talking. While I am writing a single sentence, I may have ten sentences' worth of thoughts. In the long run, the thinking is kept on track by the physical existence of the text, but my thoughts burst here and there in the midst of words and sentences. For every sentence I write, I examine a dozen options, so that while the line of the writing may creep, my thoughts rapidly spiral around it. Like any writer, I have to manage the bottleneck behind my mind, my eyes, and my hands, formed by this variance in tempo. The very act of creating a text that will outlast this moment creates thought patterns with a combination of tempos and relationships unique to writing.

Writing can give us the feeling that we are becoming more real, that experience is no longer quite so transitory. Ironically then, the very experience of writing—what it's actually like to *do* it—flees our minds. In order to stabilize that experience, we write about our writing. Ultimately, writing constantly places us at the juncture of stability and change. While we bring our best selves to the page, we are at the same time outgrowing them.

4

Moving from Private Thoughts to Performance

Having decided that *talking* about the move from notebooks to pieces written for readers would do no good, I wasted no time in giving the whole class a shove to try to help them make a transition, to use their notebooks to come up with a topic they would spend more time with and develop into a final draft. As Donald Murray has said about writing in general, there is little to say about it in advance of doing it. One day I arranged the desks in my room so that the students would be as close to me as possible as I talked to them; I would quietly persuade them of the importance of the shift we needed to make.

Finding a topic

When they had taken their seats, I said, "Let's get started, because this is a really important day for us, and we have a lot to do. You know that I've been telling you all along that the reason you were writing in your notebooks was so that you could use all that stuff to make pieces for readers. I know that hasn't been clear, so today I want to explain a little more about that. In about a month, we are going to be making a class magazine of your writing, and everybody, unless you come up with some other plan for how you want to publish your piece, will put something in that magazine. Every person in the class will get a copy, and any teachers or other people from the community who ask for one will also get a copy. Now, all the writing you've been doing in your notebook ought to help you figure out something you'd like to work on for other people to read.

"The real question for you is, *What have I been thinking about a lot? What, if I look through my notebook, can I see to be my passions, my obsessions, my favorite things to think about?* I'm going to help you with ways to figure that out.

"A couple of nights ago, I was reading through my notebook, the way you do a lot of the time when you're rethinking old issues, and trying to get new ideas to write about, when I came across an entry I had written about my best friend in third grade. His name was Billy, and we were together all the time. Anytime anybody saw one of us, they'd ask where the other was, and I can remember liking that, liking the feeling of having a friend so close that people thought we should always be together. The image that sticks in my mind of Billy was the way he looked when he laughed—his face turned bright red and his teeth seemed really big—and I guess I remember that because we were always laughing together.

"Then, when we were in sixth grade, a guy named Matt moved to our town, and we thought he was funny, too, and again I just remember the three of us giggling all the time when we were together, spending the night at one another's houses and just staying up all night laughing. People started thinking of us as the three musketeers, Billy, Matt, and Randy, always together.

"And then, as I read on in this entry, I came to this one spot where I wrote about this lingering picture of the three of us together. In San Antonio, where we lived, the sidewalks were just about wide enough for two people to walk side by side, so whenever the three of us walked together, someone would always be walking lopsided, half on and half off the curb, or else jogging backwards, working really hard to stay in the conversation—and I don't remember either of those other guys ever having to do that. As I read that in my notebook and thought about it again, it seemed like it was always me who was trying to figure out a way to be in on the conversation, like I was always having to work out how to fit into this friendship. So I wrote that in the margin beside that entry, and I also wrote, 'Even in that close friendship, I was an outsider.'

"As soon as I wrote that, I realized how much being an outsider is part of my life. I had a hunch that I was going to find other entries about that as I read on. A few pages later, sure enough, I found an entry about Thanksgiving with my relatives, where I had written about how when I was a teenager, the men always sat in the living room at my great-grandmother's house all Thanksgiving Day watching one football game after another and not talking to each other. I know a lot of you probably like doing that, but I didn't, so I would get really bored and wander into the kitchen, where the women were all, well, doing all the work, cooking and everything, and pretty quickly I could tell that I was underfoot and they were all wondering what I was doing in there anyway. So I would wander from room to room until I couldn't stand the discomfort anymore and would go walk around outside. And, again, it struck me as I read, that I was an outsider in my own family—so I jotted that in the margin.

"Then I found an entry about buying our house, and I hadn't written this, but I realized that since all of our neighbors are retired people who have lived up there on that hill for years and years, I'm an outsider in my neighborhood. So I wrote an entry about that. Since then, I've written several more entries in my notebook about feeling like an outsider here at the school in some ways. It seems to me that I've found something that is a kind of pattern in my notebook, something that comes up again and again, even though sometimes it's not that obvious.

"So that's what I mean when I say you're going to begin looking for passions or obsessions in your notebook. Maybe it's something you've written about again and again, as I did about being an outsider. Or maybe you'll have just one entry that you feel pulling you like a magnet; you know you *want* to write about that again and again, even if you haven't yet. So today, we're going to begin writing time by reading—reading our notebooks and looking for possible topics to stay with and build into something other people will read. Then, after you find your topic, you'll build it up in your notebook for a while, by writing more about it. So—in just a minute you'll start rereading your whole notebook in search of where your head and heart have been taking you the past few weeks. Let's get started."

I looked down and started reading my notebook. I didn't want them to ask me any questions. I had said enough; now they just needed time to read. In this crucial move from notebooks to projects, things get harder and harder the more you delay and discuss; you just have to *do* it. Everything was quiet, except for a few pages turning now and then. I looked up; a few kids were staring around the room. I repeated that they should be reading their whole notebook and then went back to reading mine.

After about five minutes, I took my clipboard with my record-keeping form on it and got up to see how they were doing. First I just strolled around, and everyone seemed to be reading their notebook. Wondering if the instructions were clear, I asked a few what they were doing, and they answered, as if I were not altogether right in the head, that they were looking for things that came up several times in their notebook.

That day and in the few days that followed, I conferred with them individually as quickly as I could, getting students to commit to some topic or other and helping them plan how they were going to use their notebook to research, rethink, and enrich that topic before beginning a draft. Using my ever-present pen and clipboard, I conspicuously noted in my records both their topic and their plan as we talked, so that they would feel bound to what we said. I also asked them to write, immediately after our conference, a page or so in their notebook about their topic and their ideas for ways to investigate it and live with it for the next week or so. For the past few weeks, I had been encouraging them to drift from topic to topic even within a single notebook entry, so it needed to be especially clear that now there was something they should stick to.

Naturally, I could not talk to every single student before he or she began collecting entries. Squeezing that hard on one spot in the writing process would have created a strict bottleneck of teacher attention, would have resulted in kids' sitting around waiting for me to get to them, which would not do. A couple of times I met with groups of four, five, or six to discuss some shared problem, such as not being able to find anything in their notebook or the reasons we were not simply going to recopy an entry as a draft. Also, from the records I kept of conferences with individual students, I developed whole-class minilessons about problems and breakthroughs I had learned about from one student but with which I assumed many were wrestling. In this way, I tried to make sure that teaching moments went a long way among as many students as possible.

Developing the topic in the notebook

It was perhaps during this phase of sticking to a single topic and writing over and over about it in different ways that the notebook seemed best to be doing its job as a writer's tool. Now my students were using their notebook in the way I was in working on my novel, rather than as a journal, and by the same token, their work more resembled that in the notebooks of Dickens, Dostoyevski, and James. The notebook was now, more than ever, a workbench for pieces of writing as yet half-conceived and unassembled.

The notebook was now a different tool than it had been, more like note cards for a research paper than a journal, and I needed to talk to the kids about that difference often to make it clear. I helped some students (only those who seemed confused) to make some concrete division in their notebook, the clearer to delineate the difference in function. Some simply folded over a page to indicate the spot where the notebook moved from being about everything to being about one thing. Others inserted sticky notes as tabs, color-coded the corners of pages ("purple corners means it's the section about competing with my brother"), or simply wrote their topic in large letters on their new section's cover sheet. Other kids didn't need such a clear separation, even continuing occasionally to write on some other topic that had their attention at the moment. That was fine with me, so long as on balance they were focused on something they planned to turn into a first draft soon. I encouraged these writers to try, even when writing about other topics, to see them through the lens of their main topic.

As always, there was a tension at the heart of my teaching. On the one hand, I insisted that the kids stick with one topic; on the other hand, in order to facilitate a spirit of exploration within a topic, I still stressed variety and playfulness in their notebook: a tether, but a long one. Ed chose hunting as his topic, and in his notebook he wrote entries in the form of poems about how the woods looked when he first walked into them early on an autumn morning; information about weapons, animals, and habitats; narratives of his first memories of hunting with his grandfather; summaries of magazine articles; and diatribes against people who disapprove of hunting. Leah, writing about her uncle's death and its impact on her family, collected specific stories about her uncle, including whatever actual quotes she could remember in his voice; notes from interviews with her sister and aunt; entries written in direct address, almost like letters to her parents and other family members; scenes she thought of as landmarks in the dissolution of her extended family; a groundplan of her uncle's house with annotations of what she remembered happening in each room.

Those who were successful at this casting about within a topic sometimes found themselves disoriented: *Now what was I trying to say about all this?* When I heard them saying that, I scheduled whole-class meetings that took up much of the period around just one student's notebook. Leah, for example, read to the class everything in her notebook past the divider, and students listened and offered readings of what sounded important. This gave Leah a sense of both where the center of gravity might lay in her thinking and also what was of interest to an audience. Obviously, the better part of a class period spent on Leah's notebook gave Leah a lot to think about, as well as specific help in how she might focus her work toward a draft. It also helped the other kids who were having a hard time understanding how they could write a variety of entries about one topic. I thought of these days as expensive but worth the cost in moving the whole class along.

During this phase of students' work in moving from notebooks to projects, I had three main purposes in my conferences: refining topics by both focusing them and enlarging their significance; helping the writer construct a sense of purpose and audience; and helping the writer build a vision for this topic as a piece of writing (a sense of genre, structure, and language).

Most teachers will not be surprised that I found myself reiterating again and again, in minilessons and conferences, that good topics for writing were usually not the hugest ones the kids could think of. I knew that topics like "my family" or "childhood" or "love" or "success" were most likely not going to be successful for student writers. Their adolescent propensity for abstraction and vagueness would feed directly into such topics, and I predicted a terrific struggle in helping them be specific or clear in such murky thought. This was, however, thanks to the notebooks, an easier problem to cope with than it had been before. When I conferred with a student who had declared "winter" as his topic, I simply asked to see the entries where he had written about that. Almost always, there was something particular about winter there, and the problem lay in the kid's jumping to a too-high level of abstraction. The topic was not winter, really, but "preferring to stay outside in the winter rather than inside where it's warm." Once we had more accurately defined what the writer was really interested in, the business of collecting around that topic was considerably easier and more interesting for the writer, and I worried less about troubles down the road.

Teachers and students in authentic literacy classrooms everywhere invent new words to describe what goes on in writing, and I and my students developed our own ways of talking about focus. Saying "focus, focus, focus" quickly became meaningless. Yes, I wanted them to develop a writerly vocabulary eventually, but for now I was more concerned about their doing it than saying it just the right way. It was important for them to develop their own language to confer with each other, to be able to say, *That's an* everything-in-the-whole-universe *topic; I don't think you've found your* bull's-eye *topic yet.*

In addition to working with students to help make their topics smaller, I tried to make them bigger. I wanted to complicate the writer's sense of the topic and to expand the range of meaning the writer could build there. Many times, I'd begin a conference looking over the writer's shoulder at an entry, and then I'd turn my gaze away from the page and look directly into the writer's eyes and say, *So, what was that like for you?*

Jeff had written several entries about building his own pickup truck, summarizing how he'd acquired the parts, explaining how long it had taken to assemble it. "I felt proud, like a sense of achievement," he muttered, shrugging.

"I can see why; I mean it's very impressive to me, because I don't know how to do that. But since you do know how, why was it impressive to you?"

"Because—I mean I know how—but I'd never done it before. I never really thought I could do that. I could remember when I was in second grade, and my father got a truck—it was just like mine is now—and I couldn't even climb into it then. Now I can build one. I felt accomplishment."

"Jeff, that will be so important for your readers to understand in order for your truck to have as much meaning to them as it has to you. For the next couple of days, keep thinking about that in your notebook, about second grade and your father's truck, and why this felt like such an accomplishment to you. I have a feeling that might be important in writing your piece when you get to drafting it."

Some readers may object to my focusing on the more emotional aspects of Jeff's truck ideas, and in some ways they will be right. My instructional purpose was to get Jeff to reflect, and there are numerous ways he might reflect on the experience of building a truck; for example, he might consider how next time he could do it better, faster, or less expensively. But I was thinking about this as a potential piece in the class magazine and therefore for a general readership of people who, like me, were unlikely to want details on the building of trucks, who would prefer to hear about the person doing the work rather than the work itself. I do not think, then, that I was unnecessarily sentimentalizing Jeff's truck, but rather that I was helping him focus on the human side of his story, so it would be more interesting to the people who would be reading it.

Using the notebook to plan content and form

Figure 4–1 presents some of the typical ways I conferred with writers throughout their move from notebook to project. Often, my purpose was to help the writer focus on the demands of the reader even now, while still working in a notebook, before beginning a draft. I thought if he could get a loose sense of a reader, he would better be able to decide what he needed to gather in his notebook. Sometimes, as in Jeff's case, that purpose was implicit in the direction I took the conference. Other times, I tried to get the writer to think deliberately about the reader. I asked, *Who are you imagining reading the piece you are going to write? Picture it. Someone is sitting down with our class magazine and reading your piece. Who is that person?* It turned out to have been a good decision to announce the class magazine ahead of time. In each class, we even voted on a name and appointed an editor, to try to give the idea reality. I referred to the magazines by name as often as possible, to build up the concreteness of our move from private to public writing spaces.

Sometimes, the writer needed more time with the topic before she would know from what angle she would approach it. Other times, when I felt a writer seemed to know what she wanted to do to her readers, when she had a purpose beginning to form in her mind, I asked, *What's the attitude you want your readers to have toward your topic? How do you want them to respond to this?* Trying to answer this question guided the writer in figuring out what would be helpful to have in

FINDING A TOPIC	
If I see this . . .	**I might ask this . . .**
The student seems to be reading each entry as a separate "story" or thought.	What idea, thing, or person seems to come up often in your notebook?
There are some entries with potential in the notebook, but the writer doesn't see any connection between them.	As you reread, which entries pulled at you like a magnet, making you want to think more about that topic? Find one that you feel that way about, and point to it. Now start making more entries about that.
The writer has had trouble finding anything in the notebook upon which to build a piece of writing.	Since this time you're just going to have to brainstorm a topic and start writing your piece, what have you learned about keeping a notebook so that it will be most helpful to you next time in preparing to write?

DEVELOPING THE TOPIC	
If I see this . . .	**I might ask this . . .**
The writer has found one entry she likes but it's not connected to anything else yet.	Are there other entries in your notebook that are about this same feeling or idea?
To the writer, the entry just "is what it is." He has not yet constructed its significance.	Why do you think you've chosen this to write about? What does it mean to you?
The writer seems distant from and underinvested in the topic.	What in your life right now led up to your thinking about this topic?
So far, the writer's thought seems global or general and she has not collected specific examples or support.	If you were going to tell one story that would show just what you mean here, what would it be?
The writer is having a hard time knowing how to write over and over about a topic in the notebook.	What kinds of information do you think your reader will need to get your point about this topic? Let's make a list.

PLANNING CONTENT AND FORM	
If I see this . . .	**I might ask this . . .**
The writer has developed the thought broadly and has lost the focus necessary for a unified piece of writing.	What do you think is the most important thing you want to say about your topic in this piece of writing?
The writer's attention is still primarily on the topic and needs to begin to move toward a reader.	Who do you imagine reading this?
The writer has not begun to imagine the notebook entries cohering into a single piece of writing.	What kind of piece of writing do you think this is: a letter, a memoir, a poem, a nonfiction article, or what?
The writer is seeing the material as all one blob, rather than manageable subunits.	How is this going to go? Talk this through for me. First you'll write what? Then what after that? How else could it go?

FIG. 4–1: *Some questions to ask in writing conferences during the move from notebooks to projects.*

the notebook, what entries she still needed to write. When Victoria was writing about her bedroom, knowing that she wanted the reader to sympathize with the security and independence she felt in that room helped her know that some entries, like those about the care she had taken in decorating it or her memories of seeking solace there, would probably be more helpful than entries about, say, the height of the ceiling or a list of friends who had been in her room. A writer's purpose with respect to an audience, "what I want to do to these readers," is one of her most basic criteria for selecting what's important from the chaos of experience.

The thrust of many of my conferences was to make sure the writer was not only enriching his topic, but also beginning to imagine the piece of writing he was going to make. It is one thing to be thinking, reflecting, picturing about your grandmother and quite another to be thinking, reflecting, and picturing a memoir about your grandmother. Beginning to build a vision-in-progress of the piece you might write is another way to select what kinds of entries, out of everything possible, will be most helpful in writing this piece.

One kind of conversation I had with students, and they with each other, was speculation on what genre (poetry, memoir, fiction, nonfiction, letter, essay) the piece would take. When I conferred with a student who was in the middle of elaborating a topic, writing about it from every possible angle, I would sometimes ask, *What do you think this could be when it's time to make a draft? What form do you think it could take? Just a hunch—you don't have to stick to it.*

When Juliana said, "I'm pretty sure it's going to be either a memoir, or I'll change some of it and it'll be a short story," that helped her know what kind of collecting in the notebook would be most helpful for making that thing. Since Juliana was thinking toward a narrative, she collected, from memory and from present life, details of scene and character in preparation for her draft. The material she was working with centered around her grandmother, so Juliana wrote descriptions of her old hands and skin, interviewed her mother about what her grandmother was like at a younger age, wrote some of the stories her grandmother told about her life, jotted and later elaborated her own memories of how her grandmother walked, talked, and cleaned. She also wrote several entries about her grandmother's apartment, the furniture and knickknacks, the smell of the place, the emotional associations she had with different rooms. She selected these types of entries as the material she needed to write well in this form. If, from the same set of notebook entries in which she thought about her grandmother, she had chosen to write nonfiction about how families in America deal with their elderly members, she would have required a different kind of preparation.

Naturally, kids sometimes could not say offhand what genre they were planning, so I asked the question differently, sometimes leaving it with them to think about for a couple of days: *Have you ever read anything that is like the piece you are thinking of writing?* If I could get them to name a piece of literature, then that piece could serve as a teacher for them both now and throughout the writing process.

For this first attempt at using the notebook to choose and enrich topics, students wrote in many genres. I had to accept that with so many students writing so many different things, I could not be their mainspring of information about qualities of good writing in every genre. Even if I knew enough to help them all, there was simply no time. Particularly difficult was conferring with a student who was writing a poem when she had no idea how to do line breaks, when there was no attention to sound or image in the words, when so many other things were missing that I thought were important in poetry but that I could not teach in one conference. For now, I had to let go of my hyperactive concern with the excellence of the writing and be satisfied teaching a process. Learning the new technology of using the notebook to work on a piece of writing took up the writer's energy and attention—and mine. Later, there would be time to pay the proper attention to learning from literature to write well. As I would again and again, I was learning to ask, *What's my exact purpose here?* and then to teach in a more focused way.

I also encouraged students to consider voice and organization in building a vision-in-progress of their piece. Even before they were ready to write, I often suggested to individual writers that they try out a few different voices with their material. I kept a photocopied sheet handy on which I had assembled writing about a single topic (trees, in this case) in different voices: a passage from an encyclopedia, a formal but vividly descriptive passage from a novel, a chatty paragraph from a column, and a warmly reflective lead to a memoir. The differences between these texts helped students understand what I meant by voice, and though I didn't ask them to imitate, they did get some ideas for the kinds of voices they might assume. Sometimes they tried out these different voices on some chunk of their material, without worrying about where in the piece it would come, and sometimes they tried three different opening paragraphs.

After students had collected quite a few entries about their topic, I often recommended that they try out several possible informal outlines in their notebook for how their piece would go. Doing so helped them see the draft they would make as only one of many possibilities, and it also facilitated more purposeful collecting of information since they could see what they might be needing to write a whole and cohesive piece. I kept several copies of Donald Murray's *Write to Learn* in the reference section of the classroom, so that I could refer them to his chapter on ordering, which lists several different types of outlines. In this way, I tried to counteract the years of training they had had about formal outlining, with Roman numerals and all that, which had at best limited them to one structure that will not work for every piece and had at worst left them feeling totally confused and inadequate for what should be a thoroughly individualized process of organizing information on paper.

Predictable problems—and what helps

Naturally, that first year of moving from notebooks into projects, there were problems: some kids abandoned topics when I wasn't looking; some rushed through a first draft that they also saw as their final draft; some were reluctant to make a first draft; some first drafts were recopied entries; kids chose glib and superficial entries as the seeds for their project, rather than the ones I saw as more meaningful; sometimes, students wrote more poorly in their draft than they had in their notebook entries; so much writing with no audience seemed to make some students sloppier about conventions of writing, so that I had to talk about them later more than I would have wanted.

From my own teaching and from working as a consultant in other teachers' classrooms, I've learned four footholds that help me avoid some of the pitfalls of the process. The first is that everyone has to complete a project by the deadline for publication. It doesn't help anyone to learn the writing process when the process is so complex and lengthy that the vision of the product is lost. Second, I have to remember that I am not the author of all these pieces of writing. If I don't admire the craft of every single one of them, wishing I had written it myself, so what? What's most important is the students' experience of the writing process. Elements of craft are much easier to teach in later projects out of the notebook, such as those that occur within genre studies. Third, as I have mentioned, for this project only, I try to keep my standards low, accepting and celebrating what students come up with as approximations of the use of the notebook and the rest of the writing process. Fourth, I try always to hunt for ways the notebook can remain a valuable tool throughout the process of collecting, drafting, and revising. I am not ashamed in conferences with individual students to collaborate on an assignment on which I do expect the student to follow through. Overall, the teacher's energy and resolve to complete the exodus from notebook to project is the key to success.

Making early drafts

Because kids are used to bringing only their notebook to class, I make sure that by the time anyone is going to be writing a first draft, I have paper available in the room. I have sometimes been given money for it, other times I've "obtained" it from the supply closet after hours, and other times I have bought it myself, because it sends such an important message to the writers in my classes when they write on a new kind of paper as they come out of their notebook, rather than writing the draft right in the notebook. I even walk around with this paper in my hand as I confer so that I can slip it onto the desk and say, *Okay, start your draft.* This simple move provides a concrete signal that the writing they are doing on their draft is different, something they could more easily hand to someone else to read than the more writer-based, backyard kind of writing they've been doing in their notebook.

William Faulkner said that writing a first draft is like trying to build a house in a strong wind. That is the feeling I try to instill in my students as they work on their first draft, a sense of urgency in getting it quickly hammered down, whether it's from beginning to end, or middle to end to beginning. This is just one of many possible guesses at how their piece should go, and I push them to fly through it in one or two sittings, so that they can then go back to the notebook and see what they need to add or rethink: Lucy Calkins long ago suggested that in writing nonfiction students could write their draft without looking at their notes, and that is how I encourage students to work on their draft here. This piece does not necessarily consist of the same words as those in the notebook; it is something new, made out of the thinking the notebook made possible. The vision of the piece of writing as an artifact has to emerge without being swallowed up by bits and chunks of information. Later, if they choose, they may add stuff from their notebook.

Yes, many students do feel that I'm rushing them, and I am. I'm hurrying them past trying to solve all the problems of their piece in the first draft. I want them to be unsatisfied with what they can do in one draft, so that the possibility of revision remains open, so that they don't think that the making of a piece of writing begins at the top of page one and ends at the bottom of the final page. I am trying to hold open spaces of possibility by pushing them through the first draft.

As the kids are working on their first draft, I stress an image of the piece. They've already gotten down a lot of information about their topic. Now they need to think about it as a piece of writing, a poem, a memoir, a story, an essay. Not that I dictate orthodox formulas about any of these forms; rather I want each student to pay attention at this stage of the process to the emergent form of their particular piece: What does this piece want to be when it grows up? For now, I hope they will focus on what is on the page, more than on their topic out in the world. Now is when it has to go from being a part of life to a piece of writing.

Another thing I emphasize heavily while kids are working on early drafts is the reader and the reader's needs. In fact, I talk about getting a sense of your reader so much that many students end up writing letters, either the more formal kind they plan as a gift to someone to memorialize life they've shared, or else open letters that more than one person would read or hear. I accept this slight distortion of what I mean because, for many, it clarifies and makes concrete the shift from writing for yourself to writing for someone else.

The notebook as a tool for revision

As writers finish their initial draft, they usually begin for the first time to realize exactly what information they have and what they will need to write this piece. More often than not, much of this information, whether in the form of facts to be acquired from the world or reflective explorations, is not yet in the notebook. And so, many of my conferences involve sending the writer back to the notebook, sending the worker back to the workbench.

The rethinking that writers do in the notebook can involve a number of different types of cognitive tasks that writing and rereading can facilitate. For instance, some students go back to their notebook to try to *see* better, to describe a scene or setting that they have not yet completely fleshed out either in their draft or in their mind's eye and that without such work in the notebook might remain sketchy or underdeveloped. Other writers make organizational decisions in the notebook: sections of the draft that aren't yet working may need to be outlined several different ways to discover the easiest or most logical flow of ideas in the piece. Figure 4–2 shows some other ways I have seen writers use their notebook after they already have a draft.

Conferring during drafting and revision

When I circulate and confer as the class is revising, I sometimes very gently and carefully suggest activities to the writers whose work they might benefit. However, if my suggestions are too gentle and careful, the writers will not do them. Work in the notebook such as I am suggesting slows down the writing process and forces ordinary people to think in the disciplined ways writers think. When my teaching works best, I'm not being that tentative and gentle, but rather what some writing process teachers might consider fairly directive. In conference, after hearing what the writer is trying to do and understanding what I believe the writer needs to accomplish that purpose, I come up with a plan. If the writer comes up with a better plan that's fine; often these plans are collaborative, but just as often, they are not. I jot this work plan in my notes, because if I don't I will not remember it, and I expect the writer to carry it out by the next time we speak. I check back with any writer with whom I've made such a contract to see how work has progressed and whether the plan needs to be revised in some way.

In many writing process classrooms, we've become afraid to teach. We are timid about telling the kids what to do, in favor of allowing the kids to "own" their work. Naturally, I'm all for ownership because it preserves the motivation of the writer to write and preserves the authenticity of the literacy event, but I do try to keep a balance in my mind and work between ownership and my clear and explicit ambition for the writer's growth. The best writing teachers I've known hold very high expectations for the writers in their classrooms and are not tentative about making those expectations clear. For twenty years now, our profession has known that even young children can revise; however, too often our lack of faith in our students' abilities to think critically about their writing leaves us publishing doctored-up first drafts. Even after all this thinking in the notebook and hard, if fast, work on an initial draft, there is still work to be done, and even the weakest writers in the room are capable of doing it. Revision, both in writing and as a way of thinking, is not expendable for me, because it involves the ability to imagine that things might be otherwise. That ability to re-imagine and re-create is central in my teaching. To me, it represents power: the ability to accept your initial thoughts and then transform them into something else. It is the habit of revision that makes new ways of drafting possible.

Because revision is so important to me, I try to set a tone in the classroom that encourages it, mainly by adopting an attitude toward writing that always

CONTEXT	STRATEGY
She has written a beginning and can only imagine the piece going this one way.	Writes three very different possible beginnings for this piece.
He wrote it in an order that no longer makes sense to him.	Outlines what he's done and rearranges the chunks.
She is having trouble deciding how much background she needs to explain.	Lists what she assumes the reader knows and what the reader needs to learn.
He can't decide what should come next.	Outlines what is to come four different ways.
Her character is really just a name on the page, and the reader hasn't gotten a chance to know the character.	Makes at least three pages of notes about each character as a person.
There is no way the reader can imagine the place he is writing about.	Draws the place in detail from different angles, or describe it for two pages.
A story seems sappy because it only has one simple feeling to it.	Writes the incident from several different points of view.
She hates what she has written—the whole thing. It's not saying what she means.	Writes a page of the piece in two other possible genres.
It's hard to make decisions about what is important because he is just stringing together entries.	Writes "what I want the reader to believe about my topic" at the top of a page and writes a half page in response to that.
What she is trying to say seems too simple, too obvious.	Interviews someone else who feels differently about her topic. Writes down what they say.
He has blurted out everything he has to say in the first two paragraphs and has nothing left to say.	Divides a page into three sections, corresponding to sections of the piece, and jots notes about what information he will release to the reader and what he wants to remain a mystery for now.
She is explaining too much and is having a hard time helping the reader to "see" what she is writing.	Writes a section of her piece as if someone were going to make a movie of it, including directions to designers and dialogue for actors.
He feels like he doesn't have anything else to say.	Reads and responds in writing to literature about his topic.
Her writing feels flat and boring, and she can't think of how to make it better.	Reads, copies out good bits, and makes notes about the craft of pieces of literature she admires written in the same genre.
The whole experience just is not working; it's hard and boring and he hates it and has no energy to write.	Writes about a time when he has written successfully (compared to now), especially if it was a similar kind of piece, and thinks on paper about what worked for him.

FIG. 4–2: *Some smart ways students have used a writers notebook as a tool for revision.*

assumes revision. I talk about any writing on paper as indicative of potential, rather than as a product to be judged either as good or bad, to be praised or blamed in the initial instance. When a student shows me a piece, I'm not interested in discussing whether it's "good" or not. Rather, our conversation needs to be about the author's plan for this piece and what this draft can tell us about the next stages in that plan. While it is true that such an attitude isn't inborn in our students, nor is it easy to instill, especially when the rest of the school day and the student's school history work in the opposite direction; it is an attitude that students can only learn by being in new kinds of conversations. And if it takes until June, it's worth it. I don't mind that it's difficult; if I could successfully teach everything about revision in September, there would be little else to do for the rest of the year.

Editing

As the time approaches when their piece will be going out for readers to see, students' concern about the correctness of their grammar, spelling, and punctuation intensifies. When students are working on making their writing conform to conventions of written language is the best time to assess what they really know about those conventions. What, really, are the conventions to which they are trying to conform? Of what do they think "correct" writing consists? What have they learned, mislearned, or not learned? Often, especially when many of the students share an instructional history, there is a particular problem rife in the class. My eighth graders, early in the year, were mystified by comma placement. As far as they knew, commas occurred anywhere one might pause, and so were matters of interpretation. They were astonished to learn, when I began to do a series of minilessons about comma use, that there were predictable and systematic ways of telling where a comma went. At first, they didn't even believe me. When I do such a series of short lessons, I instruct the kids to take notes in their writers notebooks. That way, when I am conferring with them individually, I can refer them to the minilesson I did on such and such a day, so they can retrieve the one or two examples we discussed. I see no reason to assume my students will remember everything I've ever said in minilessons, but I do need those lessons to count—that's why I make them write things down and then why I refer to their notes often.

In my conferences with students who are editing, I locate just one convention of language a student seems ready to learn or particularly needful of learning. I decide what to teach her by looking at the errors she has made on the page, by listening to her talk about her decision making as she edited, and selecting the one principle of sentence construction, spelling, or diction most essential for this student at this point in her history as a writer. If this is a principle I think most of the class needs to hear, I jot it down for a minilesson. If several students seem especially hung up on, say, subject-verb agreement, I arrange a time when I can have a group conference with them, allowing me fifteen or twenty more leisurely minutes of teaching what that small group most needs to hear. I never expect to clean up a whole draft in a conference—it will take too long, and I'll never get around to everyone. I focus on basic things like comma placement, sentence completeness, and agreement, before concerning myself with more infrequent problems like misplaced modifiers or errors in verb tense. For me to take on dangling participles, I have to see four or five of them on a page. And even then I assess whether what really needs attention is the participles as such or a larger issue of logic or sentence completeness.

Whenever I teach someone a linguistic rule, I write it down in my records and tell the student to write it down in his. Editing is relatively fast, a brief stage of the writing process, and so the opportunity to teach conventions of language is too rare for me to waste it spilling words into the air that are going to count only for this one piece and not for the student's learning over time. It at least has to be recorded, so there is the possibility of returning to it. Naturally, this means that editing rules are dispersed throughout the notebook—admittedly not the most organized way to keep them, because students have to flip back through their notebooks each time they edit to find the rules we've discussed. Many teachers I know have used an editing checklist stapled or otherwise attached to the student's writing folder or notebook. Atwell suggests such a list in addition to an editing conference form the teacher keeps and stores in a separate binder. I tried that but found I prefer to keep the number of instruments I use to a minimum. The fewer tools I have for my teaching, the more apt I am to use them well. A number of different forms floating around the room, receiving infrequent and inadequate attention, result in confusion, for both me and the kids, about when and how we are going to use them.

For the more extensive editing work of correcting all the errors in student writing, we have a choice and can do different things at different times. Sometimes, I am the editor of the class publications, correcting all the errors with formal editing markings and returning them to students to recopy for their "final final" draft. Other times, I highlight the word or phrase containing an error, leaving it to the student to use whatever resources are available to figure it out or correct it. Both of these methods are time-consuming and rarely result in perfect recopied drafts. Copying is boring, so kids make errors they haven't made before. They also often correct errors into a different error. Often, students, especially as the deadline draws nearer, just skip correcting the errors they don't understand. The only way to assure perfect final drafts would be to type them myself (assuming I don't make any errors), something I would never, ever do. Since getting perfect products is a problem impossible to solve, I simply don't worry about it. Obviously, kids work with each other, and we all just do the best we can for our public.

When I work as a consultant with people whose political climate surrounding language conventions is particularly hot, whether because their populations are particularly rich or poor, racially mixed or purely middle-class white, I suggest that they append to their students' publications, whether they are distributed as a magazine or hung on a wall, a letter to readers:

> Dear readers:
>
> We hope you take pleasure and insight from reading our writing. You might notice some mistakes, but please don't think it's because we don't care about making our work as perfect as we can. We proudly admit to being learners still in some areas of our work, so please read with a forgiving eye. If any of these mistakes get in the way of your reading, we apologize and hope that they don't take away from the meanings we are exploring. It's more important for us to get our writing out to you than to wait until the day when it would all be absolutely free of mistakes.

When the teachers I know use a letter like this, they explain to their students that its purpose is only to cover their butts, not to provide them with an excuse for never learning to edit.

Sometimes, for those few students who need extensive help in spelling, I create groups that meet after school, in which they enroll voluntarily, but for which attendance, once enrolled, is mandatory (by a contract between me, the student, the assistant principal, and the parent). Most students who have serious spelling problems are fully aware of their difficulty and are eager to have help, believing even to the point of delusion that their spelling ability will make or break their success in later life. In these groups, students categorize the spelling errors I have marked in their drafts—-tion endings, for example, or homophones. Then, they work either to learn the rule that applies or unlearn the distorted version of the rule that has lodged in their memories.

The entire final phase of the writing process, from later revision through editing, is intimately connected to the way the piece will be published. Wrestling with a writer to correct the spelling and punctuation of writing that will only be read aloud or placed in a folder or marked by a teacher and that will never meet the eyes of real readers is forcing us all to spend a lot of energy on something we know is nonsense. Significant numbers of significant others must be looking at a piece of writing for it to be worthwhile for the writer to give much attention to many literate conventions.

The cyclical writing life

On the publication date, the long awaited day when the magazine finally comes out, I and the students are ready to bask in the relief and relaxation that follow a big project completed together. The people who will read the magazine constitute a "them," an outside, evaluating public for whom we in here are performing. As a result, we are a tighter community; I've been able to function as a coach rather than a judge; the students have made a collective artifact that says to the world, *This is who WE are.* While the work is in process, their attitude to the magazine, like their adolescent attitude toward most things, is a study in casualness. But on the day of our celebration, as I watch them reading one another's pieces of writing, jotting notes to each other on the small sheets of stationery I provide, exchanging meaningful glances, slapping each other five, I know the experience has been packed with important learning.

Much of the knowledge they've gained, I know, is tacit knowledge, personal knowledge like that of how to breathe or walk, which lives inside each of them and can't easily be named as, *I know X or Y.* However, I do want them to name it as much as possible, so that they can have control over it when they are on their own and I'm not there to help. So there is one more phase of "writing to think" I want us to explore together. I ask them to write in their notebook, reflecting on the process they have just gone through. In order to nudge them toward a few questions to which I want them to attend, I write on the board or distribute on paper something like the following instructions:

> In answering these questions, think back to writing in notebooks before you had your topic, finding a topic, collecting around your topic, your first draft, the literature that helped you get an image of your piece, the significant revisions you made in your piece. Where in all of that was writing the easiest for you? In what ways does that mean you are strong as a writer? What were the most important things you did that you had never tried before? How do you think you can use that in the future? What parts of the whole process gave you difficulty? What does that tell you you need to work on in the future? In what ways can you use the strengths you've written about here to buoy up the areas in which you felt less strong?

Obviously, during the periods of editing, reflecting, or working on the actual publication of a piece, there is less for a writer to do in the notebook on that particular piece. In my teaching, that does not mean that the notebook stops. If I let it die, I would have to jump-start it all over again. Toward the end of the process of writing a particular piece, the notebook reaches forward to the next piece and the continuance of the writing life that pays a different kind of attention to the world. In other words, the kids go back to collecting, either extensively from life or intensively for their next project. Figure 4–3 diagrams the relationship between the notebook and the project throughout the writing process.

Writers' notebooks are compelling tools in writers' lives and in the classroom, and when they work well, which is often, students and teachers are moved by the honesty and spirit of experimentation that permeates the classroom environment. But a classroom focusing exclusively on writing for the writer's eyes only would present a picture of the writing process and the use of literacy

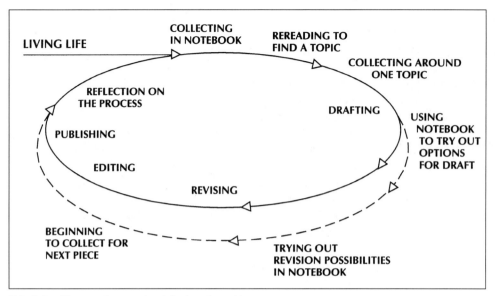

FIG. 4–3: *How a writers notebook fits into the writing process.*

almost as incomplete as that in the traditional classroom, in which all the writing is done for the teacher. Writing is both a tool for thinking and an instrument for engaging with other people, for extending one's thought into the social world. A literacy classroom ought to be a place where students explore varied uses of writing, as both a facilitator of their own thought and a transaction with readers, so that they learn to unlock and control the power of the word.

TIME AND MEANING MAKING

I sit down to write this and reach for memory. Beside me, I have some notes to help me re-create last week's thinking, but they simply taunt me: *What did I mean by* that? The only part that makes sense now is the general idea of the essay, the way the past and the future inform a present act of making meaning in reading or writing. I try to think of where I have seen the idea demonstrated before and remember Donald Murray writing in front of two thousand people at a conference, thinking aloud. I search my memory for where I have seen something like it written and vaguely remember some of Murray's pieces in *Expecting the Unexpected* but can't recall exactly how he started. I could look it up but don't want to because his voice is too compelling, too contagious. I can't remember how to write this, but I can imagine it. So I begin by looping back in memory to how I was thinking when I first sat down, and I write, "I sit down to write this and reach for memory." There is always a present moment when my fingers are touching keys, but my mind is rarely there; much of the time, I am reconstructing the past in new ways.

At the same time, I am thinking of you, and please don't be insulted, but you are at present only a ghost of possibility to me. I am, throughout this book, writing from past experience, for others' futures about which I can only guess. The writing has taken longer than I wanted, and I have often wished to give it up, but the promise of a time when it might be finished, read, and of use to someone has made me write through many present moments when I would have rather been doing something else. Each time, like today, when I begin one of these time pieces, I wonder whether they will be helpful to the book or only distractions, whether people will read them or skip them. I worry about taking on philosophical ideas about time in a book like this, and I concentrate on keeping these essays short and easy to read. At each moment of writing, especially for a reader, I am projecting into the future, guessing, anticipating, predicting, fearing, hoping. In the real work of literacy, the meaning maker stretches out both arms, reaching both backward into what was and forward into what might be, and pulls the partially known past and the only-guessed-at future close in a brave embrace.

Likewise, whenever a student is writing, he is constructing a past and a future that converge in the present moment, and the concentration required for this construction is what gives writing or reading its "lost in thought" quality. When I talk with a writer in the midst of writing, therefore, I rarely focus the conversation on what he is doing in the present moment. Rather, the talk is usually about the past or the future, either the wellspring of memory on which the writer is drawing or else the plans for how the piece will go and who will read it. I do this because, first, it is the most natural thing to talk about with a writer—that is where his mind is—and, second, this double vision between what was and what will be is what I want to try to build, through this conversation, into the writer's consciousness. Afterward, when I stand up and look at the whole room again, it is a wondrous place: thirty people seem to be in one place at one time, but in another way, they are in thirty different places in thirty different rivers of time. My respect for what we are doing together swells, as the richness of these lives and times dawns on me.

5

Corridors of Meaning
Classroom Arrangements for Becoming Better Readers

I've described my own classroom for a while, and now I would like to show you some others, especially because I believe that in helping our students become better readers, we are best served by diverse arrangements for diverse purposes. Let's take a walk down a corridor with four doors, each opening into an English classroom. If they were empty, these classrooms would be identical, since the school was built in the 1930s to house the lecture-centered model that prevailed then (as it still does in most places). However, these classrooms are not empty and no longer contain one uniform vision of what English teaching looks like. They are different in both grand and subtle ways.

These four teachers, along with the assistant principal, a custodian, and two parents, have been in a reading group for a couple of years. Together, they've read books like Joyce Carol Oates's *Because It Is Bitter and Because It Is My Heart,* William Perry's *Montgomery's Children,* Norman Rush's *Mating,* and Annie Dillard's *An American Childhood.* They meet at a restaurant once a month for dessert, coffee, and book talk. They have devised routines for getting conversations started, such as writing a few pages of reflection about the book before talking or choosing passages to read into the circle at the beginning of the meeting. As their group spirit and trust has grown, their discussions have become more and more honest, and they've allowed the books to provoke personal memories that deepen their connection to the literature and to each other. If you listened to one of their converstions now, even if you'd read the book, you would only understand some of it, since their shared history allows talk to flow between texts and to refer to earlier episodes in their continuing dialogue.

Out of that experience, they've also talked a lot about creating environments for their students that mirror the conditions they've created for themselves as readers. At any moment in the school year, their classrooms will look different, since they are different people teaching in reponse to different students' needs. All their classrooms, however, are places in which students make meaning, become communities of readers like those an active reader would want to construct for herself to support her literate life.

If you peek into the first room on this corridor, that one right there on your right, you'll see that the kids are getting settled pretty quickly, because this teacher, Lynn Samuelson, always starts the day's whole-group meeting while the bell is still reverbrating. Naturally, there are stragglers, but she wants to get the class started, so she'll try to remember to deal with them later.

"Good morning! Let's get out our books, so we can get started reading as soon as I finish what I want to say to you today."

This is also part of the class's regular routine, so most of the kids have followed this instruction before she even says it. Like most of her colleagues on this corridor, Lynn has tried to establish predictable routines in her classroom so she doesn't constantly have to explain to kids what they are supposed to do on discrete short-term assignments. With only forty minutes in the period, the stability, clarity, and permanence of its segments allow the students maximum time to work; they don't have to figure out the teacher's expectations anew each day.

Lynn sits on a stool at the front of the room, holding the book she's been reading and her writers notebook.

"You all know I've been reading Richard Selzer's memoir, *Down From Troy.*"

"How is it?" a student asks.

"I'm really enjoying it. He writes so beautifully. Anyway, I wanted to share with you something I'm trying in my notebook in response to the book. The thing is, I've been noticing from *your* notebooks that most of you are getting really good at writing about your own memories that come up as you read your book. Remember last week when Shari read hers? But I've been thinking that if we try to go back and forth more between the book and our memories, then we might be able to do more thoughtful writing about both the book and our lives. So I've been trying to do some of that in my notebook, and I'd like you to try it, too."

She goes on to describe an incident in which Selzer, then about ten years old, walking down the street with his mother, giggles at the sight of a man shouting out his misery to a maple tree. His mother roughly draws him close and says, "Listen to me, boy, one day you will be walking along the street talking to yourself out of misery, I promise you that. And some very cruel boy will gape at you and laugh." For Selzer, this is an example of his mother's passionate teaching "by precept and example, seizing each occasion as it came."

Lynn then reads from her notebook:

Richard Selzer's *Down From Troy,* p. 164. Couldn't help but think of that time when I was fourteen and I laughed at Aunt Emma's wig that looked so fake it reminded me of the solid plastic wigs I'd played with as a little girl. What was more, anybody could see it was on crooked. It really did look funny to me, and even knowing what I know now, when I see it in my mind's eye, I can laugh or at least chuckle. My grandmother, always Emma's older protective sister, dragged me into the bedroom and told me that Emma had a brain tumor (you'd think they might have told me before that) and that her chemotherapy was causing her hair to fall out. Of course, I was destroyed with guilt. I spent the rest of the day on the porch, unable to look at my aunt, now not because I was afraid I'd laugh but afraid I'd cry.

Some students smile and chuckle at her portrait of herself at their age, others glance at each other and grin ironically, rolling their eyes. Lynn pauses here in her reading and says, "When I'd written that much, I realized I was pretty far away from Selzer's story. After all, he isn't writing about illness, though there's plenty of that in the book, since he's a doctor. I wanted to discipline my response to be about this section of the book rather than to go too far off into my own life. If I wanted to, I could come back to the Aunt Emma story, but for now, I decided to go back and forth between my experience and the book, so I could understand them both better." She goes on reading:

What seems similar between my experience and Selzer's is the education-by-guilt quality of his mother's, my grandmother's, actions. These weren't lessons learned in a relaxed discussion by the fire, with the wise elder saying, "Never laugh at what seems foolish in someone else, since it is almost always the result of their pain, and in laughing, you'll just add to their pain." These teachings were in response to kids who had already screwed up, so that guilt was involved, and it must have been the power of the emotion that made the experience so memorable for Selzer and for me. Do such hard lessons have to be learned through painful mistakes? His mother was tougher with him, though, telling him that he himself would someday experience the very condition he giggled at. After all, my grandmother didn't say, "You're going to get a brain tumor, too." I can't imagine telling my ten-year-old son that he would be so miserable. She was a tough mother, and more accepting than most of us of the idea that life would be difficult, even for her little boy, that pain and grief are a part of everyone's life. That may be an important idea in the book, this acceptance of pain and death as part of the picture for us all.

Lynn finishes reading and looks off thoughtfully. The classroom is quiet for a minute while she thinks. "It was interesting to reread that," she says. "I'm going to have to think about it some more, and write about it. Can you see how I didn't just tell my story, but I went back and forth, trying to think through how Selzer and I are the same and how we are different? That made me think better about what Selzer meant by writing that, and also what my memory says about me. It helped me to be more reflective about my own experience, saying not just that this happened, but that this happened and here's what it means to me. That's going to make the memory so much more useful to me in my own writing, if I use this entry sometime later to make a poem or a memoir or whatever. *So*—I would like you to try doing some more of that in your own notebook over the next few days. See how it goes. Any questions? Let's get started."

The classroom seems to sigh into reading as kids open their books to where they've placed their bookmarks and slump into more relaxed postures in their desks. A few sit still for a few minutes, apparently deciding whether to read or write first. Lynn sits in a student desk and starts writing in her notebook. We are ten minutes into the period. Lynn's going to write for about five minutes and then have quiet conferences with about five students in a corner of the room. Let's step into the hall so I can fill you in on how the class operates.

You may recognize that Lynn has adapted her classroom structure for this part of the year from Nancie Atwell's *In the Middle*. Most of class time is spent reading silently and writing in response to reading. Students choose their own books (they can choose to read magazines occasionally but not exclusively). The main differences between Lynn's classroom and Atwell's lie in the roles of writing and talking. Because Lynn uses writers notebooks as containers for students' thinking on paper, she asks the students to write only for their own thinking, in a way they could use in pieces they might make later for readers. (Lynn found that when students wrote in dialogue journals for her or for other students, they naturally had to tell about the book before they could begin to explain any reflective or interpretive thoughts they had about it. By the time students finished summarizing, though, they were bored with writing and so never got around to anything else. Also, with one hundred and twenty students, Lynn could not keep up well with writing back to kids; she found she became perfunctory and arbitrary in what she said in their journals, especially since they wrote so much plot summary.) The kids are used to writing to think, because of their work earlier in the year in their writers notebook. They still write five nights a week in their notebook for homework, but only two of those entries have to be in response to their reading. Lynn has kept up her schedule, too, of collecting the notebooks, one class at a time on a biweekly rotating basis, to monitor the work and to research what kids are doing so that she knows what she needs to teach in minilessons. No one, including the teacher, writes anything in a writers notebook except the writer. If Lynn wants to recommend a book, an author, or a reading strategy to a student, she does it orally or by handing him a note. She often then asks the student to jot the suggestion into his notebook.

What Lynn liked about Atwell's idea of having students write to each other about their reading was that it provided kids with a way of collaborating on agendas for reading: good books to read next, authors to investigate, genres to try. It also raised student energy for reading and formed a reading community around the idea of choosing and finishing lots of books. Lynn's class accomplishes this through talk. On Tuesdays and Wednesdays, for the minilesson, Lynn tries to have students share something they have been doing in their writers notebook. Her primary purpose is to publicize useful strategies for notebook writing in response to literature, but she knows that student sharing also gets book titles, authors, and habits of reading into the classroom air. On Fridays, the first twenty minutes of class is devoted to small groups of kids talking to each other about their books, giving brief commercials for the title or author, comparing the book with others or with movies, passing the books around the group. She doesn't expect these conversations to be deep investigations into literary thought. The collaboration is for constructing a reading life, not for determining meaning in individual texts. Another structure at another time of year will focus on interpretive work. Different structures for different purposes. Trying to kill two birds with one stone leaves you with, at best, two dead birds. So that's it: what I've told you is all this class is doing at this time of the year. They've been doing it for four weeks, and they'll probably keep it up for three or four more, after which they will probably study a genre, as we'll see another of these English classes doing later.

Before this period ends, let's step into the classroom next door. Here, ninth graders are doing something you seldom see in school after about third grade, reading together in pairs. It's odd that we let go of that so early in school: there's nothing inherently elementary about it. You sit with someone you like, you read for a few minutes, then you say what's on your mind, you say something about the sense you're making, you have a little conversation about it, then you read some more. It's a relaxing way to be with somebody and a text. But it's also much more than that.

When they stop and talk out their thoughts as they read, students put into the air what might occur in their minds if they were reading silently but actively, the internal monologue of reading that Wolfgang Iser calls "the virtual text." When their partner answers, often in discord or at least from a different perspective, this monologue is complicated, becomes more dialogical and therefore more interpretive. Each reader sees that she is reading the text one way as opposed to another way, and the text isn't "just what it says," it's what you make of it.

The kids have chosen partners with whom they'll read for this entire chunk of the year, probably about four weeks or so, because it allows them to build a common history, and because if they shifted, some kids would have to wait around for a new partner. The pairs may not finish the short text they're working on by the end of the period, but that's all right; they'll take it home and write out their thinking as they read through the remainder, pausing in about the same rhythm they did in class. Then tomorrow, they'll read each other's logs and talk about the differences in how the reading went for them. If they finish the first reading in class, they'll write tonight anyway, some reflections about not only the piece, but the experience of reading it together. They'll spend most of tomorrow talking about what they thought about the text before choosing another short story, poem, or essay from the fifteen or so manilla envelopes taped on one wall. Or they may begin work on a text they choose on their own. Because they know that they will write tonight as an extension of their classroom talk, regardless of whether they "finish" the story, and that they can work on the story until they are ready to leave it, they don't feel pressured to finish before the bell. This is essential because their teacher wants their talk to be developed and elaborative rather than perfunctory.

This team of girls reading "Welcome" by Ouida Sebestyen (in Donald Gallo's *Sixteen*) has just started to talk, after a short burst of silent reading, so let's listen in.

First girl: Boy, her mother's a bitch.

Second girl: Well, she's *being* a bitch, but maybe she has a reason.

First girl: I mean about the friend, what's her name, Sharon, not letting her stay with them.

Second girl: I don't blame her. I wouldn't want a pregnant friend of my daughter staying in my house, or friend of mine either. I don't know why this girl wants her there. She's got enough problems with her parents getting divorced.

First girl: They're not getting divorced yet; maybe they'll patch things up, like she said. And what do you mean you wouldn't help out a friend? You wouldn't put me up if I didn't have any place else to stay?

Second girl: Not if you were pregnant! I don't want to take care of you and your baby.

First girl: I can't believe you! Thanks a lot!

Second girl: Well, maybe I would. I don't know, because I'm not in that situation. But I'm just saying I can understand the mother's point of view, especially if she's already got her own problems.

First girl: Anyway, I don't really understand why they keep talking about Sharon. What does she have to do with the story? It's about *them* and their problems and their relatives, not about her.

Second girl: Let's keep reading.

They've plunged back into another bout of silent reading, so let's walk around. As we scan the room, you'll notice that not all the talk right now is as constructive as theirs. Here one boy summarizes a couple of paragraphs, and his partner says, "Right," and they go back to reading. There a boy and a girl seem to be reading the entire poem silently before talking at all. Another pair, whom we can hear from across the room, seem to have strayed from the story completely and are talking about how much they hated a movie they both saw. It isn't surprising, though, that kids don't do perfectly right away the complex things we ask them to do. I've done this same type of reading with English teachers who had the same "problems." The point is for students to start doing it, so that they can get better at doing it, so that the activity can teach them in the ways it was designed to do. You don't begin golf lessons with a perfect stroke; that's why you're taking the lessons. Too often, we give up on structures that demand effort and learning from students because they "don't work" from the first few days we try them.

The teacher in this classroom, Sue Jacobs, is moving around the room, conferring with pairs of students. She listens to them talk for a while, then asks for an elaboration, a more developed thought. Sometimes she tries to slow them down so that they are really listening to each other and responding—having a conversation instead of two isolated reports of what they are thinking. When this talk gets better—a little deeper, a little more connected—she points out the difference between what they are doing now and what they were doing before she intervened. Then she goes on to another pair across the room, pausing en route to get a couple who seem to have drifted a little too far back on task. Let's interrupt her and ask why she has the students reading this way.

"I noticed when they were reading independently, based on what they wrote in their writers notebook and what they said in my conferences with them and in their groups, that a lot of my kids seemed to be lying back, waiting for meaning to come and get them or hoping the book would wash over them. Sometimes it went so far as their eyes just going across the page and their not knowing what they were reading. For other kids, they got the barest sense of the plot but didn't seem to think anything consciously about the story. I mainly wanted to force them to think as they read by having them speak their thoughts to a listener, and I thought this activity would help them concentrate on meaning. I had read Jerome Bruner's *Actual Minds, Possible Worlds,* where he has these think-aloud protocols for studying readers, which I guess a lot of reading researchers have used. And I'd read *Creating Classrooms for Authors* by Jerome Harste, Kathy Short, and Carolyn Burke, where they describe this one strategy they call Say Something, which is sort of the same thing. I just adapted those ideas and am trying to give the kids enough time to learn from them, with whatever help I can give them by conferring. But right now I've got to warn them about the bell, so they won't walk out of here without deciding what they're going to do tonight and plan for tomorrow. Sorry."

Having been shoved aside by the demands of a high school schedule (that's all right—we're used to it), let's get a drink of water during the break between periods and then check out another room.

Outside the classroom door across the hall, a group of four guys have pulled chairs into a circle and have started talking. Each of them holding a copy of *Slake's Limbo* by Felice Holman. Just inside the classroom door, we get a sense of the bigger picture of what is going on in Tom Dayton's room. The other groups are dispersed about the room, mostly, it seems, to allow as much space as possible between them. Tom doesn't tell them to do this; they've figured out that they can't hear their own group members if they are too close to another group. They've chosen the groups themselves, though those decisions obviously involved lots of difficult social negotiations, and they will stay in these groups for the whole year, except when they decide to shift. Tom's thinking, based on his experience in his own reading group, is that only by being together over a long time can a group build enough common history to be able to make connections among texts and develop a shared knowledge about one another's lives. Also, part of Tom's agenda is to put the students in a situation where they have to learn to get along and collaborate on ways to work together without his solving those problems for them. What is worth doing takes time. They've been at this for about six weeks.

The groups decide together what books they will read together. Tom has sets of six books each of twenty or so titles in his room. He considers these books to be productive of good talk, in that they open the students to questions with which they wrestle in their own lives and are interesting on several different meaning levels. When the groups were choosing their first books, he talked to them during whole-class meetings about these qualities. After explaining his criteria, he told the groups they could choose other books they thought met those criteria if they could find enough copies. Obviously, this means he often hasn't read the books they are reading, but that doesn't matter, since he's serving as a consultant on ways to proceed as a group rather than "teaching the book" to the group.

Each group decides how it will work with each new book. Tom decided that it was important to let them do what they thought best at first, and then try, through consultations with the groups and whole-class meetings, to nudge the groups toward practices that would better enable them to build meaning collaboratively. At first, many of the groups simply read aloud and then summarized orally, so Tom announced that most of the reading had to occur outside the group's time together. The groups' response tended to be to summarize what they had read independently in the first five minutes of their meeting, then go on reading aloud and summarizing orally.

Tom began explaining strategies for using writing to facilitate discussion. He asked the groups to assign, as homework, broad write-to-think entries in their writers notebooks: memories evoked by the chapters they read, opinions about certain characters, ideas about how the place where the characters lived seems to condition their actions, or connections between this book and something else they've read together. He was careful never to give any one such assignment monolithically to the whole class, since, first, one question cannot apply equally to all books and readers, and second, his main interest was in teaching his students to ask *themselves* questions about their books, not to perform for him. He circulated among the groups, advising them on their homework assignments, and pushing where necessary. Such prediscussion thinking allows students to select out some element of the section of the book they have read independently, which is a necessary step toward being able to have an interpretive discussion. Eventually, the groups began to have discussions he recognized as the same sort of collaboration for meaning he and his adult reading group engaged in. Most of the groups still need help developing strategies for sustaining good talk—galvanizing issues often fizzle after fifteen minutes or so—for moving back and forth between other texts and this text, for getting back to the book after someone tells a personal story. But since they have come this far, Tom is not discouraged about the possibility of pushing them farther through whole-class meetings and consultations with individual groups. Let's pull Tom away from this group to tell us how it feels to be him.

"At first, I just wanted to quit this. Every time I could come up for air, in prep periods or after school, I'd think, This is crazy. Some of the kids don't have the first idea what it means to work together, or even just be together. It would be so much less painful if I just took over and made the decisions for them. But then I'd think, No, this is exactly what they need to be doing, precisely because they have so much trouble doing it. The kids I teach, maybe more than anyone, need to learn how to get along, how to work out differences democratically and diplomatically. It felt so socially charged for the kids that I asked them to write to me about how they felt, doing reading this way. They were overwhelmingly positive, basically saying that they never wanted to read any other way. They had particular complaints about this one or that one not doing his homework or being a pain, but what that said to me was that they were really engaged in identifying and working through the problems they were having getting things done. Then I'd go for a few more days and get disgusted with the low quality of their conversations: They aren't even listening to each other! They're not doing anything with reading; they're only focusing on the social dynamics! Then I'd think again that that's why they need to work on it. What I want them to learn is to collaborate, to work together to do more with their reading than they could alone. Also, I'm learning so much about reading by seeing what they don't do that I do, and trying to put into words some strategies for getting more mature as readers. So now, I don't care how hard it is or if it takes all year. I've relaxed about it—a little bit—sometimes. I think for them, it's become a really important part of their day. In a way, it's more real for them than most of their other classes. The mix of socialness and work is more like their extracurricular activities. Obviously, I just wish the class period was longer—Excuse me just a minute."

But before he can say anything to the whole class, the bell rings.

"Everybody freeze for just one second. If you didn't figure out your homework for tomorrow, see each other later in the day, at lunch or after school or else call each other on the phone. You know you're responsible for making those assignments and for doing them. See you tomorrow."

While that trio of girls presses around Tom to air some grievance against the fourth member of their group, let's talk a bit here in the corner before we go on to our final classroom on this tour. In the rooms we've been in so far, the teachers have brought reading into focus for a season of the school year lasting from four to twelve weeks, with writing receding a bit for this time. There is still writing going on, but for now it is primarily in support of the reading, while it also accumulates in the notebooks, as any other entries would, for possible future use. This next classroom, however, is involved in a study of poetry, where the kids are both reading and writing in the genre. (See Chapters 7, 8, 9, and 10 for discussions of genre studies and of the ways reading and writing receive relative emphasis throughout the year.) Let's take a look.

The minilesson is over, and students are working individually. Most of the time in here, students decide how they will spend the bulk of the period, reading or writing. They know there are several things they have to do: collect at least twenty poems and responses to them into a personal poetry anthology, submit three of their own poems to the class magazine, and submit three poems (maybe or maybe not the same ones that went into the magazine) to their teacher, Deb Farris, for evaluation. There are deadlines for each of these posted on the wall, but today, they're still about three weeks away. In addition, Deb meets with a group of six students each Tuesday and Thursday to study intensively a poem she chooses for them. These groups rotate, so most students will have this experience three times during this course of study.

There's a lot going on. Since today is Wednesday, Deb is circulating, conferring with students either about their own poems or about their responses to poems in their anthologies. Usually, she tries to tie these together, asking students how their reading of poems is informing their writing. At this point in the year, her main purpose is to get her students reading like writers. After each conference, she makes notes in a spiral notebook about the poem they discussed.

But Deb is only working with one or a few students at a time, so we need to look at what the rest of the kids are doing if we want to understand this classroom. The desks are arranged to create separate areas for various activities. Over there, against the chalkboard, are Deb's bookcases, with about twenty or thirty books of poetry on the top shelves. She's gathered together the anthologies from her classroom library, a few of her own books, all the poetry from the school library, and several from the local public library. She wasn't picky, since these books are for the students to read in widely. Everything is here, from "classics" to children's poetry, with a preponderance of poets who are still living, men and women of all races, people the kids might imagine seeing at the grocery store or the library, people they, like Holden Caulfield, wish they could phone whenever they felt like it. The desks near the bookcases are arranged in several clusters and are used for reading, researching, copying, and collecting.

On the opposite wall is a line of desks facing the windows, for students who are generating first drafts or putting bits and pieces into their writers notebook. Nearest us are two rows of desks, the "workshop" for revising, for writing responses to collected poems, for editing and cleaning up final drafts for submission.

Here's a young woman who has her anthology folder open to a poem while she's working on her own draft. Since we want to understand this as a reading classroom, let's talk to her about her thinking, about why this poem, "Homage to My Hips," by Lucille Clifton, attracted her enough to anthologize it.

"I like it because it's funny and happy and kind of serious at the same time," Sheila says. "It's like, she's got these big hips, and maybe some people think she's fat or whatever, and sometimes maybe she doesn't even like these hips but she writes this poem that says, well here's what they are and I *do* like them. I think everybody, well maybe not everybody but a lot of people, have things on them they don't like, and this poem could kind of help them. Like I don't like my hair, but I'm thinking about writing a poem about it anyway. I wrote that in my writers notebook last night.

"But what I'm looking at right now, the way she writes it, it's like she's saying these really loud things with these little quiet letters and words. That's why I like the no capitals, it makes the poem look quiet and it makes you pay more attention or else you'll miss the period. And her line breaks, like, sound right to me. So in the poem I'm writing right now, which is not the one about the hair, I'm not using capitalization, and I'm trying to make my line breaks sound right, just like the way you'd say it, if you meant it."

Reading like a writer, as Sheila is doing, directs the reader's attention to the writer's craft. Consequently, Sheila's description of what she likes about the poem is more technical, more attentive to the marks on the page, than it would be if she were not making poems herself. Why would she think so deliberately about Clifton's conventions, the lowercase letters, the sentences, the level of diction, the line breaks, if she were reading it only for pleasure? These are details of craft, and only a craftsperson really cares.

Now that we've stood up, Johnny, sitting in front of Sheila has turned around to joke with her about her hair (he heard what she said about it). Deb looks over from a few feet away, where she's been conferring with another student, and says, "Johnny and Sheila, let's get writing, please. You still have quite a bit of time." Johnny sighs and returns to his draft. He's done some work on it this period and wants to stop but hasn't decided what to work on next. It's in these seams of the process that the kids tend to look up, just as I might get up for a cup of coffee. Deb understands this and accepts her role as the voice of getting-back-to-writing discipline, though she wants to try to figure out ways to put that voice into the minds of the kids. Like the rest of us, she hasn't discovered the perfect answer. She does need the classroom to be quiet, though, for the most part, since reading and writing poetry are generally not activities one would choose in a crowded roomful of chatting friends.

The room is quiet now, except for occasional low comments and the flipping of pages as students browse for poems that strike them as interesting. We are, as a matter of fact, the only ones making noise in the room, so let's slip out before we cause any more trouble.

As I told you they would, these classrooms look different in their approaches to reading. However, what is really different is the social arrangement of readers in the classroom and the particular combinations of reading, writing, and conversing; these teachers share a set of essential notions of what reading is all about.

They all believe that their priority should be helping their students read better, that is, to become more flexible in the range of ways they can make meaning from texts, and that their attention should therefore be on what their students do with texts, rather than on particular texts that all students should read. That initial assumption cleared the decks of their literature curriculum and allowed them to build from there. They have no list of books they have to "do." Rather, their decision making is built entirely on purposes they construct from reflecting on what their students can do and what they need to learn to do.

Like Rosenblatt, Bleich, and others, they believe that reading is a transaction between reader and text, that all we really know about a text is what we make of it, and that what we make of it depends on what we bring to it. A reading is not a static artifact but a dynamic event in time, from before the text is chosen to beyond the echoes of the final discussion about it. To any reading event, the reader must bring knowledge from a wide range of sources, including personal life experience, experiences with other texts, personality, culture, values, the context in which the text is read and the political relationships of the people involved, and the reader's purposes and projects. The text is one important contributing agent to this exchange, among others. Each of these contributing agents brings pressure to bear on the reading event, and the meaning of the event is determined by the exact way they come together. Figure 5–1 diagrams these relationships as axes or open corridors feeding into a single hub.

Reading, then, even within a reader's mind, is a collaborative act. Moreover, the context for reading, the purposes and projects for reading, and the cultural background for reading are such powerful constraints on meaning that the teachers whose classrooms we have been visiting give them primary attention in establishing environments for readers. Reading is social, and different social arrangements make reading a different kind of experience. What these teachers are trying to do is put into the air of the classroom the kinds of conversations they hope their students will internalize for their independent reading. Decision making in the teaching of reading is always a matter of asking, What do these students need to learn to do? (the answer to which always reveals our values about reading), and then asking, What kind of conversations best support that and lead to independence? and structuring opportunities for such conversations in the classroom.

Believing that strong readers are flexibly empowered to construct and control meaning in many different situations, these teachers, at different times of the year,

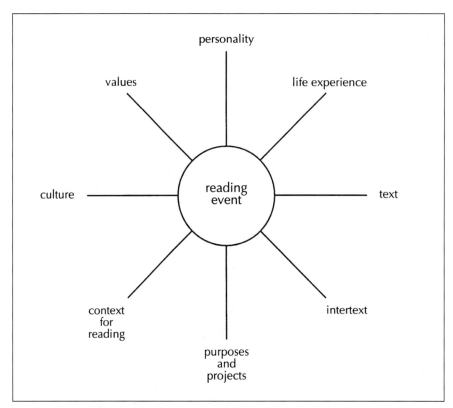

FIG. 5–1: *Things a reader brings to a reading event.*

establish varying social arrangements for varied purposes, as they described when we heard from them. Different social structures accomplish different things in a reading life. "Independent" reading of self-selected books, like Lynn had going today, gives students private ownership over their reading, allows the teacher to get to know each kid as a reader, and encourages energetic reading agendas. Students come to prefer some authors and genres and build a mind's shelf full of books they want to read someday. Partnered reading, with frequent conversations in the midst of the text, like Sue has established in her classroom, almost forces students to be poised more actively as meaning makers while they read. Reading groups like Tom has, where students collaborate on selection, discussion strategies, and interpretation, allow students to internalize interpretive conversations, develop the habits of mind that allow critical reading. Genre studies make reading writers insiders in the ways of a certain kind of text and help them pay attention to the craft of writing, which was Deb's purpose in her classroom for this chunk of the year. Whole-class texts, on which no one on this corridor was working at present, give students the opportunity to be mentored to their teacher's ways of reading. Because of the varied strengths of the available structures, these teachers seek to move through different arrangements as the school year progresses. No single structure would do the job for them.

In each of the above classrooms, writing plays a different role in supporting and extending the reading work. At any time in the year when reading is on the front burner, writing might play one of three roles: a tool for thinking in preparation for oral discussions, a transactive form of written discussion between or among readers in the community, or an answer-in-kind, where the response to literature occurs in the making of literature (see Chapter 6). In the classrooms we've looked at, only writing as preparation for discussion (in Tom's and Sue's classrooms) and writing literature in response to literature (in Lynn's and Deb's classes) were in play. Written discussion may take the form of dialogue journals such as Jana Stanton and Nancie Atwell describe, or it may be extended into a more essayistic form, as I will describe in Chapter 10. What is important to remember is that most of the time, writing in a reading classroom is primarily accomplishing one or the other of these purposes and not all three at once. If students are writing literature in response to literature, it will usually not sound like a written discussion, with explicit claims, evidence from the text, and other markers of expository prose. If students are writing for each other, the language will not necessarily contain the seeds for beautiful pieces of literature. There is no point in getting frustrated when student writing doesn't accomplish something that wasn't our main purpose in structuring the writing opportunities. As in designing the social interactions, we teachers are well served by keeping our instructional purposes for writing unified and clear in our mind and in our classrooms.

Because we have these diverse purposes for the readers in our classrooms, and because different social arrangements for reading are appropriate for each of those purposes, I believe that students are most helped by moving through different structures during a school year, sometimes reading explicitly in order to inform their understanding of the craft of writing, sometimes reading in preparation for collaboration about meaning with peers, sometimes in pursuit of their personal interests and obsessions. Any single structure, whether it's a whole class marching through a full-length work or individuals reading self-selected adolescent literature, must be insufficient. However, no one school year could ever be long enough or full enough to exhaust every possible purpose or social structure for reading. That's why it is so necessary to assess, early on and continually, what kinds of reading situations students have experienced before, so that we can choose either to build on prior strengths or to provide students with a new kind of experience. The point is not to inject them with, for example, paired reading so that they have "had that," but to provide an experience that will add to their repertoire of situations into which they can put themselves, and perhaps to situate them in a conversation that will change their mental habits—get them to actively construct sense, test a text against their own life, or formulate questions as they read, for example—when they read on their own.

When we construct classrooms that place a high value on the strategies and habits that make up our best and most generous vision of a reading life rather than on a narrow canon of literary works, we teach our students to fish instead of catching them a fish. We give them opportunities to develop adaptable, supple minds that can, given a new situation, learn to engage with any text and any community while still drawing upon the familiar strength of their own experience, personality, culture, and values.

TIME AND GROWTH

Time is inherent in education. Doesn't education always involve a person changing across time? Isn't learning always about change? Alfred North Whitehead tells us that "the lack of attention to the rhythm and character of growth is the main source of wooden futility in education." For John Dewey, education *is* growth, and growth is the reorganization, reformulation, and transformation of experience in the light of the present environment toward future situations. Within the temporal process of the teaching/learning transaction, the teacher and student have to use the present moment to transform past experience toward a future vision. They build upon their shared and individual memories and try to create a new experience, and in doing so, they're deliberately trying to move at least the student, and preferably the teacher as well, to a future understanding, which is not yet. The whole enterprise is a light shining into the future, a time when the student will know what so far he can only mimic. Lev Vygotsky wrote about the "zone of proximal development," which is a crucial idea in my teaching. He's referring to the realm wherein the learner can accomplish with help today what she will do alone tomorrow. We cannot talk about education without couching every concept in time.

Most of the progressive revisions of educational ideas we have seen this half-century have involved, at heart, the restoration of time as the central reality of learning. Think of how time is embedded in our words *process, development, memory,* and *reform.*

Moreover, it is when we have ignored the temporal dimension of our educative and learning actions that we have made our most egregious errors, such as favoring written products over the processes by which they are made, privileging static interpretations of literary works over readers' strategies in constructing readings that are persuasive to others in their community, caring more about our language's frozen rules than the dynamic ingeniousness with which people *use* language, assuming that curriculum consists of a fixed body of content rather than socialization into a community's ways with words. Ignoring the fact that language is action that happens within specific contexts, we have then accrued a pile of static facts we can write on a chalkboard, and it is on those temporally stripped bits that we spend our time. In service to those bits of information—rather than serving the growth of students—we chop up our own attention so that we can manage to talk for a few minutes about each of the items on the board. How absurd! How did we come to despise education so much?

I need to make sure that I stay focused not on the knowledge that now, for me, seems outside of time, but rather on the growth of the people with whom I work. I honor both knowledge and growth when I make sure I keep on learning about writing, reading, literature, language, culture, and then carefully watch and assess students' growth. This way, I don't worry about what I am going to say to them, since I can only speak out of my own learning anyway. A teachable moment, after all, is only the intersection of two or more people's lines of growth. It can never be absolute truth. But what could be more exciting or rewarding than the electric meeting between two vital learners' growth lines on a particular rainy morning in March?

6

A Place in the Conversation
Writing Literature in Response to Literature

I t's late: the time of night when all the news has been related, all the gossip glossed, and the conversation gets meaty—the hour of confidences. Imagine a conversation: Larry is talking to Vivian, his slightly younger sister, in an all-night coffee shop.

Larry: It's been a year already, but I just can't get over it. If he hadn't kept badgering me: "Sell me your Camaro. Sell it to me. It'll do us both good. I'll pay you more for it than you could get for it in trade; plus I'll get it for less than I could buy a used car." But I had a bad feeling about it, about selling my car to my best friend. I mean we were counselors at Camp Happy Hills for three years together, fought with those bratty kids and cleaned their noses, made them take their showers. Stayed up late after they were in bed and laughed about it—got silly, giggling out there with the crickets. Four years we worked there. Then we chose colleges within an easy drive of each other so that we could get together on weekends, sit on lawn chairs up on his roof and laugh some more—and talk about our lives. When he met Sarah, I drove her every weekend to his place—and stayed in a hotel so they'd have privacy. Paid for it myself. Lots of money. Lots of time. And after all that, because of this stupid Camaro with its damned broken transmission, we haven't spoken in—what? A year? Can you believe that?

Vivian: You recapitulated some of the highlights from your friendship with Tony, using those moments synecdochically to represent the whole relationship. Specifically, you mentioned your camp experience, the rooftop talks, and your sacrifices for his girlfriend Sarah. This was all in a flashback, after which you returned to the present and closed with some dramatically ringing rhetorical questions.

Larry: (*pause*) It's not just the car. It's not losing a friend. It's not even losing a best friend. It's that, in losing Tony, I've lost my memory. He's connected to all those moments in my past: he *is* those moments, to me. I feel like there's this chasm in the shape of a Camaro between me—now—and my life up until now.

Vivian: Tony is symbolic of your youth, and he's been corrupted by the American Dream of a nice car that works. The theme is loss of innocence.

Pretty strange conversation—not much like a conversation at all, since Vivian is obstinately refusing to respond as a human being to what Larry says, to take anything he says personally. Unfortunately, the conversation that goes on in most English classes—the reader-writer intercourse with literature, the one in which students converse with writers—is often like this one: immediately analytic, essentially unresponsive. That's because students write—when they write in response to literature—almost exclusively *about* literature rather than talking back in any kind of language that would be appropriate in what we normally call conversation.

Even in classes where part of the year or part of the week is a writing workshop, the study of literature tends to employ the critical essay, expository writing, as not only the primary but also the exclusive mode of response. Writing in response seems always to mean writing to *explain*. (This may even be true of the dialogue journals Nancie Atwell describes in *In the Middle.*)

You know the usual form: students focus on one particular assertion (if the teacher can urge them this far) about the text they've read, and they seek to prove that assertion by several supporting assertions, which are, in turn (again, if the teacher prevails) supported by specific references to the text. The form is rhetorical, argumentative, combative, in that it seeks logically and rationally to prove its point, its assertion, its thesis, to prove the writer's control. In that sense, it's an objective mode of writing, positivistic and scientistic. It treats the text as an object outside the reader, to which the reader *cum* critic *cum* writer makes reference—and over which the reader *cum* critic *cum* writer exercises dominion. This type of writing is good at achieving abstract unity and focus, and it ought to be a good way to teach students to recognize assertions that can't be supported because they aren't true. (Of course, if requiring expository writing were an effective way of buttressing a student's crap detector, then, given the uniformity with which exposition has for so long dominated all academic writing in this country, Americans ought by now to be very good at recognizing assertions that can't be supported because they aren't true. I leave it to the reader to judge the effectiveness of one hundred years of essay writing in engendering critical thinking in the populace.)

In *More than Stories: The Range of Children's Writing,* Thomas Newkirk critiques what he terms "the Great Divide approach to literacy," where children who have written nothing but narrative and description for seven years are suddenly and without transition forced to write nothing but exposition for six more years. Newkirk cites two flaws in this pervasive split: one, most students never achieve expository competence because they are inadequately prepared for it in early grades, and two, "secondary students do not get enough opportunities to write the kind of discourse that they read and are thus denied the insights into reading that writing can provide" (p. 5). Moreover, the Great Divide also separates teachers from each other, prohibiting community between elementary and secondary teachers, persuading us all that we have nothing to learn from one another. Newkirk attributes the schism in the faculty, in part, to "the ideology of distinctiveness that claims that the interests and abilities of young children differ fundamentally from those of older students" (p. 6). Newkirk's project in his book is to expand the range of opportunity for young children's nonnarrative writing. I contend that we secondary teachers need to do our part to balance school discourse, and we might start by reconciling our theories of reading with the types of response writing we occasion for our students.

Poets have always been singularly aware of the inadequacy of expository prose for understanding and living with the meaning of poetry. A. R. Ammons points out that literature is a different form of discourse from logical exposition. The distinction isn't superficial; it's essential. Poetry (and, I would add, other literary modes) "leads to the unstructured sources of our beings, to the unknown, and returns us to our rational, structured selves refreshed. . . . [It is] a verbal means to a non-verbal source. . . . Nothing that can be said about it in words is worth saying" (p. 8). Yeats claimed, "Man can embody truth but he cannot know it," and D. H. Lawrence asserted, "Art-speech is the only truth. An artist is usually a damned liar, but his art, if it be art, will tell you the truth of his day."

As teachers of writing, we know that different modes of writing spring from and contribute to different modes of thinking. One kind of thought gives rise to and rises from expository writing, another to and from narrative writing, another to and from poetic writing, another to and from dramatic writing, and so on. When we talk about reading and the ways readers respond to texts, we often say that readers respond subjectively, but that seems dissonant with the ways we always have students write their responses.

James Britton, in *Language and Learning,* postulated the diagram in Figure 6–1 to describe kinds of experience of language. In the center is expressive language, the common kind of talk we do at home and informally around friends, the home base of language. To the right is transactional, analytic language, which we use to objectify and explain to others what we understand to be logical and rational. To the left is poetic language, which is more indirect, more subjective. How does it happen that the reading of literature occurs left of center, somewhere in the subjective realm, and that writing from that reading inevitably moves right? Is it natural and necessary that this occur, that the resymbolization of a symbolization be analytic? If it is natural and necessary, why then does it only occur in the writing of people who draw either a report card or a paycheck from the academy? Why is

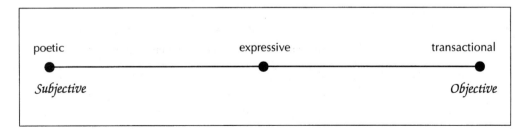

FIG. 6–1: *James Britton's language continuum.*

it not part of the life of all exceptionally literate people? Why doesn't A. R. Ammons do it all the time?

Clearly, transforming a notion from literary to explanatory will result in a different notion altogether. As soon as you say A is B or A means B, then A no longer has the same integrity, and art-speech yields to a less accurate kind of utterance, pretending to know truth rather than embodying it. The poem is flattened out, and possibility, which was myriad in literary indeterminacy and readerly subjectivity, seems reduced. Accepting and maintaining the integrity of the poem *as a poetic utterance* might require leaving it alone—not transmogrifying it into an essay.

What we teach students in limiting them to the exposition of literature is that though their first impressions may be subjective, ultimately they must squelch their response in favor of genres of writing that aspire to more objectivity. We teach them, even if we don't believe in the objective reality of meaning in a text, that their discussion of either the text *per se* or their written response (as a text itself) must refer to the objective existence of the text or response—or must seem to. Their subjective response is still preempted. By creating an environment that values essayistic modes of response, we, to some extent, force reductionist, scientistic ways of thinking, however contrary to our intent that may be. With school's shooing of kids' literate experiences out of the subjective realm, no wonder student regard for poetry is minimal. They don't see it as useful—even for emotional response—because *we* don't. No wonder when they do write poetry, it is so often sloppily felt, sentimental drivel—they think intellection is necessarily expository.

There are good reasons to write essays in response to literature, and the very explicitness I have been criticizing undoubtedly has a place. But the tyranny of the essay in secondary English classrooms ought to be questioned. There are other ways of responding to literature, and these other ways, involving as they do the reprocessing of response into new literature, are the paths most often traveled by practicing authors of literature. Many of us spend much of our year trying to help our students view themselves as authors; yet, in their relationship to literature, they are still "merely students." They never respond as authors, taking full responsibility for their gut-level response to the issues raised by the texts they read. They look at literature as if it were a mountain, something perhaps beautiful and awesome, something they could study and climb if they only had the inclination and the skill, but not something they could ever make themselves.

Who are our students? What is the purpose of teaching literature to these particular people? As Robert Probst points out (and he isn't telling us anything we aren't faced with every weekday morning), they are not all going to be literary scholars or even English majors. Our purpose, rather than having them jump through the hoops of academe, ought to be something more like opening opportunities for what Frank Smith calls "membership in the club," helping them to see themselves as "that type of person" who would meaningfully engage in and with reading and writing. The processes of literacy have to be seen as lifetime processes, habits of mind that students can carry with them into joyfully literate lives. What is the nature of a joyfully, exceptionally literate life? Maybe we can get some idea about the nature of such a life by looking at what authors do with their reading, how writers respond to literature.

For one thing, writers are constantly in search of clues to their craft, reading with a heightened awareness of how literature gets made. Thoreau said, "The works of the great poets have never yet been read by mankind, for only great poets can read them. They have only been read as the multitude reads the stars, at most astrologically, not astronomically." Faulkner found out how to write *The Sound and the Fury,* among other things, by reading Joyce with the eyes of a practitioner.

I am a very bad carpenter, but occasionally, when the house needs a set of bookshelves, say, I build something. When I am thus engaged, I have eyes for carpentry; I notice every joint of every cabinet I see, constantly telling myself, *Oh, sure, I could do that,* or *Maybe if I had the right tools,* or just, *Wow.* That's what it's like for authors to read. Responses analogous to mine about carpentry go into their notebook, and from the accumulation of such noticings, art grows.

Moreover, to writers, the ideas in literature are not just "themes"; they are blood. Authors take the ideas in literature personally. Thoughts matter. Robert Browning fell in love with Elizabeth Barrett without having met her because of what he read. He wrote to her, "I love this book, and I love you, too." Malcolm Cowley and others relate stories of fist fights over style and themes in Paris cafés in the thirties. Americans! Fighting about style!

Authors, in response to what they read, enter into conversation with ideas or worldviews. They "choose" their topics because they can't help it; their strong feelings about what they read—whether sympathetic or oppositional—compel them to write. Robert Coles, in *The Call of Stories,* quotes from a conversation with William Carlos Williams, where the poet-physician said:

> I'll pick up a good story or novel and . . . I'm in someone else's world, thank God. I'm listening to their words. My own words become responses to what they say—the novelist or one of my patients. We're on stage! . . . I'm thinking of the moral seriousness [you can see] on the stage, a certain kind of exchange between people, where the words really are charged.

Writers who take themselves seriously engage in arguments, not always in so many words, but through the forms they employ—arguing and concurring with other conventions. They demonstrate their understanding and appreciation for form through conscious and unconscious imitation. Their formal innovations can be read as part of a conversation. Occasionally, poets and writers do engage in literary criticism, usually when they need to pay some bills, or when they wish to support the work of a friend, or when they need a bird's-eye view of their literary world. At any rate, critical essays are far from their primary mode of response to the literature they read, and often as not, their criticism serves as thinly veiled justification for the literature they've already made.

Once we understand what great writers *do,* we need to find ways of building classroom structures to contain that doing. If authors keep notebooks wherein they store jottings about craft learned from reading and engage in arguments with other authors about ideas, then notebooks need to become similarly important and thoughtful structures in our classrooms. If writers' topics evolve in opposition to or in concurrence with ideas they read, we need to provide, and consider as prewriting, productive and open-ended discussion of the ideas and personal emotional associations students make from their reading. If reading informs authors' ears in deliberate ways, we need to open the possibility for students to read and hear language that feeds their writing. Our classroom structures need to offer opportunities for students to accomplish four crucial purposes: *to learn to be affected by literature; to write response statements out of the subjective ways it touches them; to allow their thinking in response to what they read to feed into a continuous writing life; and to apprentice themselves as makers of literature to the literary artisans whose work they admire.* The coming chapters in this book will provide more complete descriptions of how these purposes might guide a curriculum for English, but they require a little development before we move on.

Student writers need to learn to be affected by literature

It is obviously possible to read literature and be unaffected by it. I, for example, don't think I was ever really moved by anything I read for English class, and that wasn't the fault of the texts. It was my reading that was cold, not the stories. I was a "good reader," however, and capable of feeling powerfully connected to what I read. I was in a lot of plays in high school, and I can remember taking scripts home and standing in the middle of my room and saying the words over and over again, trying not so much to memorize them as to sink them into my personality, to take them as personally as I could, to convince myself that these sentences actually applied to me. There were nondramatic texts, too, that almost crushed me under heavy feeling. At thirteen and fourteen, I was intensely religious, and C. S. Lewis's essays shook me to my bones. During my junior and senior years, books like *The Catcher in the Rye, The World According to Garp,* and *Henderson, the Rain King* seemed to be directed straight at my identity, telling me who to become. Yet my reading of books and plays for English class was entirely different, more objective and superficial. It didn't seem really possible to take those books into myself because the teacher had read them *lots* of times before and knew them better than I ever would. Even as she tried to get us to think more interpretively, she already knew the novel or play so well that there was no point in our trying to guess at what she already knew. I think I read in a way that resisted involvement because I needed to keep to a kind of least common denominator of the text, the things we would need to know to be thought competent, to pass the tests, to write the essays, to get the grade that was only hers for the giving. Fortunately, I had that other reading life, especially in acting, which outlasted my formal literacy education. Most people don't.

What we as teachers value about reading creates the nature of reading in our classrooms. Reading literature in our class is what we make it. If we want our students to take literature personally, we have to talk up that value and then put our time and practice where our mouth is. For me, this means giving sermons and pep talks about the power of literature to move us emotionally, discussing my own responses to whatever I'm reading independent of my teaching. It also means reading with students shared texts that I don't already know, so that I'm responding to it just like they are, not pulling out my bag of fixed opinions. Also, when I discuss literature with students, whether it's individually or in groups, I ask questions like, How did you feel about that? and What do you think it is, from your own life, that causes you to feel that way when you read this? I do not choose, for the whole class, texts that I have no reason to believe can affect students personally. I don't believe my English teachers even had the same goals in mind as I do in choosing texts when they selected *The Scarlet Letter, An American Tragedy,* or *Darkness at Noon.* The kind of talk among students I value when they are working in response groups is both intellectually rigorous and personally engaged. By encouraging and entertaining personal response in all the possible arrangements for reading, I expect to create an environment in which students are used to answering back, from their resources of knowledge, experience, and feeling.

When students write in response to literature, that writing should originate in the subjective ways the literary work touches them

I have said that I tell students over and over that one of the main ways I want them to grow as readers is to become the kind of people who are moved by literature, who expect literature to affect them personally and help them see the world differently, even sometimes to change completely the way they think about their own lives, the lives of others, and their society. I would create an odd disjunction between thought and writing if I asked them, immediately after they read a piece of literature, to write about things like poetic devices they can recognize in the piece, how the text fits with the rest of the author's corpus or the literary school with which she is associated, what the author is trying to say, or any other issue that places the text outside the reader, turning the literary work into an object, rather than treating it as part of the reader's subjectivity. In fact, especially with older students, I ask them *not* to try to be "smart English students," as they may have been trained to be in other English classes. No writing is "natural"; it's always conventional, the product of what the writer has been taught socially about what writing in a given context is for and how it can go. Writing about our own experience or our feelings in response to literature is not a return to some romantically aboriginal discourse for everyone. For some students, the subjective thinking on paper I'm trying to draw from them does not come easily, but I do not necessarily expect it to. I'm inducting them into a new discourse, and I have to teach it—by talking and writing that way myself in front of them and by carefully constructing the environment of my classroom.

As I've discussed in my descriptions of notebooks, I want to narrow the gap between students' human thinking and their writing, to come as close as possible, in fact, to eliminating that gap by supporting writing as a tool for thinking. If I hope for literature to matter personally to them, then I need to demonstrate, encourage, and assist them in writing "from the gut" their immediate and visceral reaction to the text, often right after they read. The writing I sponsor, then, supports and guides the thinking I want to educate into their reading lives. Sometimes that thinking centers on memories the story brings up in them and reflections on those remembered events; other times the thinking is more freely associative. My instructions to them are usually to write "just what the text makes you think about, how it makes you feel, what it reminds you of, your honest first thoughts that in your head run alongside the words of the text."

Jerome came upon a poem by Marcia Southwick that made him think in new and surprising ways.

A Burial, Green

It was afternoon, and my brother split
a turtle's head
open in the rain; the tiny skull
glistened, and soon the ants knew
every detail of cracked shell.
For hours he sat in the blue shade
of the elm, planning a burial
for his small dead, until
the shadows knew each curve
of grass around the green and orange
spotted shell, a tiny helmet
filling with air. It was spring
and the bark on the dogwood trees
was slick and wet, the cardinals twittered
on the green feeder.
And my brother thought it was ceremony,
the way the door to our white house opened
and he entered, done with his spade
and boots, the way my mother
hovered in the doorway
and touched his shoulder
without a word
like the rain.

Jerome immediately wrote the following response in his notebook:

The poem was about the feelings of a boy who had smashed a turtle's head open. The theme of the poem dealt with the boy's feeling of remorse over what he had done, and his grief of the turtle's burial. I didn't really care about this boy's morals being rubbed the wrong way.

The underlying feeling of the organicness and wetness of the day seemed to overpower the theme.

I got a feeling of leaving the world of heat and society and entering a primordial ZONE. A basic world with basic life forms no higher than a turtle. I felt like I was feeling the cool, pure wet grass with all of my body. I smelled wet bark and loamy earth. I tasted the pure coolness of the wetness. I felt the residual warmth of the turtle's brains. The ants and worms were there in their simplicity. Every bit of life has its own slight pool of warmth, the plants and the animals. The only thing that didn't have warmth was rocks and sand. They were just there. The soil, the earth, reeked with life potential. There was no rot, no disease, no pain. It was cool, not cold, like rolling naked in newly cut grass in the shade of an early spring. Then it was over when the boy went inside and was touched on the shoulder by his mother. I felt as if the clothing I am putting on does not give me security, for it is restricting, like light spring clothes are like a strait-jacket arctic outfit. I put all this on and enter society in my newborn insensitivity. Like the boy, I am touched, and I am commited forever to the world of today. Society welcomes me, and I know I can't live without the touch, but I wish I didn't.

You can see Jerome being initially drawn toward and then rejecting his learned way of giving his teachers what they wanted, saying what he thought the poem's "theme" must be, which must of course have something to do with morality. Then he flatly states that he just doesn't care about that theme. The bulk of his response is impressionistic and emotional, personal though not autobiographical in any obvious way. He has allowed the poem to work on him, to take him on an unexpected journey of thought, which the writing supported. I don't believe he would have sustained the imagery in his mind if he hadn't written it down. And he most certainly would not have written it down if he weren't in a class where such writing was expected. The environment of my class didn't do the thinking for him, didn't put it into his head, but it provided the structure and the conversation that occasioned it.

Students' written responses to literature need to feed into a continuous writing life

Even subjective response statements can become a kind of "schoolwork," just another disjointed thing the teacher makes the students do. They go to history class and take their test on the Revolutionary War; to science, where they fill in the spaces of their "lab report"; and to English, where they write their personal responses to literature. It is possible for none of that to add up to anything in the student's life as a thinker or writer. If Jerome had only responded the way he did once or if each of his responses was automatically turned in to the teacher or even if he just did the responses and never went back to them for further thinking and possible use toward a larger project, his writing in response to literature would amount to little more than a set of exercises. However, because his response statement was an entry in his writers notebook, he could return to it, write again about those thoughts, develop them, and eventually choose to form them into a poem.

I don't believe that Jerome should write a poem every time he reads a poem, or that he should write any kind of piece, literary or expository, as an immediate response to a text. Jerome and his classmates read lots of literature, occasionally responding to it in their notebook, either because I asked them to in class or because they wrote in their notebook for homework and chose to make an entry in response to something they read. Those entries stayed in their notebook, along with all the other entries they made there, and sometimes were seeds for larger projects. To me, a mechanistic read-a-poem/write-a-poem approach to literary response would be inauthentic, in that it no more reflects what writers or readers do outside of school than does a more traditional read-a-poem/write-an-essay mode of response. The way I see the process, rather, is that reading literature significantly feeds the writer's thinking, which is concretized in the notebook, which, quite naturally, may along with everything else in the notebook contribute to the making of a piece of literature for readers in a genre of the writer's choice.

Jerome said to Marcia Southwick, just as she presumably has said to other poets she's read, Yeah, that, and this too. His reading process was transformed because he habitually formulated a comeback to texts, and his writing was transformed because his thinking became, in response to literature, more metaphorical, more instantiated by the big life issues with which literary writers grapple. Very often, these entries that stand on the shoulders of good literature do carry embryos of thought that grow into poems, short stories, memoirs, or nonfiction feature articles. Not surprising, Jerome, after writing more in his notebook about the same feelings, images, and memories he worked with in his initial response and after rereading older entries with those ideas in mind, eventually made a poem:

Earth and Rain

Naked, spinning in mud,
as if on a spit, roasting in earth,
the boy thrashes his head, diagonally—
    back and side
    back and side
gnashes his teeth, lips pulled back,
eating the warm, dark paste of soil.

Spewing moss from his nose, he rolls
and feels the mud fill the spaces
under his toes, secret between his legs,
    coating his throat,
    sealing his eyes.
Suddenly he stops and, rising,
animates his cocoon like a boy.

Bouncing his upright brown cell,
heavy springs in his ankles,
he lunges his homeward strides:
    a plunge and stretch
    a dip and reach
In no hurry but no doubting his step
Homeward he silent moans.

Tracking his way up the cool gray steps,
he reaches a caked hand for the screen door
and listens alert to the creak of its yawning
    his grandfather's knee
    a rocking chair.
Like the kiss of rain, his mother's hand
Glides its welcome across his back.

Students need to apprentice themselves as makers of literature to the literary artisans whose work they admire

The coming four chapters provide extensive examples of classroom environments that invite students to acquire a sense of craft in writing by attending to that of their mentors, just as they first learned to speak by attending to the lips of their parents. This is too big an idea to be developed only as a subsection of a chapter on response to literature. For the sake of balance, I do need to mention it here, however, because my point is that the reading of literature provides not only grist for the mill but also the shapes of the pans in which the flour from the mill is baked into bread.

When people read, they not only respond subjectively to the poem's or story's content, they also learn new possibilities for ways of saying things. Each reading experience has the potential to educate our own ways of saying, our imagination of formal possibilities. Too often, the word *form* is thought to be restrictive. A sonnet has fourteen lines, and that's that. But all language takes some form or other, without our experiencing its forms as prescriptions. In speech, for example, we greet each other, negotiate, and take turns talking according to cultural forms we have learned from people around us. Our parents explicitly coached us in most of these speech genres at an early age; the rest we have picked up with experience in society, only paying conscious attention to them during the process of learning them. Similarly, in literate language, we learn forms or genres by reading them within communities that value those genres.

From beginning to end of the writing process, students can apprentice themselves to literature. We have seen that the thinking that leads to the initial topic may be a product of the student's engagement with literature; also, literary works the student admires may coach the crafting of the student's own text. Thinking in collaboration with literature can tell writers not only what to write but how to write it. Jerome went back to Southwick's poem and others he had read for help making technical decisions about things like line breaks, diction, even punctuation. His decision to write a poem, moreover, was governed by his knowledge, formed in his reading of literature, of what genre would help his thought develop into its most appropriate shape. Because he already saw himself as someone like South-wick, someone capable of answering back, it was a logical move for him to look at how she and other poets use language and space on a page to form their thinking. Anybody who's going to develop the *chutzpah* to write has first to be invited to develop an identity in a horizontal relationship with authors of literature, rather than in a submissive relationship to the texts they read. A democratic sense of being an equal with writers who produced the objects of study is the cornerstone of students' empowerment.

Literature makes us think and feel in certain ways. The best way to grow those kinds of thoughts and feelings is through crafting them in the forms we learn from that same literature. A sense of craft is not mere ornamentation and window dress-ing, and it isn't just a container for previously formed thoughts. Writing in a par-ticular genre and crafting those texts helps us think in specialized ways. Learning to write poetry, fiction, drama, and other literature opens possibilities for the kind of thinking we can do—and for what meaning we can make of our raw material, what Lucy Calkins has called "our not-yet-precious particles of life." By inviting students to become makers of literature, artisans with the material of their own lives, we make them strong enough to imagine their own lifelong literacies. And if that isn't our reason for being literacy teachers, I don't know what is.

TIME AND A SENSE OF PROJECT

I once saw a movie on television in which two married, terminally ill older people committed suicide by sitting in their car in the garage with the motor running. They had planned their deaths for weeks and made extensive arrangements. In the scene just before they went into the garage together, the man, who had spent his life as an English professor, said, "Oh wait. I forgot my book." He got the book he'd been reading and carried it in one hand, holding his wife's hand in the other, out to the garage.

The idea of reading a book while you are dying (though I suppose, in a sense, we all are) struck me as mildly outrageous and more than a little troubling. I saw this movie years ago and can't remember anything else about it except that scene, that one instant of getting the book. I have thought of that moment often over the years, and I'm quite sure now that it would never have occurred to me to take a book with me. Even if, realizing I was going to be waiting in a car, the idea had flitted into my mind, I would have snickered and shrugged it off, thinking, *Why read? I'm going to be dead in a few minutes.*

My point is not that the movie was unbelievable; I've talked to a lot of people about it, and many of them would take a book with them to the gallows. For me, though, a big part of reading has to do with growing toward a future. I always read with a sense of project. I suppose I *think* with a sense of project. I'm always getting ready for some conversation that's yet to come, putting an anchor down in some point in the future and dragging my life's thought and energy toward that anchor. And so removing the future from the picture completely would seriously confuse my meaning making and probably render me illiterate in some dread way.

When I read a text, the text means something because it connects to what I've encountered in the past and in subtle, sometimes invisible ways, modifies what I've known before. While I'm changing my mind as I read, I'm doing so in anticipation of new experiences still to come. I'm getting an answer ready for my life. Then the next time I read and make connections similar to those, they'll be a little richer and more complicated for my having read what I had before. The experience of meaning is always one in which past, present, and future are brought together. Contrast that to the attitude toward time implicit in more traditional ways of thinking about literature: *learn about this now so that you can repeat it later; you should know how to comprehend it because you've been in school long enough to have learned those skills.* The difference lies, in part, in where past knowledge is assumed to come from and where the fruits of reading are bound in the future. For me, as a reader and as a teacher, the source and destination of a reading experience is a whole lifetime, not just school, the engine is the learner's purposes, not a performance for authority. Consequently, what I most need to teach students is how to use both memory and planning as strategies for making sense at every level of reading: decoding, comprehension, interpretation, and beyond.

Our projects are what give our lives meaning, what allow us to keep striving, what keep us alive. We should keep that forward-looking mindfulness and committedness vital in all that we do and all that we ask others to do in the name of their learning.

7

A Curriculum for English
Seasons of Inquiry into Making Things

We hold our little lives in our hands like clay for the shaping and accept that this is what we have to work with. What we are able to mold of that clay depends on how many shaping options are available, how many different kinds of things we can imagine making of this stuff, how many forms we can bring to it. From here on, it's a question of craft. To see the future of this lump of clay as taking some new shape requires an act of imagination, a projection of possibility. As writers, our clay is what happens in our lives and the meaning we have so far been able to make of it through reflection. All of that is in our writers notebooks. The notebook's purpose is to get out the clay, to see what we each have to work with. To do something with this stuff is the work of an informed imagination, which comes from our experiences with different types of things writers write and readers read. The most basic tool for a literate imagination, the fundamental shaping force, is genre.

If this chapter were a television show, the opening music would be fading right about now. When we watch television, we expect a piece of music at the beginning. They can't skip it; it has to be there. How else would you be sure you were seeing the beginning? And if we wanted to make a sitcom with our own video cameras, we'd put a song at the beginning, too. Because a sitcom has to have a song. That's how these things go. Our sense of "how this type of thing tends to go" could be called a genre schema, a *scheme* for a *kind* of thing. We have thousands of them: for restaurants and school days and knock-knock jokes and football cheers and New York City taxis and family relationships.

Our students know how TV shows go, too. If they were making a sitcom, they'd put a song at the beginning, too. Just as adults do, they have lots of genre schemas, some we may not even share, like those for Nintendo games or interviews with professional wrestlers. The also have a sense of how things go with written things—they have literate genre schemas. We sometimes act as if they don't, because we don't always value the literacy that is present in their daily lives. We complain about how the kids never read, forgetting about all the practical texts

116

that flood the attention of anyone in our culture: street signs, letters, shopping lists, comic books, magazines, newspapers, checks, food stamps.

When I was four or five years old, the first things I could read were gas station signs. I grew up in Texas, where you have to drive a lot, and my father was a car dealer, so it's sort of fitting that these were my primers. A gas station sign seems like a pretty simple text: just one word. But to pick out that kind of text from others required dozens of complex bits of information: the shape of the sign and its pedestal, the colors, the presence of gas pumps, its distance from the street. The first texts of several generations of American kids have been McDonald's signs and Burger King signs, which very young children can spot on streets crowded with other kinds of signs, for dry cleaners and clothing stores, for example. Eventually, most can generalize from those particular joints to all places that have their kind of crap to eat. They just have that look. How early they learn kinds!

It isn't long until they are aware of many different kinds of texts: they know about bills and checks and receipts, they recognize video boxes and cereal boxes and Nintendo boxes, they know picture books and books with lots of stories in them and phone books. I carry a pad of sticky notes in my car, for sudden ideas—but of course I can never find it because Jake has used it up, filling the car with more of the literacy he already sees there: parking tickets. They're stuck on the windows, shoved into the glove compartment, pasted to his sister's forehead.

We aren't born with these genre schemas. We learn them socially, by reading and hearing them. In fact, what we learn, what stays with us, from all of the texts we encounter—stories, jokes, newscasts, shopping lists, tests—is not what's in them, not their content, but their type, that sense of "the way this kind of thing goes." Margaret Meek, the British literacy researcher, has written, "The most important single lesson that children learn from texts is *the nature and variety of written discourse,* the different ways that language lets a writer tell, and the many and different ways a reader reads (p. 21, italics mine).

When as readers we come across a text, one of the first things we do (automatically, unconsciously) is assess its genre and create a stance for ourselves as readers based on its kind. Often, we don't have to look at the text at all, since the situation in which we are reading it cues us as to its genre. If a thick piece of paper is placed under my windshield wiper in New York City, it's either a parking ticket or a flyer for a 900 number. The pamphlet handed to us by the usher in a Broadway theatre is most likely a program, so even before we look at it, we have oriented ourselves to ways of reading that genre and will read it only with those questions in mind that are usually answered by a playbill. Every piece of writing, every *text* we read, comes to us as both a text—the piece it is—and a *kind* of text—an instance of a genre. And what kind of thing it is puts some limits on what we expect to find there. Genre, an oft-overlooked cuing system in reading, constrains our prediction, lays down a track for our reading.

A sense of genre is one of the most important mental frames we use in our writing, too. There comes a point in the writing process when we need a sense of "what kind of thing I'm making." The fiction writer and teacher John Gardner writes: "The artist's primary unit of thought—his primary conscious or unconscious basis for selecting and organizing the details of his work—is *genre*."

Whether writing a fantastic tale, a grant proposal, or a research report for a scientific journal, a writer must necessarily adopt some template for "one of these," and it is that template that provides the writer with the basic outline of the thing he is making. One of my mistakes early in my life as a writing teacher was constantly and almost exclusively to refer to what my students wrote as "pieces." What is a "piece"? How is it put together? Where in the world is it found? Who writes "pieces" and under what circumstances? It was an umbrella term, meant to encompass all genres, but I think its very generality kept even their personal writing confined to school-based inauthentic nongenres, the same category that includes "reports" and "book reports."

I do not want to be confused with a camp of Australian educators who, motivated by convictions about social justice with which I do sympathize, advocate quite traditional direct instruction in "genres of power" (see Cope and Kalantzis), a practice to which I am not sympathetic. These theorists believe that the linguistic features of the genres most favored by the culture of power ought to be taught explicitly as content to students throughout school, especially those from marginalized communities. They see a progressive focus on literature, personal experience, and student choice as the hegemony's way of keeping the disempowered in their place. While I think this is an interesting idea, the theory of learning that underlies their pedagogy is the old conduit metaphor: students are empty vessels who need to be filled with, in this case, rules about genres of power.

The trouble with such a curriculum is that it assumes that people can learn to do things with language when they are not actually *doing* them, that people can learn to write in the discourses of power when they are not really members of the communities who use words that way. As I've already discussed, such a doctrine of incremental preparation has always prevailed in American high schools, where teachers strive valiantly to teach students to write in ways that have nothing to do with their present lives, because those ways of writing might be demanded in college. But most people do not learn to do in school what they can never imagine themselves really doing in the world outside school. So instructing in genres of power will not bring hope to the disenfranchised, but rather, like all pedagogies of preparation, will simply provide more explicit tools to those students already destined to be part of the powerful discourse communities.

Even if you could ensure that students would learn all they need to know about genres of power, by the time they got to use them, the forms would no longer be valid. Genres come about because certain social situations in which they are useful recur, so genres are always located in contexts and communities. Therefore, the precise forms in the genres are constantly in flux. A particular discourse community values very particular genres: "report" may refer to texts that are used at IBM, and those "reports" are significantly and structurally different from those at Kodak, which are widely different from those used in the *New England Journal of Medicine*. "Report" is not a stable genre across society. The world of literacy is too intricately diverse to assume that we can bank into students' minds all the possible genres they might require to negotiate power in a rapidly changing world.

So much for what I am *not* suggesting in the way of genre studies. I have in mind, rather, that a class take a particular literary genre for a time as a broad object of inquiry and allow that genre to become a lens for making meaning of their own experience. Focusing on *literary* genres, as opposed to texts like business letters, legal briefs, or procedural descriptions, allows kids to write *about* what matters most to them, their own personal lives, the human matter of love and death, solace, isolation and betrayal, while also developing a flexibility with the forms their writing can take. When writers take the raw material of their lives and make something of it, a poem or short story, they move from the privacy of their writers notebooks into the social world. Genres are conventions, and that means they are social—socially defined and socially learned. Every community of people determines which kinds of writing count to that community. Helping students learn how to learn about different genres of writing empowers them to find a way of writing that counts in the different communities they will move through in their lives. I don't teach poetry so that kids will remember all about writing poems and be able to do it forever. I want them to develop habits of mind related to learning in a genre, so that they can learn in whatever genres they need.

Literacy education might, from the perspective of genre studies, be viewed as a history of experiences that allows the reader/writer to move through many different houses, each with its own architecture. Through these experiences, people develop habitual ways of exploring a house, ways of coming to feel comfortable living there, ways of learning about its architecture, and ways of constructing similar houses. When they have finished, they may have learned about so many different houses that they cannot remember just how to build the one they want—but they will have developed the habits of thought that will allow them to rediscover it. Our students can learn how to learn about a kind of writing, so that they can always use their habitual ways of reading, thinking, collaborating, and composing to master whatever new forms they encounter.

I didn't always think this way. For a long time, in my writing workshops, students always chose their own genre for each piece of writing they made. I believed that somehow the piece would speak to the writer and tell him what form it should take, and then the writer would use whatever he knew of that form, with a little help from me in conferences, to draft and revise. I valued the originality of each author, as if each person created wholly new formal possibilities for each piece he wrote. Occasionally, I would try to help them learn about craft, so that their readers would admire their work, by bringing in a short text, having them read it at home, and then using it for several days' minilessons. The relevant points I could make about craft in using a short story, however, were limited by the fact that Marcy was writing an essay, Jose a set of poems, Joy a nonfiction article, and so on across my classes. Meanwhile, there was never enough time to work with Marcy on transitions between points of her essay or on voice in writing about ideas rather than events. Only rarely could I gather a helpful batch of readings for a particular student, and since I had a hundred and twenty something, such help was haphazard or absent. Just as rare were their opportunities to collaborate with a group of peers in order to glean from a set of texts the features unique to the genre in which they were writing. I was able to give them opportunities to learn, but I was not really able to teach.

When I first dared to do a whole-class study of nonfiction writing in order to satisfy my department chair that I was teaching my kids to "do research," I did so with guilt, trepidation, and worry that I was depriving the students of "ownership." To a certain extent, I was, since they could no longer write anything they wanted in whatever way they wanted. However, though ownership and autonomy are important in my value system, I do care about some other things, too: community, for example, and inquiry, mentorship, collaboration, and a sense of craft. Teaching decisions are always sites of tension among the different values we hold. I discovered that my students and I could share an investigation of genre while they maintained ownership of their topic choice and their decisions about which elements of craft to attend to when, and ultimate control over what went into their articles.

Meanwhile, the class together could explore strategies for interviewing, data management, organization, and other tasks unique to the process of writing in this particular genre. Groups of students gathered to look at good pieces of nonfiction by professional authors to discuss exactly where on this page the author achieved writerly effects they could admire and emulate. My minilesson on any given day made sense for a large portion of the people in the room. Around the classroom, more conversations than ever sprang up, with or without my presence, about qualities of good writing. What was even clearer to me than all that, however, was that this shared study brought new energy to my classes. Even though students before were always trying new things on their own, what they were doing together was always pretty much the same. The genre study gave them a new shared journey, and it reinforced the spirit of community I had been after all along.

After that, I became convinced that the writing workshop should move through seasons of shared inquiry into genres, with other times of the year reserved for students to make their own decisions about what kind of thing they would make, to revisit familiar forms and experiment with new ones based on their enlarged understanding of the options available to them.

It took me several years to come to terms with the term *curriculum*. Too often, it means that the decisions that need to be made by teachers and students have been displaced into the hands of people in district and state offices. (God save us from that ever being a national office.) But in fact, what my students and I were doing as we moved through seasons of inquiry into reading and writing was constructing a curriculum. Every year was different, and often the same year was different for different classes, but I no longer saw the school year as one monolithic chunk called "reading/writing workshop," but rather as a course to be run, with turns, obstacles, and landscapes distinguishing one segment from another. The curriculum is negotiated between me, representing the interests of social norms and conventions, and the students, with their interests, agendas, and experiences. I bring the form, and they bring the content. The year might take an infinite

September	*Establish community (see Chapter 2) *Launch notebooks (see Chapter 3)
October	*Notebooks and first project (see Chapter 4)
November	*Begin poetry study
December	*Finish poetry study *Independent reading (see Chapter 5, pp. 88–91)
January	*Whole-class novel alongside independent reading
February	*Begin memoir study (see Chapter 9)
March	*Finish memoir study *Begin nonfiction study (see Chapter 10)
April	*Finish nonfiction study
May	*Writing workshop without shared genre

September	*Establish community (see Chapter 2) *Launch notebooks (see Chapter 3)
October	*Notebooks and first project as a memoir study (see Chapters 4 and 9)
November	*Continue memoir study
December	*Independent reading (see Chapter 5, pp. 88–91)
January through April	*Small-group reading and genre study of literary criticism (see Chapter 10)
May and June	*Poetry study

September	*Establish community (see Chapter 2) *Launch notebooks (see Chapter 3)
October	*Notebooks and first project (see Chapter 4)
November	*Begin memoir study (see Chapter 9)
December	*Finish memoir study
January	*Poetry study
February and March	*Nonfiction study (see Chapter 10)
April and May	*Fiction study (see Chapter 8)
June	*Writing workshop without shared genre

FIG. 7–1: *Three examples of ways a school year might go in a class focusing on genre studies.*

number of specific shapes, with either writing or reading moving onto the front burner at different times. Figure 7–1 shows three examples of ways I could imagine my year going, depending on the students' needs, interests, and purposes. The dates are approximate: things, as they say, take longer than they do.

Authentic inquiry does not follow a lockstep, prescribed procedure, but rather occurs only when we break out of the paths we already know and begin exploring new routes and new territories. However, in order to keep at bay the habits of mind school tends to lock us into, it may be helpful to keep in mind a few principles that seem to cut across studies of different genres. In any particular season of work with students, some of the principles below are more important than others. I don't follow every one of these guidelines every single time I lead a class in inquiry, sometimes because of my own oversight, sometimes because of the time pressures I have chosen for our work, sometimes because they just don't feel right given the particular students I am working with or the texts we are studying. In principle, though, I think they are always good ideas. The next three chapters provide some more fully developed descriptions and examples of what I discuss below; here, I'll explore some general themes that inform planning the time and work of a genre study, using poetry as an example throughout.

The genre is carefully chosen and is authentic

The only genres I choose for whole-class study are, first, those that students may encounter in an authentic reading life. They have seen this kind of thing in the real world, or, at least, if they look, they can find it. Second, I keep the boundaries of our study wide, so that students have plenty of choice about the particulars; that is to say, the shared genre is poetry, short fiction, or memoir, not a subgenre like haiku, science fiction, or family stories. I avoid genres such as sports writing that assign a topic as well as a form, since no matter how much I may want to reach the five who would thrive on sports writing, there will always be at least five who would feel oppressed by it. If I know there is a passionate interest among several kids in sports writing or science fiction, I may set aside a part of the year, after we have done a couple of genre studies together, for students to work in small groups on self-sponsored genre studies. That way, we can have the sports writers, the romance writers, the sonneteers, and the film critics all working at the same time.

When I am deciding which genre to study with students, my focus is first on them and their work so far. I go over my records to get a sense of what they are doing well and what characteristics are missing from their writing. Of course, this diagnosis and prescription process cannot approach pinpoint precision; it's only an impression. No one genre will be just the thing for a hundred and twenty students, and besides, a genre study is a very broad, open kind of work and so can't surgically improve student writing. But generally, if I have a sense that many students need to concentrate on imagery, the sound of language, or structure, I may choose poetry. If I want to work with them on character or planning before a draft, I may do fiction. If students seem to need more of an engagement with the world outside the classroom or if I feel like they need to bring their own expertises into their writing, I may choose nonfiction. Very often, because their notebooks are full of material from their personal lives, we work on memoir fairly early in the year.

Other considerations also inform my decision. If I have only four or five weeks, I am much more likely to do poetry, picture books, memoir, or drama than fiction or nonfiction. If energy seems to be flagging, I may do picture books or drama. If I were teaching in a situation where a centralized curriculum was carefully monitored, I would (after signing up for the curriculum committee) teach nonfiction in the "research paper" slot and would use some of the required short stories in a fiction genre study, poems in poetry, and so on. In other words, I adjust my interpretation of the curriculum to match my students' authentic work.[1]

While I am willing to listen to anyone who has evidence that I am wrong, my experience has shown me that students in an English/language arts class ought not to be attempting something of book length as their work for class. It is simply too difficult to plan, revise, and keep in control, and it generally takes longer than a school year to complete. If a student wants to write a novel, I encourage him to go for it, at home, while he continues to do other work for class. Therefore, the genres we study together, the kinds of texts on which we focus for most of the year, are short texts, which is a significant shift from the bibliocentric habits of traditional English classes whose curriculum consists largely of a list of novels.

The teacher is a colearner

While I may be a more experienced reader and writer than my students, it does not help them learn how to learn if I present myself as someone who already possesses ready answers about the qualities of good writing in any genre. My primary responsibility is to demonstrate inquiring habits of mind and some of the processes and actions that may accompany those habits. That means I do not have to put off doing a genre study of poetry until I have a folder full of poems for my students and notes about how to write poetry. Instead, I can choose, from a couple of anthologies, two or three poems which I like and in which I think my students will be able to see themselves, bring them into the class, and then study them alongside my students, individually, in small groups, and in the whole group, to try to figure out how these texts do what they do. I, like they, can pick out the parts where I think the poet has written particularly well, the bits that please me, and can try to find the words to describe what he seems to be doing there.

---

1   In my experience of consulting in many secondary schools across the country, I have found that rigid curricula are usually imposed by members of English departments upon themselves and kept in place by a tense peer pressure, not required by state law, district policy, or school administrators. More often than not, "they make me do it this way" is shared mythology among teachers, even when administrators directly state that it's not so. I have seen a few exceptions to this, but it's still important to be honest with ourselves about how much responsibility we have for the curricula we enact in our own classrooms.

I also work on my own writing in the genre we are studying, which is the only way I know what to say in conferences and minilessons. Often, I make overheads of my drafts for minilessons or even try to compose or revise right on the transparency in front of the class, allowing the work to progress a little from class to class as I go through the day. Writing in front of people while you think out loud is an odd thing to do, something that requires practice to get used to, but it seems to me to be a helpful skill for anyone who teaches writing. I do not always finish these pieces, but I do the notebook work, the rereading and selecting, the initial draft, and some revision. If we do not demonstrate the decision making that goes into writing, what voices will occupy our students' minds when they write? What will fill the awful silence of writing?

Teaching into my own uncertainty is not the same thing as an irresponsible lack of preparation, if I deliberately and constantly make my own learning processes explicit to my students and we collaboratively build a shared base of knowledge about the genre. We don't stay ignorant, keeping the question of how you write good poems fearsomely open, but rather try to build, from the experience of reading, some list of strategies and characteristics. I am still the teacher, so my voice will carry extra clout in the community, but I do not want to mystify "good writing" by handing out a list of a good poem's attributes that seems to have been composed by the gods. Rather, I want the kids on the journey of inquiry with me, collaboratively creating shared knowledge about the genre.

Students participate in selecting and evaluating materials

One of the reasons our folders don't need to be bulging with examples of every genre we might teach is because it is so valuable for students to be included in the process of finding examples of the genre and evaluating whether they fit into our study. Learning from models does not have to mean that the teacher is the only one bringing the models into the community. Having students search for model texts not only ensures that our choice of genre will indeed be authentic, but it also demonstrates that authenticity, in effect saying to the students, *This isn't just a school thing; this is the real thing. You can find this in your world.* As they comb through newspapers, magazines, anthologies, and other sources, the kids have a chance to work out their own conception of the genre, building an image of what kind of thing this is as they try to recognize it among other kinds of text. I've mentioned that very early in childhood, children learn to pick out print from the other signs and symbols in their environment; so this later selection process, separating out one kind of text among others, is an extension of that early discrimination.

Seeing what students bring in allows me to assess their conceptions, values, and tastes about the genre we are studying. I can see which schemas they are drawing on when they think of "poems," and I can thus more intelligently meet them where they are and extend their knowledge. Casually mentioning, *You might want to look around the house for examples of this genre,* doesn't seem to produce much, so I organize this work into a kind of assignment. I tell students to bring in more than one example on or by a particular date when I will plan for response groups to meet. (I have tried to work out some way to provide a copy of the texts they bring in for each of their group members, but this has proved logistically difficult, except in communities wealthy enough to simply require it of the students. I keep searching for a solution, though, because it's a good idea.) I also ask them to write a letter to me and their group in which they tell the story of their search and the decisions and difficulties that arose on the way and defend their choice of these texts as examples. I stress that they don't have to bring in only "good" ones; negative examples can be just as helpful in drawing the distinction between what we hope to make and what is outside the boundaries of our ambitions. In the days before they bring their examples in, I bring in a few, which I hope will inform their looking, and we also begin collecting in our notebooks toward our work in this genre. On the date assigned, students meet in groups to discuss their examples, working out whether or not these texts are in or out of the category of this genre, whether they think they are or are not "good" examples, what the characteristics of this kind of thing are, and what makes one "good." Someone in the group takes notes, so that the next day, they can report to the class on what interesting questions or problems arose during their conversations. Therefore, our whole-class discussions about the nature of the genre rise out of questions the kids have developed through their reading.

The class takes a very few texts as touchstones, to which students and teacher make frequent reference

With everyone contributing to our stock of examples this way, obviously we quickly have many more texts than we can study deeply together. More shared texts is worse, not better. So, a few days after the small groups have met to discuss students' independent examples, I cull through all the texts we have accumulated together and select two to four (depending on the genre and the length of the texts) for us all to share in our inquiry into how these work. Usually, because I have several classes, a couple of these touchstones are taken from my examples, and at least one of the texts has been brought in by a kid (this text varies from class to class). Every single class doesn't have to have its own unique set of poems, but I do need to send the message to the students that they are contributing to the shared corpus. I make a class anthology of photocopies of everything people have brought in, with several copies in the room, so that in conferences I can refer students to examples that pertain to what they are trying to do.

I select the shared models based mainly on the diverse ways they get the job done, the differences between the textual strategies they employ. In poetry, for example, I select poems with different lengths of lines, different kinds of topics, different ways of working with sound, different uses of metaphor and image. I want students to think of poetry as something made by people living in this world of ours, with its cars and grocery stores, music and brand names, so I favor living (or only recently deceased), even relatively young poets, not all men, not all white. When I am working with students who speak Spanish at home, I try to include some poems that switch at least a little between Spanish and English. This is a lot of pressure to put on such a small number of poems, and obviously no tiny sampling like this can represent the full diversity of possibilities, but I worry about it and do my best. In principle, I need to help my students become aware of the wide options available to them as they work with their own life material in this form.

The first lesson in any genre is its power to matter to readers

A danger in reading texts connecting to genre studies is that we may become so concerned with technique, with *how* these texts do what they do, that we forget to let them *do* it. Before I engage my students too much in analyzing elements of craft or qualities of "good" writing in the texts we share, it is important that I open up space for them to respond to these texts as readers, as human beings able to be affected by literature. For this work, we can't be seeming to run through the texts to spoon out a quick response. Rather, time has to open into a big bowl for thought in collaboration with the text. I do this in any of several ways, usually as minilessons combined with some student work at home. Sometimes, I read the poem aloud, or get a student to, and ask them to write and then talk about how the poem affects them, how they feel when they read it, what it makes them think about in the world, in their own lives, or in other literature (including movies, TV, songs, and so on). Other times, I ask them to read the poem for places in the text where they feel pleased by the writing itself, where they think it's pretty. They might mark these sections in the text or copy them into their notebooks. Some students may even choose to try to imitate them, or we might do that together, with me taking dictation on the chalkboard or overhead. These two types of response, the first to the content and feeling of what they have read, the other to the writing as writing, are both important in the lives of writers. We keep language whole by remaining focused on meaning first and allowing the grammar of how texts work to unfold from what the texts do to readers, the ways they matter.

The class develops its own metalanguage for describing the textual features they see in their examples of the genre

With subsequent readings of the touchstone texts, the class conversations turn from our responses and interpretations toward the writers' craft. Of course, our aesthetic and emotional responses are still present and are still a part of the conversation, since the real question in examining a writer's craft is, *What did he do, as a writer, to help me have that response?* In poetry, I can predict that this will mean looking at such issues as the way the poet uses line breaks to organize the reader's attention and cause the poem to sound in the reader's ear; the metaphors the poet has constructed; the images the poem is built on; the ways the poet either sustains one metaphor or image or else shifts rapidly among several different ones; the poem's movement in time, between the present moment and memory; the way the poet pries open feelings to tell a more accurate truth and avoid sentimentality; the word choices that create the poem's music; the repetition or variance of rhythms; the organization of the poem into stanzas, or verse-paragraphs; indentations, centering, and other constructions of white space on the page. It's my experience as a reader and writer of poetry that helps me as the teacher predict that areas like these will come up as we read. This knowledge, which John Dewey called "the logical organization of subject matter," allows me to see the significance in what students notice as they read. If someone says, *I like the way this line sounds,* I can develop a hunch that if we dig deeper for what the kid likes about the line, it will follow one of these paths. My knowledge about poetry serves this purpose: to extend and build significance of students' initial noticings, to help them name the techniques they see, so that they can use similar strategies in their own poems.

If I decide to provide the name of something students see, the way I explain it to them is simply to say, *Oh, you noticed that? Here's what it's called. Let's see if we can find some more of it.* I try to teach like a parent on a hike through the forest rather than like a pedagogue. I do not need to hand out a list of terms that students are "responsible for," mainly because if I did, I would really have taken upon myself the responsibility for discovering the ways with words to which those terms refer. The learners need to find them, point to them, discuss them, and then name them. That's what they are responsible for—the whole ball of wax.

Naming what we see in the poems we read, in fact, does not require that the students and I ever arrive at the standardized scholarly names of poetic elements. Communities always make up their own metalanguage (language about language) for what they are studying and making. Maintaining the words they originally used to describe what they saw when they saw it helps also to ensure that their knowledge of technique holds close to their existential experience as readers, remaining dynamic and usable rather than becoming abstracted and inert. Therefore, "that looping thing" is a fine way to describe a structure where the first line of each stanza is the same; "a shoelace structure" can describe rapid alternation between past and present images; "MTV cuts" describes juxtaposition of surprising, surrealistically connected images; "comparison" is just as good as "metaphor"; "like a movie" just as accurate as "imagistic"; and "four beats" easily replaces "tetrameter." We often post around the classrooms lists, written on chart paper, of elements of craft in the genre, things to consider as we write, and as often as not, it is students who write the items on the list, and they do so in their own terms. In fact, students' own terms for naming what they are trying to do are most often better than standardized terms, since a class's adoption of this language shows the students are really engaging in collaborative inquiry into the genre and constructing their own personal knowledge.

A genre study involves a deliberate interweaving of reading and writing

To me, a genre study is the most sensible way to unite reading and writing, which is so essential for those of us who have a single period for English/language arts class. Even if we did have one period for reading and one for writing, genre studies would still be important in themselves and also as ways to obtain more temporal flexibility. People who are used to equating reading with whole-class study of novels may see genre studies as mainly about writing, with reading taking too much of a backseat. While it is true that genre studies condition reading—in the emphasis on short texts, in directing readers' attention explicitly toward the writer's craft, in valuing responses written in literary modes over expository writing about literature—still, reading in a genre study is no less reading than in any other curricular arrangement. There is no such thing as "pure reading"; the context of reading, as I discuss in Chapter 5, always exerts pressure on the reading event and always changes the nature of reading. Inquiry into kinds of written text that gives priority to students as makers of literature simply brings reading and writing together, which perhaps is so unusual in English class that it looks to some as if reading has disappeared, though it's far from the case.

In a genre study, for the most part, my classes follow the same writing workshop structure I describe in the second chapter of this book. When we first get started and are reading a lot of examples of the genre, the student work time might include discussions in small groups or independent reading, rather than writing, but the basic structure remains as predictable as possible. The students need to see that whether we are mostly reading or mostly writing, the point of the class is still their work in this genre, not whatever lectures or clever activities I may be able to come up with.

Writers notebooks are tools for responding, collecting, thinking, and rehearsing

From the beginning of a genre study, while they are still searching for examples of this genre and examining touchstone texts, students begin keeping a notebook *as a maker of this kind of thing*. When studying poetry, students begin noticing the world and reflecting on their experience as poets, which may cause them to keep a notebook somewhat differently than they have done before. As they begin to understand what poems are made of, they will become better able to collect the kinds of entries that will prove most helpful to them when they make drafts of poems. They may start staring at the world more, trying to capture images in their mind's eye and on the pages of their notebooks. They may return to stories they have already told in their notebooks, and focus on small objects or fine details they have previously glossed. In rehearsal as poets, they will turn over their thinking in different ways, experimenting with form and with the kinds of language they are beginning to hear in the poetry they have read. Naturally, they respond personally to the poetry they read, and make notes on what has pleased them in that poetry and how they think the poets did that. They reread everything in their notebooks, but differently this time, because they read with a poet's eyes.

As they move toward drafts, they use their notebooks to plan out how the poem might go—making several different outlines, trying out different leads, experimenting with the perspective from which they will tell their material. Then, in the midst of a draft, they can use their notebooks to visualize the options they have about what comes next, to try lines in different rhythms and words, to play with line breaks. As they revise, they can continue to do these things in their notebooks, as I discuss in Chapter 4. The point here is that a genre study, far from supplanting notebooks, rather makes them much more valuable and important for writers, as they try on the form, and hold onto their most important material.

Students are likely to revisit "old" material

Having written about something from our lives doesn't mean we are finished with that topic, never to return to it again. Working writers know that each of us only has a few central issues to which we return again and again, one way or another, in our writing lives. F. Scott Fitzgerald said:

> Mostly, we authors must repeat ourselves—that's the truth. We have two or three great moving experiences in our lives—experiences so great and moving that it doesn't seem at the time that anyone else has been caught up and pounded and dazzled and astonished and beaten and broken and rescued and illuminated and rewarded and humbled in just that way ever before. (In Winokur, p. 67)

Truman Capote agreed:

> I think one writes and rewrites the same book. I lead a character from book to book, I continue along with the same ideas. Only the angle of vision, the method, the lighting, change. (In Winokur, p. 66)

Donald Murray (1991) has said:

> We all have two or three or four themes we go back to again and again. My own have been war, school, and the mystery of writing. . . . Students shouldn't have to keep getting a new subject; they should be able to keep turning over their material, writing what they don't know about what they know.

But such thinking doesn't come naturally to students in a school system that attempts to march them through ever-new material in linear progression. Most kids have been miseducated to believe that rereading a book is cheating and, by the same token, that it must be cheating to write again about something you've already written about before. It's too easy; it must be wrong.

But if we want students to write what they care about, if we value their interests and obsessions as the bedrock of their learning, then we need to encourage—loudly and clearly—the continual unashamed reuse of those bits of life that are most precious and familiar to our writers. After all, dealing with life material in a new genre transforms that material and makes new meanings possible. Of course, this is only possible if we avoid choosing class topics in addition to the class genre, which is not then a genre study at all, but an assignment: *Everybody write poems about winter.*

One of my students, Cheryl, had lots of entries in her notebook dealing with her passions about her family's farm, the outdoors, and the environment. (She's the same girl whose entry about her farm I include in Chapter 3.) All year long, her entries threaded through these obsessions, and so did her pieces of writing in different genres. When she wrote nonfiction, it was about the greenhouse effect; one memoir she wrote was about her special place, a tree bent over a creek, where she retreated at times in her life when she needed to get away by herself and think. Her poems too grew from these same passions:

Fearing Myself
Behind my house there lays a woods.
And in that woods is a magical land.
It's nothing technical or anything big.
I go there for the Peace.
Peace.
I see the deer run into the woods,
And it reminds me of what this world is
Supposed to be.
The deer are free and unharmful.
If only the world were like deer.
Everything would be so much better.
War.
Enemies.
Hatred.
Selfishness.
Pollution.
Crime.
The list goes on and on.
I go to the woods to sit by the creek.
To look around and see myself.
I think about the wrongs,
And look for the rights.
The way everything is now,
I wonder.
I'm so young and it scares me to no end
To think about what it will be like when
I'm older.
I'd rather sit in the woods, by the creek
And watch myself and the world fade to
Darkness.

And this one, untitled:

> As I tasted the polluted air of the meadow,
> I realized how far away I was from the cruel,
>   vicious society.
> I stood there in the waist high weeds and grass
>   with a breeze slightly blowing my blonde hair.
> A single bird cried out a precious tune.
> Where was this god-like whimper coming from?
> There were no trees for it to perch on.
> No sky for it to crash through.
> No earth for it to bury itself in from this
> Sweet World.
>
> I see a future yet unknown
> A past I'll always cherish
> A present I'm unsure to say
> And a world about to Perish
>
> The sun shall rise no more again
> I hear my distant cries
> But when this place crashes to the ground
> I can at least say
> I tried

Someone asked me recently whether Cheryl, now in college, is still as interested in the kinds of things she was in eighth grade. I'm sorry that I don't know; I hope and expect she is. But that's not really the point. As her teacher, I was hoping she would learn that whatever her present passions are, they can fuel her work in whatever discourse to which she sets her hand.

The classroom environment is a concrete reflection of the genre's peculiar modes of thought

The idea of a writing workshop, ever since Graves, Calkins, Giacobbe, and others first conceived it, has always been that the mental actions and needs of a writer's mind are somehow projected onto the environment of the classroom and made concrete. Writers need intentions and purposes, so teachers, rather than assigning topics, teach strategies for finding them. Writers need time and control of that time, so the workshop leaves a large chunk of space for students to manage their own work. Whether or not every writer in the world keeps a notebook, students' work in notebooks makes concrete and clear some important processes in writers' minds. The principle of making a writer's mental work concrete remains true in each genre study, but being more specific about what kind of writing work we are doing together suggests many more possibilities for what the environment might include. I try to ask myself, *What do writers in this genre do? What are the conditions under which they do it? What are the main things they have to pay attention to? How can those things become part of my class, both in the physical room and also in structures of time and activity?*

One of the requirements for thinking in poetry, for example, is an attention to the sound of language, so I set up opportunities for my students to read poetry, their own and others', aloud, singly and in chorus. I also set up as many tape recorders as I can find, ask students to bring their Walkmans to class, and bring in tapes of poets reading their own work. I keep blank tapes on hand so that students can add their own recordings of their readings to our audio library. I get the auditorium as often as I can, so that some students can go there to rehearse their lines in a more declamatory voice, which sometimes helps them identify slack sections.

Poets also try to hold an image in mind, so I gather into the environment opportunities for different kinds of looking. I invite (or direct) students to bring in photos and objects, ones that hold special personal significance or that they just find interesting or beautiful. Taking an idea from my friend Georgia Heard, I put frames on parts of the windows in the classroom where students can go to look and daydream. I encourage those students who like to draw to sketch in their notebooks, either before starting a draft or as they start to revise. As with all of these strategies, I let the kids in on what I'm trying to do, so that they bring their own ways of looking into the classroom and take them out into their lives.

A more technical aspect of poetry involves the arrangement of lines on the page. Poems say things on different levels, of course, and one of those levels is simply the shape they make on paper. I'm not talking here about concrete poetry in the shape of a swan or whatever, but more ordinary decisions about the arrangement of lines, such as whether they form a single solid block of text, whether the lines skitter down the page or sprawl across it, whether indentations dance the reader's eye from left to right and back again. Because poets keep in their mind's eye the options available to them, I get students to make large posters of the poems they admire, and I do the same, so that the walls of the room offer a visual repertoire of possibilities, to which we refer frequently in our conversations.

The next three chapters give fleshed-out descriptions of how particular genre studies have gone, in my experience, so that each of these principles will become more concrete and clear. My purpose in this book, however, is not to provide prescriptions for specific genres, but to share the principles that have informed my decision making in a constantly evolving conversation with the community of educators with whom I learn. Genre studies are inquiry, so the answers cannot be fixed in advance, in this book or anywhere.

SCHOOLTIME AND LIFETIMES

When I taught second-semester seniors who were, for the most part, not college bound, I was struck by how precious and potentially significant this time was. Oh, sure, they were eager to be gone and occasionally hard to keep calm and all that—but they were also very reflective. For them, there was no question about the need to value their pasts, nor about the need to examine who they were in order to imagine their futures. Given where they were in development and circumstance, they were especially engaged in the work of my class. They didn't have much patience for the details of neatly finishing their projects and getting them in on time, but they found the process of interrogating their lives and making something of their experience very interesting. When we did a genre study of memoir, therefore, our work was more focused on making meaning of memory than studying the craft of the genre. At this moment in their lives, school agendas were only important as something they had minimally to answer for a few more weeks. But figuring out their lives—that was important.

A member of their class, Joseph, had died four years earlier in a car accident. When Brian read aloud his memoir about Joseph, who'd been Brian's best friend, most of the class cried. Their tears seemed to be prompted by more than loss. It seemed important for them to show one another that, even after all this time had gone by and they'd all grown up so much, Joseph was *still* important to them all, they *still* missed him, they hadn't forgotten. Through their tears they were sharing not only their grief but their sense of community and their commitment to old friends.

When things like that happened—or when Jimmy had to leave the room several times a day while he wrote about his grandfather or when two girls in one class were writing about their abortions or when Jamie wrote about sex—I was, to say the least, not always comfortable, socially. After all, I had arrived very late on the scene, had never known them before they started writing these pieces. What was I to say, how to respond as a teacher, in the face of all this rather intimate self-exploration?

I hear a cynical voice saying, *What were you trying to do? Be their therapist?* And to that cynical voice I can only answer, *Give me a break.*

Is any context in which people talk honestly therapy? Is therapy the only place in your life where you think about your life? Is it really possible to live such an unexamined life? I wasn't doing therapy because I wasn't trying to help them fix their psyches. I was helping them make better pieces of writing out of their life experiences than they would have done had I not been there. I possibly helped them discover in writing a tool for thinking about life. These were the students I was most likely to meet after I left the school, working in stores, taking their kids to the mall. Several of them told me they still wrote, still kept a notebook, just to help them live. I could do worse in a life's work.

My real point in telling these stories right after discussing curriculum planning is this: what we can plan in a curriculum—and then only to a certain extent—is schooltime. But schooltime always meets lifetimes. What we plan to *do* with students always has to *be done* by real people living real lives. And it is that doing, the real people in their real lives meeting the actions we can set out for them, that comprises the substantial curriculum. Before the lifetimes, the schooltime plan is only words, only potential.

Education is always part of a life history. A class is a certain number of weeks together as a community, and if the people in that community can bring their real lives to that place, those weeks do have the capacity to change the course of those lives. And the curriculum is only worth the paper it's written on if it does affect the course of students' lives. Even our limited time together in a room can create in students' imaginations new possibilities of "what my life might be like." And if that happens, far from robbing the curriculum of its power, we have released its values into real peoples' minds and lifetimes.

8

Fiction
Building a World of Possibilities

I knelt beside Luke[1] for a writing conference. He kept writing, but I knew he knew I was there.

"What are you working on, Luke?"

"My story."

"That's good," I said, tolerating the stall. "What about it are you working on?"

"Well, my character, he's in a baseball game, and he's about to come up at bat."

This is just the kind of answer that would have made my heart sink, once upon a time. I would have remembered all the horrible pieces of student fiction I'd read: strings of events tumbling into events, with no connecting through line of feeling or theme, hollow characters, barren landscapes. I would have pictured this part of Luke's story as going something like this: *Then the Blue Jays came up to bat and it was Jerry's turn. He hit a double and got onto second base. When the next batter hit a double, Jerry rounded third and slid into home, just in time. The score was now 15–13. The next batter struck out and the Astros came up to bat. They managed to get one run, but the Blue Jays still won, 15–14. The next game was the championship. . . .* In the past, my students had tried to write fiction the way they read it, from beginning to end, without first building the world they were trying to create for readers. Consequently, their process had never been like that of the fiction writers I admired, and their short stories had borne no resemblance to anything I'd ever read and liked. So I had hated their fiction and just hoped any student I found working on a short story would hurry and finish and get on to something worth writing. Obviously, these were not my proudest moments as a teacher of writing.

This time, though, I was working in a classroom where we had studied short fiction as a genre, both by reading the kinds of stories we wanted to write and by

---

1 Luke and the other names in this chapter are pseudonyms for students in Sue Schmitt's class at Geneseo Middle School during the 1990–91 school year. Most of what I've learned about teaching fiction is the result of a collaboration with Sue, along with Cindy Schmitt and Bill Brummett, that year. They are bold and exquisite teachers, and I thank them.

exploring a process akin to that of the fiction writers we admired. Because we had a conversation going about how fiction worked, my conference with Luke could be in the discourse of fiction writers, as it had taken shape in this class.

"Your guy's name is Jerry, right? And he's coming up to bat. Is this time up important?"

"Yeah, the score's tied, and he never gets a hit, and . . . um . . . everybody's mad that he's up at bat now."

"Did you just think of that?"

"Yeah."

"Make a note of it in your notebook so you don't forget." I paused while he jotted. "So you've really turned up the heat on the situation here. What's at stake for *him?*"

Luke looked at me for the first time. He was a small, thin boy with sandy hair and wire-rimmed glasses. He wasn't thinking along these lines, and I could see his mind shifting tracks.

"Does Jerry care if he gets a hit?"

"Sure," he said.

"What does he really hope for?"

"A home run."

"Why?"

"Because he wants the other players to like him and respect him. He doesn't want them to call him a nerd anymore. Also, his parents are there. They're divorced, and they're never together, and he wants them both to see him get a home run."

"Jot that down." I paused again while he wrote in his notebook, *wishes he could get home run because of his parents—other players won't call him nerd.*

"So, Luke, it sounds like, if Jerry can do well this time at bat, he can bring things together. He can feel like part of his team, and he can also feel like part of a family. That's pretty powerful stuff. It's more than just a game, then, isn't it?"

"Yeah, it is."

"How can you show that in your story, though? How can you get those thoughts onto the page? Any ideas?"

"No. Well, I could write it before he comes to bat."

"How? What would the words say?"

Luke looked at his draft. "Jerry wanted to get a home run because . . . No . . . Jerry was thinking about . . . I don't know."

There are several strategies for revealing a character's thoughts, and I had a choice of either directly telling those to Luke or else helping him find them in literature I knew he'd read. This time, I decided on the latter, because, as he had tried to compose orally, he'd seemed to need not only a technique but an aural image of how the technique would sound. He needed the language, the tune, of storytelling.

"Luke, get out three or four stories—or for this you could use your novel— where you remember an author revealing what a character is thinking, and see how you might do it. Get Sharissa or Clarence or somebody to help you if you want. Study how those authors get you inside a character's mind, and that will teach you how to write this part of your story. Then you can tell the class what you found out."

In this conference, which is representative of the conferences I tend to have with kids who are writing fiction, Luke and I were able to dwell on values that I see as more readily available in a study of fiction than of another genre. First, the writer has to reach with his imagination into the consciousness of another person, has to empathize with someone whose experiences, values, and situation may be different from his own. Moreover, this person into whose skin the writer has to project himself is someone he actually has to build, out of his beliefs about how people work. Because complex motivations and feelings make better characterization, the planning, drafting, and revising of what makes these particular people tick is part of the craft of writing stories. (I realize that complex characterization is not an attribute of all fiction. Counterexamples range from epic storytelling to postmodern fiction. However, most of the fiction students have read or will read in my classes will be of a more "realistic" subgenre, in which the construction of characters' interior lives is part of the craft.) I cannot think of too many other places in a secondary school curriculum where understanding why others do what they do is a focus of inquiry; yet I do see such inquiry as potentially helpful in educating students to be more compassionate, thoughtful, and democratic. If they can imagine the world through the eyes of someone who is not themselves in constructing a story, there's a chance they may be a little less likely to see other human beings as objects or stereotypes. For that reason and others, I do not see fiction writing as frilly and unrigorous playtime but rather as a hard rehearsal of valuable habits of mind.

Furthermore, in imagining life stories other than his own, Luke had to open his mind to possibility. Mario Vargas Llosa has said, "A wondrous dream, a fantasy incarnate, fiction completes us, mutilated beings burdened with the awful dichotomy of having only one life and the ability to desire a thousand." If Luke could make up someone else's life, then he could imagine his own future as possibly different from his present. Whenever we make plans for where we want to go or who we want to be, we are, in a way, making a fiction, composing possibility. Possibly, writing fiction, even more than reading fiction, provides experiential roots for that kind of essential thinking in life. One of John Dewey's definitions of freedom includes just this type of thinking—freedom involves the ability to imagine that things could be otherwise. Fiction writing, when we pursue it as inquiry, gives us an opportunity to exercise that ability.

Because those are the values I have in mind for student work on fiction, I try to construct our inquiry into fiction in ways that will set up our conversations centered on those values. In the coming pages, I outline the larger moves I make to establish the environment for those conversations. However, it is not getting through the curriculum but rather holding my larger purposes in mind that informs my minute-to-minute action with students. I decide what to say or do based on those big objectives, not on a list of "elements of good fiction writing," and in that way I hope to keep the heart of fiction writing—and of teaching—alive.

Getting started—building fictional worlds in the notebooks

I've come to believe that one of the reasons student fiction in the past did not look like the fiction I like is because in writing it, students were not drawing on the same genre schema as I was. I evaluated their stories by overlaying a template I drew from reading short stories by F. Scott Fitzgerald, Katherine Anne Porter, Raymond Carver, Alice Munro. But students weren't usually drawing on reading experience with short stories as they wrote. They cannot write what they have not read. The problems with their stories were often the result of the stories' being drawn from genre schemas that they know—television shows, movies, video games, Dungeons and Dragons scenarios, and the like—but that are not necessarily appropriate wells from which to draw for making short stories I will be able to recognize as "good." Even when students have read a lot of novels and draw upon them in writing their stories, it is dysfunctional, since a novel is constructed differently. In such cases, students may have written twenty-five pages before arriving at an inciting incident, such as our hero's getting left in the woods. After that point, they will have to write perhaps a hundred more pages to unfold the story, a length impossible for them to control and revise, especially under the constraints of schooltime. In order for us to be able to converse about values and craft in fiction writing, we need to be talking about the same thing when we say "short stories." Therefore, as I discuss in the previous chapter, we need to share a few texts to which we can refer. (See the end of this chapter for a bibliography of resources for short stories I have found to be useful with young people.)

In addition to informing their sense of the genre by studying such texts together, I also need to help students become insiders in the ways fiction writers approach their craft. Given the values I attach to fiction as an inquiry with students, it may not be surprising that in my minilessons, I begin with character. I share with them some of the lore I know about writers, that Ibsen said he would never start writing until he knew his character so well that, in the period just before he slept, they could come to him and have a conversation. Faulkner said that often his job as a writer was to follow his characters around, writing down what they said and did. Harold Pinter once described his process as locking two characters in a room together. I bring in Robert Newton Peck's book about the craft of fiction, *Fiction Is Folks,* whose very title reinforces my point, and leave it where they can get to it. I tell them that I once met Robert Lipsyte, author of *One Fat Summer* and *The Contender,* and I told him I was worried that I was taking too harsh an angle with this approach to fiction, maybe because I'd been an actor. He assured me that everybody he knew began with character and that he went so far as to begin by figuring out what year the main characters were married, so he could research (or invent) what names might have been popular among people like them at that time in history. That gave him the name of his character, and he proceeded from there to make up things about that person. I see anecdotes like these as important because I need to persuade the kids not to begin work on their story at the beginning and write to the end, but rather to start planning their character and her or his world in their writers notebook. I begin with students by collaborating with them on creating a character, with kids' calling out attributes as I take dictation on the board, often pausing to make them think about what they are saying. That's what I did in Luke's class.

"Alright, so let's try making up a character together," I said, picking up chalk. "What's our character's name?"

"Johnny," someone called out.

"Okay," I said, writing it on the board, "is Johnny male or female?"

Someone called out, "Male," but then others rebutted, "Female."

"You'll get a chance to make your characters whatever you want them to be. This is just an example, so we'll make Johnny a male, since it was the first answer I heard. How old is he?"

"Thirty-eight." "Fifteen." "Eighteen."

"As much as possible," I said, "it's a good idea to make your characters at least close to your age, so you know more about what they are like. Since no one in here, except me, unfortunately, knows anything about what it might be like to be thirty-eight, let's make him fifteen. So what else do we know about Johnny?"

"He has red hair," someone called out, "and freckles."

"He plays the piano."

"He lives in a house in the city."

For a while, it went on like this, with people describing Johnny's appearance and making up vital statistics that were somewhat superficial but helpful for their envisionment of the character. At some point, someone called out, "He's a nerd." I stopped. Something like this always happens, someone always makes the character an object of mockery with a stereotypical category.

"I'm not going to put that up here, because there are several problems with fiction writers' saying their character is a nerd. First of all, it's not a description of the person, but just name calling. It doesn't give you a better, more specific idea of what this person is like, but instead pushes him away, makes him an object, and no longer a person you really have to think about. Second, as a fiction writer, you have to love your characters; you have to feel for them and know what they are like on the inside. Nerd is a name people might call someone; it's not what someone is on the inside. Fiction writers have to be smarter than that about people.

"So what we know about Johnny so far is some things about his outside, what he looks like, some things he does. Let's make up some things about his inside."

"He hates his father."

"Why?"

"Because he's mean to him."

"In what way?"

"He calls him a nerd. Can we say that?"

"It's an odd thing for a father to say, at least to me, but maybe that will make it interesting when we move on to think about the father. I'll put it down for now; we can always change it. What else about Johnny's insides? What does he love?"

"The piano."

"His room."

"His little sister."

"What is he afraid of?"

"His father."

"Being late for school."

"Getting hurt."

"Why's he afraid of getting hurt?"

"Because it hurts."

"Yeah, but everybody's afraid of that; what makes Johnny's fear of getting hurt different from other people's? We need to find out what makes him who he is, specifically."

"Okay, take it off."

"No, if we accept it, it might be something to work with. Why is Johnny afraid of getting hurt?"

There is a pause while they think.

"Maybe if he gets hurt he can't take care of his little sister."

"Maybe his father calls him a baby if he gets hurt."

"He's afraid that his hands will get broken, and he won't be able to play the piano."

"Okay," I said, jotting those notes on the chalkboard. "Do you see how, as we go along, the pieces start to connect? It's not just a list of 'things about Johnny'; you're making a person, and trying to make him as real and honest as you can. Sometimes, you think about how you would feel; sometimes, you don't know, so you make it up. You have to know about your character inside and out, because that's where your story is going to come from. Now, you notice, we didn't concern ourselves with what the story will be about, what will happen first and second and so on. We just thought about the whole character; the story will come later. Let's figure out one more thing about Johnny. What does he need, most of all, deep inside him?"

"He needs to get better at playing the piano."

"Why? Is he bad at it? We didn't know that before."

"Not real bad; just not too good."

"So why does he need to get better?"

"So his father will have to admit he's not a nerd."

"So what? What's so important about that?"

"He wants his father to respect him, not to think he's worthless."

"So he needs his father's respect in order to feel like he's worth something, and he might use the piano to get that," I summarized. "When you work on your character's inner qualities, keep asking yourself, Why? and So what? If you know what your character needs, then that might, down the road, help you know what your story should be about. Now, go ahead and get to work on your own character—not Johnny, but someone you make up—in your notebook. You can't get done; keep asking yourself, What else? I'll be coming around to see how you're doing."

I then erased the specifics of Johnny's description from the board, leaving up those parts that contributed to the core of the character, so the kids could be reminded of the kind of thinking they were headed for. They could look up and see "loves," "fears," "needs," "places he feels safe," "places that are dangerous," "important objects," "important people in his life," and so on.

As I circulated and conferred, I kept on asking them the same kinds of questions about their characters as those I had asked about Johnny. I steered them away from anything that got too close to the plot of the story, like "has been suspended from school and wants revenge," holding them rather to the real heart of the character, the qualities that made her who she was over time. Terminal diseases proliferated, but I insisted that they couldn't give their character cancer until they knew who he was and until they learned more about crafting a story. Sometimes, they got into the character's biography, and I just reminded them that though it's important to know all of this, it wouldn't all be in the story. Making up some of the events in the character's life are merely a way of getting to know the character.

In my experience, as soon as the plot begins to fix itself in the student's mind, it's much harder to teach him about the elements of crafting the fictional world. Therefore, I try to keep my students from thinking about what's going to happen in the story. Since I neither can nor would want to erase their thoughts, I tell kids, if they have an idea for the story, just to jot it in their notebooks as a possibility and then keep working on their character and other elements of the world they're creating. Also as I confer, I watch for students who seem straitjacketed by the focus on character, who might benefit more from working on a setting for a while before discovering the people who occupy that space or who might want to create a whole social group, such as a family, a group of friends, or a team, before delving into an individual. I listen for the differences in the ways they talk about entering their stories, and try to support their own ways in, while still believing that for most of the kids character is the most facile place to begin.

After that first day when students meet their characters, I talk in minilessons about connecting the initial sketch of their character with the character's whole biography, taking each inner attribute and asking, What happened in her life that made her this way? or What are some ways this characteristic has come out throughout her years on earth? I suggest creating a time line of the character's life, where they can make up the major events that even if not told in the story still inform the actions of the character. As we get nearer to a draft, the concrete time line or outline of the character's life will in fact help the writers to limit their attention to a single point on the time line, rather than trying to tell everything.

I do not require that they write a formal character biography, nor do I collect the time lines or character sketches; these entries, like the rest of their work toward a draft, are part of a writer's work in her notebook. They are not exercises nor a series of assignments. I do, however, insist that they use their notebook to build the elements of the fictive dream, and I teach them multiple ways of doing it, though they are always free to invent whatever strategies help them get to know the worlds of their stories better. If they were writing about their own lives, they would collect entries around a single topic, which deepens and enriches their thinking about the subject. Since that is important when they are writing about reality, it's much more important when they are writing about a world that does not exist off the page. How can you "write what you know" when you're writing fiction? One answer is: make up the world you are writing about, get to know it well, and then write. As they feel their ways through character biographies and other types of notebook entries, they make familiar what is possible but not yet experienced. I tell them all this, worry about it in front of them, and share with them that, over his desk, Franz Kafka had tacked one word: WAIT.

As their characters grow, students usually do succeed in falling in love with them, or at least empathizing with them. Sometimes when my back is turned, they give their characters lavish gifts of happiness and wealth. Suddenly, it's an attribute of three students' characters that they've just won the lottery. Or they've been adopted by the President. Or a rock singer has summoned them up onto the stage. Like the alternatives of a fatal disease, an accident, or the loss of their entire family, the boon syndrome gone unchecked will eventually present fiction writers with serious problems in making an interesting story. First, the naïveté about the world that young people already obviously bring to fiction writing is intensified by the need for information about finances or medicine that such situations will demand of them as writers. Second, since it is unlikely that the recent winning of six million dollars will not come into the plot of the story, such decisions rush too early toward a particular plot and return the students to the event-after-event writing I saw students do before I began teaching fiction more deliberately as craft. Third, both the fantasy situation and the horror situation create the students' characters as patients rather than agents, victims of circumstance, acted upon rather than acting. In order to figure out a plot, the main character has to be going after something, trying to fill some need. Beginning a story with the character being adopted by a millionaire makes it difficult for young writers to find some place to go, dramatically. If the story begins with a girl's discovering she has terminal cancer, we pretty much know what's going to happen in the rest of the story. Drama requires conflict, and though disease is a sort of conflict, in student's stories the character is ususally a passive victim. In a fiction genre study, as in the rest of my work, I try to keep students focused on the ordinary desires, needs, and conflicts they know from their own lives, from the lives of friends, and from most of the realistic fiction we read together. Their characters need to be trying to *do* something, they need to be agents, and writers can depend on life as they know it to give them obstacles as well as victories.

Moving outward into a fictional world

Students need to know that just because they started with one character does not mean that that character will remain their focus. Possibly, another will come into the picture at some point, and the writer will choose to center her attention upon that newer character. Alternatively, a social milieu tied to a place, perhaps a garage rock band or a street gang who hang out on a particular corner, may very quickly divert their attention from an isolated individual. I encourage students to do thorough work on as many characters as they can, and the places and objects associated with those characters, before beginning a draft, in order to enrich their imagined social world and to provide themselves later with as many storytelling options as possible.

Over the next days, I talk in minilessons and conferences about other elements of fiction that can help them flesh out their imagined worlds. We try, for instance, to become thoroughly familiar with the places in our characters' lives. I have seen students write for pages describing the character's room, what's in it and where those objects came from, what the light sources are and the quality of light that comes from them, what it smells like in here, what the furniture feels like to the character, what stories live in this place. Their entries are sometimes in prose sustained over several pages, sometimes notes and jottings over time. Often, kids find it helpful to draw a room, a field, a bus station, a basketball court, or to sketch a floorplan of the character's home. All of this knowledge will be helpful, even if all of it doesn't appear in the draft of their story, because when a character enters a room, the writer will be able to picture that room and know where the character could sit and what that would feel like. Knowing the condition of the room, they will be able to picture a character beginning to straighten up when a guest arrives.

Another day, I talk to the class about relationships between characters. No one exists alone, and even with our first experimental character, Johnny, and his all-important relationship to his father, it quickly became clear how much others mean in defining even a made-up person. To demonstrate this to a class, I either tape back up the example of our first day's shared character, or else talk about the character I'm working on myself. With Johnny, for example, I'd want first to think about his relationship to this father who calls his son a nerd. I'd want to ask about this father and son some of the same questions I'd ask about any other relationship: Why do these people (apart from biological ties) have anything to do with each other? What are the most cherished memories each holds of being with the other? What are the times that each has to forget or ignore, in order to be able to go on in the relationship? How does each meet needs the other has? How does each keep the other from getting things he needs? Then, I'd want to ask similar questions about Johnny's relationship to his mother, even if she's not still around at the time we're considering. What's more, I'd want to ask some of these same questions about the relationship between the mother and father. As the creator of this social world, a fiction writer needs to probe all he can into the complex web of relationships among the characters.

I talk about finding objects that might be important in revealing a character and her relationships to places, to other people, and to herself. I ask the kids to recall important objects from stories we've read together and novels they've read on their own, and I tell them about some of my favorites from literature, such as Allie's left-handed fielder's mitt in *The Catcher in the Rye*. Sometimes this attention to objects helps add detail to characterization, as when Liam's character had a favorite coat that he always wore or when Suzy's had a trumpet her grandmother had given her. Often, such objects evolve into symbols. Liam's character, in the midst of his parents' divorce, wore his heavy coat as a kind of protective armor well into May. Suzy, in her story, transformed the trumpet into an emblem for feminist resistance, a means for her character to make noise when everyone has in many ways told her to be quiet. It's much easier for students to imbue objects with emotion and meaning now, in the notebook, before they have a draft, than after they feel they have "already written" the story. In Liam's case, the coat was not explicitly a part of his story, so if he'd written the draft first, he'd never have found it. Liam needed to be able to scour the terrain he was creating, asking, What have I got here, and how can I use it?

During these first couple of weeks, when students are mentally reaching out for experience that is not their own, I prod them to be aware of the ways their own experience *is* informing their work. Fiction is simply another way of telling the truth about our own lives, even as we pretend to be talking about someone else. Obviously, I don't mean that everyone has to use his own life events in his story, only that our own feelings, attitudes, and life issues always find their ways into our fiction and that is a good thing, since those issues provide the engine for our work. Fiction is a projection, psychologically speaking, and we always bring our business to any story we make up. The characters, places, and plot are only masks, and as such they often free us to say clearly what we otherwise would lack the nerve to express. In minilessons, I ask students to freewrite about what situations, events, or feelings from their own lives help them know what they are writing about. I tell them no one else has to know about it but being aware of the real stuff they are working with provides an important source of energy for their work. I also frequently encourage them to reread their notebooks to see where they have written before about things that may turn out to be in their stories, so that entries about baseball, family vacations, fights with boyfriends, and such, might provide useful details for their work. Even more important, writers reread in search of some feelings, relationships, or themes that connect to their work in fiction. Once they realize the connection between their real lives and the made-up world of their characters, they can, if they get stuck for material, look to that part of their lives for inspiration. But I tread lightly in making the connections between autobiography and students' fictional worlds too explicit. In some ways, fiction writers trick the truth out of themselves by bypassing their usual defenses. For some writers, telling a deeper metaphorical truth might require keeping the most powerful connections between life and fictional work somewhat underground. Even if a student's own life history suggests to her elements of her story, eventually she may have to forget her own life in order to craft the story.

One of the unexpected by-products of studying fiction writing with students has been the opportunity to see them develop ways of taking notes on their own thinking. As they explore the complexity of a life, the web of existence spins out quickly, and not in ordered prose. Writers' jottings are elliptical, quick, and spacious, leaving plenty of room for free play between the lines. This quickness helps them capture the ambiguity and complexity we recognize as "true to life," even as they make up people and events that never happened. Each kid brings his own style of thought to note taking. Nikki's were almost all prose; Danny dashed off list after list; Ryan made boxes around the page, spatially compartmentalizing his categories; Meghan labeled her categories one per page, so that she could layer them over time with more thinking; Esoti wrote many short narratives of events from the lives of her characters. As I've watched students taking rapid notes on their own thinking, I've wondered where else in school they are likely to use writing in this way, quickly stabilizing their own fleeting thought, a practice that seems so central a part of my own literate life.

Setting the world in motion—manipulating time

Depending on the pace of student work, there comes a point (after I'm not sure how long—longer than a week) when several writers know a lot about their characters and their worlds, and they are ready to figure out what from all this they want to select for their story. By this time, they should have slowed down enough that exploring what will happen in their stories won't send them scurrying after events the way they might have without all this work in the notebooks. To help them keep control, there are still several more elements of planning with which I try to help, mostly having to do with time.

First, it is important that the kids know that not everything they have figured out about their characters will be automatically dumped into the text of their story. In fact, they probably have not yet made up the incidents that will be in the story. The question for them now is: which little bit of their character's life's time line will they pinch off to narrate in the story? A short story is usually just a tiny bit, maybe even just a few minutes, of a character's life. Packed into those few minutes, however, may be many of the issues with which the character struggles in her whole life. Writers, then, have to select carefully what bit of life will best reveal who their characters are and what they care about, what they are trying to do in their lives and what is in their way. In most cases, this means choosing moments when the character's need is greatest and most threatened. These few moments give the writer the idea for the story. From there, they can begin to figure out what happens, given what would make sense in this world they now know.

Much to everyone's frustration, knowing what happens in the story still doesn't tell the writer what to write. The story is not the plot. Plotting involves planning how the writer will *tell* the story, the order in which events will appear on the page, and therefore involves a deliberate manipulation of time. We all recognize from our reading of stories that time in a narrative doesn't simply march forward: prior events are embedded in exposition; hints of foreshadowing make us predict what we do not yet know; the teller of a story may from the first word be located in a time long after the last event in the story. But having such knowledge from our reading does not necessarily make it obvious that *our* story can be thus controlled and arranged in time. Once student writers have a story in mind, "this happens and then this happens and then this happens and then that," they will, in my experience, usually write the story just that way, unless they have the opportunity to plan their story more deliberately and craftily and help in doing so. Ultimately, they can write their story any way they choose, but I want to provide an environment wherein we are all inquiring into possibilities. I want them to try several outlines, deliberately employing some of the tools of time with which more seasoned writers of narratives are well versed.

I don't have anything specific in mind when I say they need to do several outlines. I can think of few things more destructive to the spirit of our inquiry than to use this as an opportunity to teach a certain technique of formal outlining. I just mean some sketch of the order in which they will tell their story. It may be a quick and simple list whose elements can only be decoded by the writer. It may be a time line or some other graphic map. Some kids prefer to write out sentences as a scenario or synopsis, something like: *First, Jenna is practicing in a practice room, really into the music. Then, she's walking home and she can't get the music out of her mind. When she gets home.* . . . As with their note taking, students develop styles of outlining that suit their own ways of thinking.

Making multiple outlines reveals to writers that the story can be told in a number of ways and unlaces their sense of necessity so that they are less likely to think, *It has to be this way because this is what happens next.* Their relationship to their material becomes more fluid and therefore also more controlled by the writer's will. The story is pliable and so the artist can work it into different shapes. The outlines are just guesses, not contracts. Like my plans for a class, they are loose commitments, a way of preparing for the future without determining it. As they draft, students will free their minds to play, to invent, and the outline will only provide boundaries for the playing field. I stress that they can change those boundaries as soon as they don't fit the game anymore. In fact, many fiction writers pause often in the midst of drafts to outline the next bit. Lawrence Durrell described it this way: "It's like driving a few stakes in the ground; you haven't got to that point in the construction yet, so you run ahead fifty yards, and you plant a stake in to show roughly the direction your road is going, which helps to give you your orientation" (in Plimpton, p. 188).

When students make their outlines tighter and more authoritative, they are likely to write quickly from one point on the outline to the next, without lingering in the moments that make the fiction most real. But when they have no sense at all of where they are going, when they don't know the ending of their stories and how they will get there, they are likely to wander aimlessly, unloading their notebooks onto a page without shaping the action. I want them to know their destination and their basic route, *then* to take the scenic route and enjoy the vistas. Like everything else, plotting is a balancing act.

Because these plotting techniques are difficult for kids to grasp without examples, I usually ground my explanations about them in students' accounts of how they made particular decisions about their stories. This means I have to use my conferring, at this point in the process, as a kind of farm for minilessons, getting kids to try things I haven't explained yet to the whole class, so that they can become examples for everyone's learning.

Even after Dana had selected the bit of his character's life that would be his short story, he still had to decide where he would start the action and where stop it. These decisions would require that much of what he knew about the character be revealed, if Dana decided it was necessary, in some way other than straight chronological telling. He was tempted just to tell the story from beginning to end, because that was easier, involved less technical trouble than starting late and having to figure out the words for going back and scooping up earlier events. But he also wanted his story to be more exciting, more urgent than it could be if he started when Derrick got his first basketball. After we had conferred about his decision, I asked him to begin the next day's class by sharing what he'd decided to do and why, using an overhead of his plotting notes.

"I wanted to tell about how basketball became important to my character, which was that his parents had given him a basketball hoop for his eleventh birthday and his dad had played with him at first, after he got it." As he spoke, he pointed to the relevant places on his time line and his plot outlines. "And then that he tried out for the team and didn't make it and then finally he did make it and that was the first time he got to be on a basketball team and now it's the thing he's the best at. And also there was all this stuff about his parents and how they're too busy to pay attention to him. They're always too busy. But I decided that if I put all that, all those years, into the story, it would be too boring and it would go too slow. I really wanted to get to this one big game when his parents finally do show up. So I decided to start at just the day before that and he has a game when they don't show up and talk about that problem there and then the next day they do show up. So I think I'm going to start the plot almost at the end of the story."

When Dana finished explaining, I switched off the overhead and said, "Dana's made a really important decision about the point of attack for his story. The point of attack is the place you start your story, the first thing that's happening in the first few sentences, what's going on when the lights come on. Dana's decided that he wants a really late point of attack, so that his story is going to take place in just two days, but in those two days, he'll show a lot of things about the character's whole life. It's a strong decision for him to make because it puts the character right in the situation he cares most about, and he's got a problem, and there's just a short amount of time, so there's a feeling of urgency, which is more exciting than a long string of events. All stories don't do that, but that's one of the options you have. You might decide to start very early, which has more of a once-upon-a-time feel to it, where you're going to tell the whole thing from beginning to end. Or you might even decide to start a long time after everything is over, and have your main character or someone else write or tell this story of something that happened before the point of attack. Try it different ways, just sketching it out for yourself in outlines, and we can talk about your options."

Though everyone does have to make decisions about their point of attack, there is no law that says it's where they have to begin. Writers can begin to craft the present action of their stories by beginning at the beginning, at the end, or somewhere in between. Tanya knew that at or near the end of her story her character would have a chance to shine as a performer with her abusive mother in the audience. She wrote that part first:

She began to sing. Her voice sounded as if she was an experianced girl, who was crying, a kind of crying you could'nt see you would just know the tears were there. Aleasha's dress sparkled from the light above. As Aleasha sang she looked at the surroundings around her. The stage floor looked like it was slippery. It was a pretty beige which also sparkled off the light. The stage curtains were a maroon color. And were also velvet. The stage curtains looked so soft and made Aleasha go with the stage. Like she finally belonged somewhere and no one could kick her out. When Aleasha was done with her song there was a short pause. Then a tramendous sound of applause. Then Aleasha went to the back of the stage. No one was back there but her. Aleasha wanted to cry but she didn't. Something stopped her and told her everything would be ok. And she listened to that voice and didn't cry.

Now, having fixed her destination, she had to plot out where to begin and the route she would take, as well as plan ways to fold into her story information about events that had happened before the story starts. No matter where they begin, writers of narrative almost always have to embed prior expository information into the ongoing action of the present story. Tanya had several tools at her disposal, which we talked about by referring to the stories we both knew. For one thing, she could reveal background information through dialogue. She found she had to be careful about this, though, because it's easy for this technique to turn into the phoniness of bad plays and movies, where one character tells another something she already fully well knows: "As you know, Grandma, my father left us two years ago, shortly after my grandfather, your husband, passed away, and since then Mom hasn't been able to get a job." Her desire to be believable made her reject these early attempts. The reader be damned, most adolescents would rather be anything but fakey, and with all the exactitude they can muster, they bring their sense of how the world goes to their fiction making. Instead, she figured out that it sounded more real to her if her characters provided exposition when they were fighting. This seemed to me to be a brilliant decision, since in arguments, people are constantly shouting over and over again things the other person already knows, because the facts, or at least the interpretations of facts, are in dispute. So Tanya had Aleasha, her main character say, "Mom, ever since Dad left you've been picking on me. But it's *not my fault!* And it's not my fault that you can't find a job, either!" Mom beat the reader to the punch in wondering whether it was necessary for one character to reveal that information to the other. "Don't you think I know that, Aleasha? Nobody ever *said* it was your fault!"

Another strategy in Tanya's repertoire was the uncovering of background through various kinds of flashbacks. Tanya favored the psychological flashback, where past events are revealed through a central character's reveries of memory: "Aleasha looked at the empty chair across the room and remembered that day two years ago when her father had left them. When she had come in the door, he had been sitting in his plaid chair, with his hands hanging down almost to the floor." Grammatically, if the story is in past tense, this kind of flashback can follow a simple formula: a past tense sentence about the character remembering, followed by several sentences in the past perfect tense, which narrate the memory with sensory detail. As many kids do, Tanya ended this kind of flashback with someone's shouting Aleasha's name, abruptly ending the memory, and with Aleasha's saying something like, "Sorry, I was just thinking."

But this is just one kind of flashback, and there were others available to Tanya, which she chose not to use. Sometimes the narrative voice can accomplish the jump back in time without the main character's thoughts going along: "Two years before, Aleasha had walked through the door of her family's trailer and seen her father sitting in his plaid chair with his hands hanging down almost to the floor." A double space between lines can also signal a time leap which omits the verbal temporal transitions. The writer just skips a line and acts like she's writing the prior story, then skips another line when she's ready to return to the story's present action. Yet another technique uses the stories behind objects or other characters to reveal important information: "She had had that teddy bear ever since the day before her father left for good, and he had taken her to the county fair." Whatever devices the writer chooses to use to expose past action, the important thing to me is that kids have a range of options, an awareness of the ways they as authors can control and craft time in stories and of the ways in which the past is always still alive in present feelings, thoughts, and actions.

Authors also craft the future, but in a more limited way. Few professional authors can say what happens after their stories are over. That entire fictional world ceases to exist after the last event. Isak Dinesen said, "People always ask me, they say, 'In "The Deluge at Norderney," were those characters drowned or saved at the end?' . . . Well, what can I reply? How can I tell them? That's outside the story. I really don't know!" (in Plimpton, p. 188). But within the bounds of the story, fiction writers prepare readers for future events and try to make the story seem, at least in retrospect, to possess the inevitability of destiny. It's a matter of planting at the beginning the likelihood, or at least the possibility, of what will happen later. Anton Chekhov said that if a gun is loaded in the first act, it's got to go off in the third. It's just as true in short fiction as in drama that important late events are usually prepared early on in the story. This requires, of course, that writers plan, that they see the time in their story as a whole, the future, as well as the past, encoded in the present action. However, there does come a time when planning must end, and a writer has to lay down prose. As important as all this preparatory work has been, we are only inquiring into fiction writing if eventually writers use their notes to make a draft, and of course, the making of a draft brings a whole new set of decisions into focus.

Opening the storyteller's mouth—drafting and revising a story

Most likely, as soon as a writer of fiction has written a sentence, he has made at least a provisional decision about point of view and voice. Naturally, I think this decision should be, if not problematic, at least conscious. The kids don't get far in their draft before I start bothering them again. I bother them about point of view because I want them at least to consider the possibilities available to them as to who is telling this story. Would it be most powerful if the main character told it, or if some other character in the story told it? Or is there information the reader can only get from a narrator who knows what all the characters are thinking? These decisions about who is telling the story lead immediately to other decisions about what the language of that telling is like, the voice of the story. If a character is telling the story, to whom is he telling it? The answer to that question may lead the writer to adopt a more distant and formal voice or a more friendly, oral style. When a writer decides to let one of the fictional characters tell the story, the *telling* of the story may become another fictional scene, and can be attended to for the definition of character and place, just like the scenes within the story. A decision that "Louis is telling the story to his son, who is the same age Louis was when the story happened" leads to a different tone and style than "Louis is writing the story, immediately after it happened, for a school disciplinary council."

Even if the story is told impersonally, by no one in particular, and the writer wants the narrator to be as transparent as possible, there are questions that, during revision, the writer may consider in rereading her story. How much, for example, does the narrator care about what happened in the story? How passionate does she feel about it? How vividly is the narrator trying to help the reader picture the action? How much does the narrator like the reader? How much does the narrator like the characters? How friendly or how formal is the storyteller? What is time like for the narrator? Is it urgent to get the story out, or is she luxuriating in a lengthy and detailed, even tangential, performance? Such questions personify some of the stylistic features of narrative text. In the context of student work on fiction, this personification has, for me, felt like a reasonable way to discuss issues about language that can otherwise be slippery, especially when the writers are deeply involved in their fictional worlds.

While students are drafting and revising their stories, my conferences are often fairly random interruptions in their work. I ask them what they are doing, and then probe into their thinking beneath the surface. Why is this character doing that? What is he thinking and feeling? Why does this matter? How does this fit with the rest of your story? Where is this happening, and what is it like for the character to be there? How should this part sound in the reader's ear? Of course, what I ask depends on what the student says he is working on. Usually, there are gaps in the writer's thinking, questions he isn't sure how to answer, and most often, I send him back to the notebook to imagine and plan that part of the story before going on with the draft. The forward motion of writing a story sometimes propels the writer too quickly through time, and the recursive process of rethinking and revising helps to slow things down again and helps the writer envision the total world of the story, rather than merely the linear action and events.

Sometimes, kids' best fiction writing is in the small moments of their stories, in the spaces between the points on their outlines. In these little details, they seem less to be gripping their imaginative worlds with tight control and more to be releasing the story to live "naturally." I make a big deal of these small, brilliant moments, publicizing them to the class as examples of how a writer creates details that reveal important qualities of character and theme, "telling details." I asked Nora to share with the class the section of her draft where her character, nervous about that day's events at school, "flung open the door to the cereal cupboard and pulled out the Trix. I usually eat them in order by color, but today I just shoved them into my mouth and ran upstairs." Danny told about the section of his story, when his character was feeling abandoned by everyone in his life, and "saw a racoon nibbling on a tree branch. I put out my hand to pet what looked like a cute, cuddly, good friend. It snipped at me. I was hurt. It seemed like anything I tried to get close to would snip, bite, and make me feel bad." Dana also provided an example; he's the student whose character had the problem with his parents not paying attention to him. When he talks to his mother in the basement of their house, "the high ceilings of the big and dry basement made Derrick's words echo." These moments, often more revealing than the rest of the plot, are spots where the kids are most immediately grasping the essence of fiction writing, doing what the famous writers do.

As I did with Luke at the beginning of this chapter, I very often refer writers to the short fiction we have read together and, when appropriate, to novels they are reading independently. This is most helpful with questions about technique: How do you shift to the interior thoughts of a character? Is it okay to be in the thoughts of one character and then to switch into another's mind? How can you tell an event from one character's perspective and then the same event, even though it's already gone past, through the eyes of another person? How can you write about someone's being really sad without just saying, "He was really sad"? Where in a scene can you break the action to describe the setting? When you're writing in first person, how do you jump in time? How can you describe a character while the story is still moving, without stopping everything to say, "She had black hair, brown eyes, cinnamon skin, and big teeth"? Any short stack of stories will have several ways of solving these and most other technical difficulties, and learning in a genre always includes researching the available literature to solve problems of craft.

I can only recognize these problems when I hear students wrestling with them if I'm working on a piece of fiction on my own. If I had not run into the selfsame confusion in my own writing, I probably wouldn't be able to translate the kids' stuttering, rambling frustrations into terms I could understand. But, because I've "been there" as a writer, just last night, I can look at the page and listen to the writer, recognize the issue, and say, "Oh yeah, that's a tricky one. Let's look at how some other people handled it." In the interest of time and the multitudes, I help the student define the question, send her to the literature, and leave her to her research, saying I'll check back later to see how she handled it. If she's found a narrative strategy that might benefit a number of the kids in her class, I ask her to share it for the minilesson the next day.

There are other times when it's not really necessary for the writer to go on a technique hunt, when I have a feeling that the kid probably already knows, from experience with both oral and literate stories, the batches of words, little linguistic formulas, that might get him through this section. I can help the student become aware of his own competence by simply asking him to tell me this section of the story, without looking at his page. Together, we use oral storytelling to run quickly through the options, and then the writer chooses which way he will take the time to write it. When Sean was trying to cut back and forth between two characters' thoughts, he told me he didn't know how to write it. He knew what he wanted each of his people to be thinking, but he was stuck on the transitions. I asked a couple of the kids sitting near him to think with us about how this section could go.

"I could just say, While Richard was saying this, Tommy was thinking that," Sean began.

"Or you could like, make Tommy frown while Richard's talking, and then tell why he frowned," Luke suggested.

"How would that sound, Luke?" I asked.

"He could say, Richard said blah, blah, blah. Tommy frowned. He had never heard anything so crazy. Ever since he'd known Richard, he had . . . whatever."

"Okay, there's another option. What else?"

"He could make the characters just be honest and tell what they are thinking. In the dialogue," said Tanya.

"So how would that go?"

"It could be like, Richard said blah blah blah. Tommy said, Well that's not what I think. I think, blah, blah, blah."

"No, that won't work, because the whole point is that they're not saying what they're thinking in this part," Sean said.

"I read something once where they put the character's thoughts in script, and the words they said in quotes, but I don't know if that will work with two characters because it would still be confusing whose thoughts they are," said Luke.

"You could have no dialogue," I put in. "You could just say something like, Even though Richard said that he blah blah blah, he really thought de-dee-de-dee-de-dee. Tommy answered that bing-bang-boom. But he was already planning dah-dah-dah. . . ." There was a pause while we all thought. "Anyway, those are some ideas, Sean. You can try one or think of some more or look through some literature if you don't like those. I'll look forward to seeing how you do it."

In this kind of conference, I am trying to scaffold the writer's consideration of some options. I want her, while I'm kneeling here, to come up with some possible suggestions. If she's working, then I'll put in some ideas too, unashamedly, to contribute to the repertoire of possibilities. It's a conversation embodying a set of thoughts I hope Sean will internalize: recognizing a problem and brainstorming several possible solutions. Sean would not have gone through that process if I hadn't been there, but I hope that because he thought through it with me today, he will be able to do so independently tomorrow.

The proliferation of options is one of the main agendas I bring to every conference, even when the student is not working on fiction. I know that one difference between a basic writer and a fluent writer is that a basic writer believes that what he writes next can only be one thing, the next necessary word. Fluent writers are always at a fork in the road, always aware of options: I could do it this way, that way, or the other way, so I'll try it this way, and then come back and try again if I don't like it. I hope, in many of my conferences, to help students see that it ain't necessarily so, to lift and complicate what they think they are doing, so that they will get used to thinking that there are always other possible routes in the journey of a piece of writing, and the act of writing is always a matter of making choices based on where you're trying to take the reader.

I believe it's my job, as the teacher, to help kids do something with me that they couldn't yet do on their own. I don't just check up on them to make sure they're having a nice time; I push them to reach for a kind of thinking that, tomorrow, may come more naturally. I want to help them work in what Lev Vygotsky calls the "zone of proximal development," which in simpler terms means the part that will come next in the learner's growth. That principle underlies my conferring with individual writers and also every other aspect of this study of fiction. The whole journey is an attempt to support writers in processes in which they are for now emergent learners but which I hope will in time become internalized and independent.

If the processes kids are learning in the study of fiction writing were just about making up little stories, it wouldn't be so important for them to grow in those processes. As I stated earlier, my real goals in teaching fiction don't center on the stories as products. There are far too many professional fiction writers already; I'm not preparing them for anything in the workaday world. I do hope they are growing, however, growing in habits of inquiry, growing in their abilities to imagine the internal lives of other persons, growing in the craftsmanship of possibility, growing in their awareness of time's warped arrow whereupon each of us bends our past toward the hope of a transformed future. And I can't help but believe that when they mature in these ways, they are becoming prepared for their own futures as empowered authors of their own life stories and as compassionate collaborators for tomorrow's society.

Resources: short fiction for kids

When I first began working with fiction, I found one of the chief difficulties was a dearth of available short stories to read with kids. Since then, I've been collecting titles everywhere I can. Categorized below are the titles of books that happened to have crossed my path and that have been helpful to other teachers. It's not an exhaustive list nor even a catalogue of great short fiction. It's a start.

Collections of short stories written for young people— more than one author

CHAMBERS, AIDAN, ed. *Out of Time.* New York: Harper and Row, 1984. Science fiction.

GALLO, DONALD, ed. *Sixteen: Short Stories by Outstanding Writers for Young Adults.* New York: Dell, 1984. Realistic fiction, mostly.

———. *Visions: Nineteen Short Stories by Outstanding Writers for Young Adults.* New York: Dell, 1987. Realistic fiction, mostly.

———. *Connections: Short Stories by Outstanding Writers for Young Adults.* New York: Dell, 1989. Realistic fiction, mostly.

_____ . *Within Reach.* New York: HarperCollins, 1993. More realistic fiction.

_____ . *Join In: Multiethnic Short Short Stories by Outstanding Writers for Young Adults.* New York: Delacorte, 1993.

YOLEN, JANE, MARTIN GREENBERG, and CHARLES WAUGH, eds. *Dragons and Dreams.* New York: Harper and Row, 1986. Science fiction and fantasy.

Collections of stories written for young people—one author

CORMIER, ROBERT. *Eight Plus One.* New York: Bantam, 1982.

CRUTCHER, CHRIS. *Athletic Shorts: 6 Short Stories.* New York: Greenwillow, 1991.

FLEISCHMAN, PAUL. *Graven Images.* New York: Harper and Row, 1982. Three longish stories about people whose lives are supernaturally affected by sculptured objects.

HUNTER, KRISTIN. *Guests in the Promised Land.* New York: Charles Scribner's Sons, 1968.

MAZER, NORMA FOX. *Dear Bill, Remember Me? and Other Stories.* New York: Dell, 1976.

MOHR, NICHOLASA. *El Bronx Remembered.* New York: Harper and Row, 1990.

_____ . *In Nueva York.* New York: Harper and Row, 1990.

PATERSON, KATHERINE. *Angels and Other Strangers: Family Christmas Stories.* New York: Thomas Y. Crowell, 1979. Christmas stories; very religious.

RYLANT, CYNTHIA. *Children of Christmas.* New York: Orchard Books, 1987. Christmas stories; not too religious.

_____ . *Every Living Thing.* New York: Macmillan, 1985.

SIERUTA, PETER. *Heartbeats and Other Stories.* New York: Harper and Row, 1989. The characters are mostly high-school aged, and the stories are excellent.

SOTO, GARY. *Baseball in April and Other Stories.* Orlando, FL: Harcourt Brace Jovanovich, 1990. Mexican-American boys and girls becoming teenagers in California.

TAYLOR, MILDRED D. *"The Friendship" and "The Gold Cadillac."* New York: Bantam, 1987. Two long short stories in one slim volume.

THOMAS, PIRI. *Stories from El Barrio.* New York: Knopf, 1978.

Collections of stories written for adults but collected here with young readers in mind—that is, they may not be easy for young people to read, but they have characters who are children or teenagers

ADOFF, ARNOLD. *Brothers and Sisters: Modern Stories by Black Americans.* New York: Macmillan, 1970.

BAMBARA, TONI CADE, ed. *Tales and Stories for Black Folks.* New York: Doubleday Zenith Books, 1971.

BARRETT, PETER, ed. *To Break the Silence: Thirteen Short Stories for Young Readers.* New York: Dell, 1986.

BENARD, ROBERT, ed. *Do You Like it Here? and Other Stories: Twenty-one Views of the High School Years.* New York: Dell, 1989.

GOLD, ROBERT S., ed. *Point of Departure: Nineteen Stories of Youth and Discovery.* New York: Dell, 1967.

———— . *Stepping Stones: Seventeen Powerful Stories of Growing Up.* New York: Dell, 1981.

ROCHMAN, HAZEL, ed. *Somehow Tenderness Survives: Stories of Southern Africa.* New York: Harper and Row, 1988. The book was intended for young adults; some of the stories are difficult, mainly because of the rich background knowledge required.

SCHULMAN, L. M., ed. *The Loners: Short Stories About the Young and Alientated.* New York: Macmillan, 1970. Includes stories by Jean Stafford, Isaac Babel, William Faulkner, Ernest Hemingway, et al.

———— . *Autumn Light: Illuminations of Age.* New York: Thomas Y. Crowell, 1978. Includes stories by Roger Angell, Vladimir Nabokov, Kurt Vonnegut, Jean Rhys, Truman Capote, et al.

ZOLOTOW, CHARLOTTE, ed. *Early Sorrow.* New York: Harper and Row, 1978.

———— . *An Overpraised Season.* New York: Harper and Row, 1973.

Collections of short stories for adults that may prove useful with some groups of kids

COOPER, J. CALIFORNIA. *Some Soul to Keep.* New York: St. Martin's Press, 1987.

HOWE, IRVING, and ILANA HOWE, eds. *Short Shorts: An Anthology of the Shortest Stories.* New York: Bantam, 1983.

SHAPARD, ROBERT, and JAMES THOMAS, eds. *Sudden Fiction: American Short-Short Stories.* New York: Norton, 1986.

———— . *Sudden Fiction International: Sixty Short-Short Stories.* New York: Norton, 1989.

Recommended reading on the craft of fiction

GARDNER, JOHN. *The Art of Fiction: Notes on Craft for Young Writers.* New York: Knopf, 1984.

MACAULEY, ROBIE, and GEORGE LANNING. *Technique in Fiction.* Second Edition. New York: St. Martin's Press, 1987.

PECK, ROBERT NEWTON. *Fiction Is Folks: How to Create Unforgettable Characters.* Cincinnati, OH: Writers Digest Books, 1987.

TIME AND STORY

The way time is constructed in a text is one of the first keys to its genre. A text ordered outside of time, as if its points are always true, now and forever, is expository, while a text ordered *in* time is a narrative. The word *then* may be crucial in either genre, but it means very different things. *Then* in an essay means *therefore*; *then* in a story means *next*. Stories, narratives of any kind, whether they refer to actual events or to made-up ones, come the closest to reflecting our experience in time. They move, as we read or write them, like life does, through time. Therefore, though essays may tell a truth, only stories can be lifelike. The truth in a narrative is conditional and situated—this murder happened on this particular dark and stormy night—and doesn't aspire to eternal reality.

But in spite of their seemingly modest pretensions about their absolute truth, the stories we tell, more than any other act of language, reveal our most dearly held theories about "how life goes," or at least "how life might go." Listening well to a person telling a story is the closest we can get to a window on her beliefs and understanding about life. What does she choose to emphasize? With what assumptions does she begin? What is left out of the story? After all, in telling her story, she is framing experience—choosing where this thing begins and ends. In order to rope off *an* experience from life in general this way, she has to select, out of all the possible seconds of her life, some bounded experience that *says* something, that shows what she means. Our experience forms us; what we understand of experience is what we understand ourselves to be, our identities. We are the stories we tell.

Our writing lives need to include many stories, not a single story, for no one story can include all the possible times we need to explore. If we write, say, only one story in a year, we are sure to be blocked about it. How could we choose? A writing life involves constantly exploring real and possible times. And in these explorations, we show what we know about how life tends to go.

9

Making Something of Our Lives
Reading and Writing Memoir

As far back as I can remember, my grandfather was made of memory. When I was little, I used to climb into his lap and ask for a story. His stories were never fairy tales but "true" incidents from his childhood in a coal-mining camp near Warrior, Alabama. Not even incidents, sometimes—he'd weave a story about the conditions of the life he'd known there, the unspoken theme always being how different it was from the life he saw people living. When I think of those stories now, I realize what a master craftsman he was with the raw material of his life, turning ordinary happenstance into magic. He was able to take an everyday occurrence from his boyhood and turn it into the first important piece of literature of my life.

When I was home in Texas during a recent Christmas break, I got to see my grandfather for a day, something that doesn't happen as often as I'd like. Papa's an alcoholic, started drinking about the time I was born. (My being born had nothing to do with his taking to drink—at least as far as I know.) He's on the wagon now. It's a bit of an uncomfortable subject, his drinking, especially for me, since I've never been an insider on those conversations, but somehow, it came up.

He said, "You know, Rand, I used to really hit the sauce—for years I did." I nodded ambiguously, hoping to suggest the possibility that I'd never noticed.

He went on, "But I stopped, I stopped. The doctor found something he could say that would scare me. He told me that the alcohol had been hurting my brain, Rand. And he said that the first thing to go would be my memory. And hell, Rand, that's all I got's my memories. Nothing was worth losing that. If my memory's gonna go, I'd rather be dead."

He meant it. And it made perfect sense to me. As far back as I could remember, memory was what Papa was made of. *Now* I know he's not just cherishing the memories that *made* the stories but the memories of *telling* the stories to four little kids sitting on his lap and resting their chins on his knees—and the memory of his now-gone wife's face when she would chime in with a detail he'd forget—and the memory of his daughter's, my mother's, voice when she would ask a question, some point of detail in the story she'd heard a thousand times, so that part of it would seem new to her, too.

I guess Papa would have to disagree with Benjamin Bloom. Bloom places memory on the bottom of his taxonomy of learning, as the least important, the least complex, the lowest level of cognitive functioning. Thomas Newkirk has commented that Bloom's taxonomy has to be seen as a "statement about the kinds of thinking valued in our culture and, particularly, in academic institutions in our culture. When we talk about . . . higher-order thinking, . . . we are making a statement about values. . . . 'Higher' shades into 'better' or most significant or most worthy" (p. 17).

Newkirk's point, well taken, is that the survival of oral cultures depends on those who remember. But the survival of our culture, too, in fact the survival of our earth, depends, as Elie Wiesel continually proclaims, upon the depth and truth of our memory—our memory of what human beings are capable of, our memory of the black smoke of Auschwitz. Wiesel says, "the fear of forgetting remains the main obsession of all those who have passed through the universe of the damned. If memory grew hollow, empty of substance, what would happen to all we had accumulated on the way? Remember, said the father to his son, and the son to his friend. Gather the names, the faces, the tears" (p. 1). In the film *The Ploughman's Lunch*, one of the characters comments, "Milan Kundera has one of his characters say that the struggle of freedom against tyranny is the struggle of memory against forgetting. . . . If we leave the remembering to the historians, the struggle's already lost. Everyone must have a memory. Everyone needs to be a historian. In this country, for example, we are endangered of losing hard-won freedoms by dozing off into a perpetual present."

Memory, particularly memory of that which I have witnessed, of my own life, may be the most important form of cognition. In *The Brothers Karamazov*, Dostoyevski says, "People talk to you a great deal about your education, but some good, sacred memory, preserved from childhood, is perhaps the best education. If one carries many such memories into life, one is safe to the end of one's days, and if one has only one good memory left in one's heart, even that may be the means of saving us." And Robert Coles, in a gloss on this passage in *The Call of Stories*, describes such a memory as "a recollected moment in which someone has tasted of life, a moment forceful enough, charged enough, to survive many other moments. . . . Without such compelling memories, we are not ourselves, but rather anyone" (p. 183). If Erik Erikson is right in claiming that the primary task of adolescence is self-definition, then, by severing students from their past, secondary schools do more to impede development than to facilitate it.

In *Composing a Life*, Mary Catherine Bateson proposes that in our culture, "the materials and skills from which a life is composed are no longer clear. It is no longer possible to follow the paths of previous generations" (p. 2). The task of composing our lives, therefore, requires more attention than it ever has before. Each individual is engaged in a process of self-*invention*—not discovery—shaping and reshaping the raw material of both the past and the future. "What we search for does not exist until we find it," Bateson says.

Where will our students learn to pay attention to their lives in this way, crafting themselves into certain kinds of persons by choosing what has been important to them, by deciding what matters? Where, in our heavy-laden curricula, do we provide students with the opportunity to cherish their remembrances? We talk often of future-oriented thinking, executive functions of planning, predicting, organizing—but when do we teach kids how to gain access to their past? School doesn't have room for that. It's too personal. And besides, how would we measure it?

Papa dropped out of school in the ninth grade and became a man who made things. My earliest memory of something he made is a small pine bust of himself he brought home from work one day when I was about three, a bust he carved during breaks at the shop where he was a welder. I still have it, and I'm looking at it now. I remember him striding into the house and presenting it to Mammaw, and both of them laughing. To me, it does look like him, maybe only because this object helped form my image of him. I remember being amazed that someone could *make* something that *looked like himself*. It's an important piece from my life's museum because it says so much about one of the central issues of my life: the making of things from the chaos of experience, a sense of craft, making something that looks like myself. These are the reasons I write.

So what is this thing called memory? How can we begin to complicate our thinking about remembering, so that we can see it and teach it as a craft? How can we gain control over the accidents of autobiographical memory?

The ancient Celts believed that the souls of our lost loved ones are captive in objects, lost to us until we happen to pass the tree or hold the object that forms their prison. Then they start awake and tremble, they call us by our name, and as soon as we have recognized their voice the spell is broken. Delivered by us, they have overcome death and return to share our life. So it is with our own past.

Marcel Proust sips tea in which he has soaked a petit madeleine, a small cookie. The taste and warmth of the sugary tea evoke in him a wonderfully familiar feeling that he can't place; it's buried in his mind, just out of reach. And from that tiny moment of sensual stimulus, his memory and imagination yield all seven volumes of *Remembrance of Things Past*.

I'm not suggesting that we march thirty fourteen-year-olds around the neighborhood in search of the captive souls of their dead relatives, and I also don't recommend launching a memoir course of study by inviting our sophomores to dunk some cookies in tea. I do hope to suggest that without ever limiting topic choice with silly exercises like "my best experience," "my most embarrassing moment," or "if my mother were a tree," we can put into our students' hands keys with which they can begin unlocking their own life histories.

When the poet Suzanne Gardinier joined the Teachers College Writing Project staff, she questioned the "personal narratives" we were all trying to get kids in writing workshops to make, because neither she nor any other writer she knew ever said they were working on a "personal narrative." She wasn't objecting merely to the term but to the form that had evolved, a new school genre, too often a simple story told from beginning to end. The conversation she began led us to study memoirs by professional writers, both those of book length and shorter texts that appear frequently in magazines and newspapers. Too often, memoir is thought to consist of the reminiscences of old people and ex-presidents. But what we were seeing in the best literature we could find were neither "all about everything that happened to me" nor the "this happened" personal experience stories we too often saw in our classrooms. Often the best memoirs explored a number of small, simple moments, linked by a common theme. Sometimes the events were bigger, but whatever the drama inherent in the event, what distinguished these memoirs from what we saw in classrooms was a reflective angle, a lens of meaning that linked the different stories or made even a single incident connect to the rest of the writer's life. The memoirs we admired seemed to say, *Here's something important about me, and probably about other people, and here's how it came to be or worked out in my life.* They also had a tone and often an explicit theme dealing directly with the nature of memory, with the ways our past is transformed and changed as we reconstruct it at different times in our life. The more we read, the more we saw a stable set of genre characteristics emerging. Moreover, when we read interviews with memoirists, and articles such as those included in William Zinsser's *Inventing the Truth: The Art and Craft of Memoir,* it became clear that the writers of memoir had some of the same habits of process. Memoir can only become a genre of writing, as opposed to stories remembered and written, when we read examples in the genre.

Reading memoir not only builds into students (and us) a sense of the genre's structural possibilities and writerly craft, it also is a powerful stimulus for memories. As Franz Kafka said, "Reading ought to be an icepick to break up the frozen sea within us." When our students read memoir and from their reading bump into memory and from remembering reach toward writing, the lines that divide reading, writing, and living blur. Distinctions collapse between literature and creative writing and composition and reading. The walls come a-tumblin' down.

Before beginning to write a memoir, Larissa, in Judy Davis's class in Manhattan, read *Homesick* by Jean Fritz, a memoir of a young American girl growing up in China during the communist revolution. Jean feels herself always out of place, living, as she says, on the wrong side of the world. She hears of America only through her parents' descriptions and her grandmother's letters, and when her family finally returns, she still feels alienated because it is now her homeland that is foreign to her. Here is part of Larissa's memoir about her return to her family's country, Poland:

Coming

Till last year I didn't know how Poland looked or hadn't seen my relatives in ages. The minute the plane touched down on Polish soil, I knew I was "home." Waiting next to the plane was a soldier with a rifle. We went through what seemed like six kilometers of customs. After, I got to see my grandmother for the first time in seven years. I didn't recognize her. When we went outside, I just stood and looked. I looked at the Polish people. I looked at the Polish cars. Cars drove around frantically. People looked very happy. All those got to see their relatives. I knew this was my homeland. A moment later, we got into my mother's friend's car, and drove and drove. On the way, I saw things you couldn't see in New York. Like a cow grazing of the side of the road.

Larissa wrote in response to memoir, but she would have responded to *Home-sick* in the same personal way even if it were fiction. Jareed, a student in Karen Rosner's Bronx classroom, read *Park's Quest* by Katherine Patterson and rather than writing a summary book report, wrote a memoir.

Private Cooper, You've been Drafted

When my father was in Vietnam I wasn't around. He sent letters home to my mother and brothers and sisters. I know they were scared.

In 1978 I was born. My father was already home. One morning my father James found his purple heart medal in his junky closet.

I never imagined growing up without a father. He could of died in that war. I never thought of it that way. I'm sure my mother did. The subject never comes up at home. But I think of it every night.

In the Army you have to get shot to get a Purple Heart. Being shot at is good enough.

I wonder what I would do if I was in the army? Lt. Craven, it has a nice ring to it.

Is this learning about reading and writing or is it paying attention to life? Is this learning or living? Does it belong to the space inside school walls or out in the world? Do such questions even make sense? If not, why have we tolerated the distinctions for so long, and why do they persist in our minds and in our practice?

Reading, after all, like writing, is an act of composing meaning, and reading memoir, like writing memoir, involves a student in the act of composing meaning from his own life. Doing memoir brings into sharp focus the truth that reading and writing and living are each most sensible when they are combined. When I am making memoir, what am I doing but writing a reading of my living?

When I write from what I read rather than about it, talking back in my own voice, reading can be a process of discovering the deep structure of what matters to me. Literature can unlock corners of my own experience that before seem to have been inaccessible.

I shared with a group of students "It Was All Over" by Zoe Gilman, a junior high student, anthologized in James Moffett's *Active Voices II*. It begins, "All was quiet at the dinner table. . . . How do you act when you're sitting at a table with a wife and two kids after they have just found out that their father/husband has cancer of the liver? The expressions on their faces were nothing that I had ever seen before. He was going to die, and there wasn't anything that anyone could do but pray that the cancer would go away." The piece goes on to describe the illness, the decline, and the eventual death of this close friend of Zoe's family.

After reading it, Cheryl wrote about an older man named Leo, a friend of her family, whose health had recently taken a turn for the worse. Words poured into her notebook in the few minutes I gave the class to write in response.

> The story made me feel really emotional. I almost cried. It made me remember Leo—the man that made me dream. In a special sense, my very best friend. He's 78 now, as foreign as ever. He has changed my life so dramatically. He made me think. About myself. You always learn to remember your neighbor before you think of yourself. He taught me to think of myself for once. What would be best for me. He's the one that brought the adult out of my childhood. I'm the doctor. I'm his angel and he mine. I'll become a doctor for him and only him. In appreciation of the 100% part of his effect on my life. Because of Leo's war injuries, I'm afraid that his death will be soon. At night, when I can't sleep, I think of what it will be like when the news is broken to me of his death. I'm scared. I really don't know what my emotions will be like. I realize that everyone dies eventually but I never thought that Leo could die. He is a superman in my eyes.

Cheryl underlined "He's the one that brought the adult out of my childhood," which she used as the basis for her memoir about her relationship with Leo, about how he questioned her and with his eyes told her that he really expected some answers.

When I saw this entry in Cheryl's notebook later that week, I said to her in a notebook conference, "Cheryl, I was really struck by this entry you wrote about Leo. He's so important to you, I wonder why you haven't written about him before." She said, "Yeah, once I'd written it, I wondered that, too, but, first of all, Leo belongs to a part of my life that's just like so far from school, I would never have thought about him here in this place. Also, until I read that story and wrote this, I don't think I realized what I thought about him."

Like the ancient Celts, Cheryl heard and recognized the voice of a shard of her own experience, and as a result, that part of her past came to live with her, to occupy a greater measure of her present.

As a writer, when I am trying to write memoir, I deliberately seek to expose myself to pieces of literature that will ignite my own memory around a particular subject. Since the day I became the father of a son, I have been writing about my relationship to my own father, and have read everything I could get my hands on about fathers and sons, the better to make sense of what's happening to me, to delineate my own experience of being a man and to understand what makes it different from others'. I claim my life by discovering how it's uniquely mine.

As a teacher, I seek deliberately to put in my students' hands pieces of literature that will butt up against their own life stories and help them in their composition of who they are. Also, they need to read memoir in order to build a genre schema for the piece they will try to write, to build a sense of memoir-ness, a mental contour image of the container they are trying to fill. This obviously poses a problem, since the literature that's ordinarily available around the average secondary school is not stocked full with short memoir pieces ready for our use. But magazines, newspapers, and even literature anthologies (especially for college composition courses) have, in the past decade or so, printed more and more good examples of memoir. We just have to read more and be wide awake enough to clip and save. I have included at the end of this chapter a list of some good memoirs that might be possible to find, especially with the help of a willing librarian. Moreover, some excellent book-length memoirs contain chapters that work well with some classes. I have known some high school classes to read one entire book-length memoir, such as Annie Dillard's *An American Childhood* or Tobias Wolff's *This Boy's Life*, or one of Maya Angelou's several volumes of autobiography, as a whole class to launch their journey into memoir. Younger readers could accomplish the same thing with Jean Fritz's *Homesick*, Gary Paulsen's *Woodsong*, Milton Meltzer's *Starting from Home: A Writer's Beginnings*, or even some of Vera B. Williams's picture books. It's always an exciting challenge to begin a study of a genre with a class, especially if it's one that's unfamiliar to me, because it pushes me to read in areas I ordinarily would not.

The main reason I teach a unit focused on memoir is because there are elements of craft I want to teach kids, to make them better at reading and writing memoir and to make them better at attending to their own lives. Having them read, tell their life stories, and write in notebooks are fine to begin, but it is important that, at some point, they come out of the notebooks and begin to craft pieces of art from their lives. Therefore, I have to be prepared to teach minilessons, engage students in writing conferences, and build response groups around the characteristics of fine and literate memoir.

Writers of memoir, first of all, place enormous emphasis on minutely particular sensory detail. The Portuguese poet Fernando Pessoa wrote, in his journal, "I find deep meaning in a matchbox lying in the gutter, in two dirty papers which, on a windy day, will roll and chase each other down the street. For writing is astonishment, admiration, as of a being fallen from the skies taking full consciousness of his fall, astonished about things." In most good memoir, it is not so much the hugeness of what happens to the subject that sticks with a reader, but the ordinary minutiae of the everyday.

Some kids panic when they begin to see this, because, well, they just can't remember every word someone said when they were three or the particular pattern on the upholstery of their aunt's sofa. What they need to be taught is that much of the work of remembering is imaginary. We as readers don't test memoir for precision, and it isn't necessary for authors to scrape the edges of their brain trying painstakingly to extract every drop of accurate detail. Rather they select and even invent details that tell the larger truth about their lives. That's why William Zinsser titled his book about memoir *Inventing the Truth*.

Frank Kermode has pointed out, as have Anthony Petrosky and David Bartholomae, that in order to interpret a text, the reader must forget most of it, since to remember every detail would result in a paralyzing overload and, very likely, madness. The same is paradoxically true of inventing memoir: we are most successful when we forget a lot. When students are looking for notebook entries that might be important in a memoir, I frequently ask them, *If you were to pick just one entry that really showed who you were, showed what your life is like, which one would it be?*

I asked Ellie that, and she turned to a page in her notebook that looked sort of like a play, with character names, colons, lines of dialogue. I said, "Tell me about this, Ellie."

She said, "It's about this fight my parents had. This is when my dad talks, and this is when my mom talks."

Stalling, buying time, I said, "So . . . this is one particular fight you remember them having?" Notice the brilliance. "Was it a really important fight?" I'm trying to get her to connect this single event to a larger life issue, by asking about the significance, which is sometimes a synonym for meaning.

"No."

Wonderful, I thought. "Ellie, I'm a little confused. You said this was an entry that really shows me what your life has been like. How is that?" I've had a hunch all along, of course, having many times gone through, as a writer, the same thought process Ellie is working through. But it's important for me not to step in too soon to connect the dots for her. The whole point of the teaching is her thinking. If she goes nowhere with it now, I may help by explaining a little more, maybe giving examples from my own writing or that of other kids in the room, maybe even going so far as to say, *If I were you, I'd be thinking, wondering whether I'm saying this is an important entry because it connects to some big deal in my life, like maybe I think they're really mad at me or it just makes my life feel so noisy and nervous or it's just like my fighting with my brother. Something like that?* I say as many possibilities as I can think of in that moment, never just one, even if some of my suggestions are downright stupid, just so the problem stays open to her thinking. This time, though, I just wait, because I can see Ellie is thinking.

"Well," she said, "they fight all the time, and I'm really scared they're going to get a divorce and that would mess up my whole life because I'd have to live with only one of them and I might have to go to a different school . . ."

"Is this something you think about often?" I asked, again trying to connect the particular to the general, the one day to every day.

"Yes," she nods and pauses. I wait. "Every night before I go to sleep."

"Oh," I say, "Now I can see how this is so important to you. It's not just a fight one day, but it's this worry, this big deal that you think about every night before you go to sleep. It's maybe even an obsession right now for you. You know, that's what good memoirs come from, Ellie, those big deals—so you're really onto something now. Do you think there's some way, if you wrote that as a project, you could help the reader understand that bigger fear?" I thought she'd say she'd tack it on to the end.

But she said, "When I go to sleep, right here." She pointed to the page. "I could dream they got a divorce. It didn't happen like that but I could write it like that."

"Great!" I said, really meaning it. "Go for it." My guess is that Ellie's narrative strategy came from movies or television, maybe even soap opera, and not from the genre of memoir per se, but it was a much more sophisticated solution than I had expected. The schemas of how feelings, inner states, or past events might be revealed through action may be informed by any experience with story. Often, as in this case, a dramatist's solutions can help a memoirist. Ellie turned to a new notebook page and wrote just the dream, postponing figuring out how it would fit into the rest of the story until she wrote her first draft. There will be, after all, other elements of her memoir she'll want to explore in her notebook before deciding how to present it to readers.

We are trying to help kids see the general in the particular, the big in the little, and in so doing, to valorize the fine fibre of their experience. It is an uphill climb, this attending to the tiny, in the culture of the action-packed splash. As Tom Newkirk writes, "Teachers of all grades hear students say that they cannot write about their lives because nothing ever happens—nothing, that is, remotely as exciting as what happens to characters on television. This is precisely the cultural message that writing-process teachers seek to countermand" (p. 194).

And then there's time, under whose thumb we school people always feel pressed. Clocks, curricula, and calendars rule our lives. Well, memoir is our chance to strike back. In memoir, an author controls time in his own life story. If I am crafting an autobiographical piece, I must be able to skip parts that don't pertain to my meaning or help to underscore the significance of the topic. Selection of this kind necessarily involves jumping around, yoking together events that in real life were temporally far apart, took place at different ages, different stages. By knocking those against one another, the writer makes clear for the reader and for himself that the subject of the piece isn't a passing fancy—or a topic grabbed out of the air so he'd have something to write about that day—but one of the obsessions that make up his life. A writer may begin at the present and skip to the past, allowing the reader to see how the present is old and heavy with history, how the writer is this person today as a result of what happened to him then.

Giving deep and careful attention to particular moments of my life often picks me up and catapults me to another place on my life's time line. Arthur Miller calls these experiences "timebends." In his memoir of that title, he writes, "Memory keeps folding in upon itself like geologic layers of rock, the deeper strata sometimes appearing on top before they slope downward into the depths again" (p. 586). Memoir, like fiction, is essentially a narrative genre; that is, its essential structure is chronological. As with fiction, then, learning to play with time is part of learning to write memoir, and when we play with the time of our own life, it can be an even more powerful experience.

Writing about my brief (but not brief enough) experience as a high school football player, I began thinking abut how dangerous was any drill that involved standing in a circle. Most often, one boy stood in the center to be charged and knocked from his feet by the other players around the circumference. The guy in the center never knew which of his teammates would hit him next: it always hurt, and, even the big guys were terrified of circle drills. I began to press harder on that point in my life, and was transported to other circles I've known, and I saw circles of prayer and circles around camp fires, a circle of friends holding hands at an orphan's Thanksgiving, the circle in which I ask children to sit when we tell stories. And it began to dawn on me that those painful circle drills under the searing Texas sun fought directly against what a circle of young men ought to be, and they started to represent for me all that's diseased about the community of men in America and how early and systematically violence and competition usurp connectedness. Here it comes again. It's one of my life's themes.

Another manipulation of time at the service of memoir authors is the relationship of one day to every day. A writer may juxtapose what happens every day against what happens one day (Every day we . . . But one day . . .). A rhythm may be set up back and forth between habitual time (Each day, we would . . .) and particular time (One day . . .). Or an author may represent a life's condition with a single day. One day stands for every day. Even as she grew beyond what could be a small-minded small town, Marcy had been writing frequently in her notebook about her need to feel connected to her community. In "The Flag Was at Half Mast" she used a single day to signify her need for belonging:

It was a cold rainy day. The kind of morning you want to stay in bed and sleep all day. I forced myself out of bed, and dragged my feet down the hall into the shower. By seven o'clock, I was all ready for school. My hair had looked quite nice, but with all the wind and rain it would get messed up anyway. I waited five minutes in the cold wet rain for the bus. By that time it looked like I had taken my shower with my clothes on, and my hair had gone flat. When I got into school I could sense that something was wrong. Everyone was walking around in a daze, one girl even had tears in her eyes. "What's happened?" I thought to myself, "everyone is acting so strange." Well in homeroom I found out.

"Will homerooms please stand for the pledge of allegiance." I stood up and put my hand on my heart, which was almost a habit. I had been saying the pledge of allegiance for eight straight years, and I was getting pretty sick of it. Couldn't they make up a new? . . . with liberty and justance for all. I sat down and waited for the announcements, but instead Mr. Elmendorf our principle came on.

"Saturday as many of you may know one of our teachers and dear friends Phil DeFavio died of a heart attack. Mr. DeFavio was more than a teacher. He was Key Club advisor and a sports instructor, but most of all he was a friend. Let us take a silent moment in memory of Mr. DeFavio."

Who's Mr. DeFavio, I thought during the silence. Being only a seventh grader I had never been in his class. Our homerooms were dismissed and we went into the halls.

I wished that I could have stayed in homeroom the halls were hecktic. People were crying and wiping their eyes, and nose. I felt guilty that I couldn't share their grief with them, but I couldn't bring myself to cry for the death of this man.

The whole day was a "blah." Teachers and students seemed different. Mr. Elder gave us a lecture on being "fine" and how you didn't always have to be fine. Mr. Wooley didn't want to do anything. And Mr. Milano was nice! We found out that school was going to be canceled Tuesday but it didn't seem to cheer anyone up. Before lunch, I was getting some books at my locker and this girl walked by. It didn't take me long to notice that she was crying. Not the "my boyfriend just broke up with me" kind of crying, tears were running down her cheeks, and her eyes were red and puffy.

"Hi," I said. She looked at me and stopped crying for a minute.

"Hello," she answered back.

"How are you doing?" I asked her, even though it was obvious she wasn't very happy.

"Fine," she said and walked away.

I thought about Mr. Elder's lecture on fine. I could tell she wasn't fine. Nobody cries if they're fine, but then again nobody tells a perfect stranger how they are really feeling.

At the end of the miserable day I was walking down the main stairs, and I looked out the front door of the school. I saw the flag with the rain beating on it and the wind swirling it. It was flying at half mast to show people that Nunda and Keshequa cared for this man. I stepped outside. I was standing under a ledge, even though I was dry the dismal day came over me. I looked at the flag again. I thought about the girls crying and the flags flying, and I cried for Mr. DeFavio.

Marcy developed meaning from a day in her life, but the craft of memoir also may involve the construction of a reading, an interpretation, of the writer's life's larger plot line. In so doing, writers have to value some things over others, since meaning cannot be made if everything has equal weight. They choose what is important, and so choose themselves—who they are, who they will be. They begin to ask what the anecdotes of their lives will add up to as they begin to look for patterns or themes that make the discrete vignettes cohere.

Katie worked through a similar process, when, as she reread her notebook, she noticed that her whole history of having friends is a history of being left behind: one friend moved away, one died, one found another best friend. Her memoir "Don't Leave Me Alone" explored her feelings both about her past and about her friendships to come. Similarly, Denise noticed that all of her strongest memories about her family revolve around her grandmother's kitchen, where they always congregated. Shelley, after weeks of rereading and writing more, decided to fictionalize her memoir about a little girl who is sexually abused by both parents, grows into adolescence allowing herself repeatedly to be a victim of abuse from boyfriends, and finally begins to choose herself as someone who will not be victimized anymore. Jim remembers how when he was a little boy, getting dirty was the worst thing he could do, in his mother's eyes, and so he loved to do it. Now, as he approaches adulthood, there are still ways he "gets dirty," doing exactly the things everyone tells him not to do, for the heady rush of rebellion.

For Jim, as for Marcy or Jean Fritz or Annie Dillard or Maya Angelou or John Updike, or me, the writing of memoir stems from this thought: *Okay, I've lived all these years, all these days, all these moments. So what?* The question itself is so terrifying that at first it stops us in our tracks. But we have a right—and a responsibility, if we are to make something of our lives—to answer it. To what better use could literacy be put? If it's not ultimately to answer the So what? of our lives and thus to make us better at the living, what is literacy for?

Not only should our living and our reading feed our writing, not only should our living and our writing nourish our reading, but also our reading and writing ought to make living possible and sensible. Crafting meaning in memoir is the act of turning our lives into projects; and thinking of our lives as projects is what makes our tenure on the planet purposeful—and thus keeps us alive. And so, gazing full face at the question So what? after a moment's faltering and a longer moment's reflection, we get busy, inventing the truth for all we're worth. Right now. We have to make something of our lives.

Resources for memoir: a beginning

ANGELOU, MAYA. *I Know Why the Caged Bird Sings.* New York: Bantam, 1969.

AUSTER, PAUL. *The Invention of Solitude.* New York: Penguin, 1982.

BAKER, RUSSELL. *Growing Up.* New York: New American Library, 1982.

DILLARD, ANNIE. *An American Childhood.* New York: Harper and Row, 1987.

DUNNE, JOHN GREGORY. *Harp.* New York: Simon and Schuster, 1989.

FRITZ, JEAN. *Homesick: My Own Story.* New York: Dell, 1982.

GORNICK, VIVIAN. *Fierce Attachments.* New York: Farrar, Straus and Giroux, 1987.

MACNEIL, ROBERT. *Wordstruck.* New York: Viking, 1989.

MELTZER, MILTON. *Starting from Home: A Writer's Beginnings.* New York: Puffin, 1988.

MONETTE, PAUL. *Becoming a Man: Half a Life Story.* New York: Harcourt, Brace, Jovanovich, 1992.

NOLAN, CHRISTOPHER. *Under the Eye of the Clock.* New York: St. Martin's Press, 1987.

PAULSEN, GARY. *Woodsong.* New York: Puffin, 1990.

PRICE, REYNOLDS. *Clear Pictures: First Loves, First Guides.* New York: Ballantine, 1988.

SELZER, RICHARD. *Down from Troy: A Doctor Comes of Age.* New York: William Morrow, 1992.

SOTO, GARY. *Small Faces.* Houston: Arte Publico Press, 1986.

UPDIKE, JOHN. *Self-Consciousness.* New York: Knopf, 1989.

WOLFF, TOBIAS. *This Boy's Life.* New York: Harper and Row, 1989.

TIME AND MEMORY

We make ourselves out of our personal histories. Right? And we make our personal histories out of memories. Now get this. Turns out we make our memories out of our sense of self! We've tended to think of memory as life that just gets burned into our mind, but that's not how it is at all. Memories, autobiographical memories, that is, are always constructions. Most of us can admit that we don't remember *everything.* But why do we remember some things and not others? The obvious answer is that some things are more important than others. And that's exactly it!

We select, arrange, and even make up our memories based on our sense of who we are, and we're conveniently amnesiac about those things that don't fit into our sense of self. The anecdotes and epics we hold in our memory, the life stories that become objects of meditation for us, are little allegories that hold our sense of self. After all, it is only in our stories about ourselves that we think of ourselves as characters, as somehow observable objects. Where else in our thinking do we get to look at ourselves like that?

As soon as we tell or write a memory, moreover, the memory is more or less folded into the telling. Though we gain the story and can tell it again in the future, we lose some of our feeling of remembering the original experience. The memory is replaced by the story, and we have made ourselves over again.

10 *Making Sense of Nonfiction*

ometimes students write texts that, let us say, don't please us. When this happens, it is partly because the genre schemas that form our expectation as we read their texts are different from the schemas they have used in writing them. We are expecting short stories, and they are writing sitcoms. When we expect poetry, they write greeting cards. We are expecting memoir, and they are writing "personal narratives," whatever that means. Besides this schematic disharmony, another root cause of our disappointment is that our students are performing for a school environment that in no way matches what people who write this kind of thing do in the world. Only students whose lives and minds for some reason allow them to transcend the constraints of their environment could hope to write well in the contexts we, as a profession, have constructed for them.

Once we understand these problems, it becomes possible to begin solving them. We can first provide an environment that reflects and makes explicit some of the elements of writers' processes in making the genres we hope to see our students write, and we can second, within that environment, steep students in reading the kind of text we mean for them to write. By rethinking the opportunities we are creating, we may not turn every student into Annie Dillard, but we can help him at least get onto the right path and then support his approximations of what Dillard and other writers do.

We have already seen, in memoir and fiction, how inquiry into a genre and the processes and thinking within the work in that genre are necessary to help students develop a clearer sense of craft, a sense of "the kind of thing I'm making." The need for this kind of work is even more essential in teaching nonfiction writing, where our thinking is more muddled than in perhaps any other field of writing. The perceived demands of schools built on a transmission model of learning have caused us to create and proliferate nongenres deeply entrenched in our assumptions about school writing, genres with no correspondence to the world outside school, genres no one ever chose to write. The research paper, the report, the five-paragraph theme, the essay test, the process essay, and other such genres make up almost all the writing that occurs in schools and very often delimit what we can even *imagine* occurring in school.

Nonfiction in American English classes typically appears as "research papers" and "critical essays." More often than not, teachers assign these papers and essays as ways of assessing students' thinking about literature. I have already argued why I believe such genres to be less useful as responses to literature than is commonly supposed (see Chapter 6). However, the problem with students' nonfiction writing is not simply that it is about the wrong topic. More and more secondary schools are trying to restructure their day to provide longer class periods, and English teachers, in support of "content" curricula in social studies and science, are struggling with student writing about westward expansion, economics, and invertebrate biology, which is just as problematic as the papers about literature they used to see more often. Regardless of the topic, the writing often resembles Jaycee's:

Sponges

Sponges are very soft. A skeletal framework supports the soft mass of the sponge are normaly two meters high.

Sponges live in oceans, sea, rivers, caves at the Bottom of the sea, or oceans, and sometimes in streams. they normally get washed to the beach. Some sponges lives in caves.

Sponges are used by people in many different ways. they use them for washing dishes or probably anything.

they are all different colors. there are yellowish brown, red, brownish yellow, and green. green ones are found in caves.

there are different kinds of shapes. Some are vase shape. Some are fan or dome. they are straight or curved.

there are all kinds of groups. Here they are:

Finger Sponges

10 to 12 inches in diameter.

long slender fingers from 1 to 4 inches in lenght.

white, yellow, grey, orange, and occasionally red.

Why I like different kinds of groups are I like the names and see how they are alike. See if they have things in common.

Reproduction

Reproduction is sexual means. the male is divided into sperm cells that goes into the water. then the ferteilized egg becomes a flagellated larva. Reproduction may also be by budding.

this is my last paragraph to sum it up here it is:

Sponges as one finds them an the beach, are brown, yellowish, reddish, or greyish, rather formless masses of soft, or dry, and harsh tissue. Sometimes they are branched sometimes in rounded or irregular clumps. In the water, and when alive. they are soft, and of various colors: bright red, brown, yellow. Often they are gelatinous to the touch.

writen by:

Jaycee R.

It is tempting, when we see writing like this, to shake our heads and say, *She can't write; hasn't got the skills. She's basically just not very smart.* But Jaycee's writing in other genres was charming, full of personality, insightful, and if not error free, then at least not as tormented as what we see here. Jaycee's problem, as is almost always the case, was not about skills but about context. Her problem, to be direct, was her teacher—I hesitate to admit—*me.* Well, not so much *me,* as my failure to teach nonfiction as a genre as I had done poetry and other literary genres. I asked myself, *What have I read, which I was hoping Jaycee would approximate?* The answer was easy. I read magazines all the time, and the nonfiction feature articles in them formed my expectations for good nonfiction about a topic like sponges. Jaycee read magazines too, I knew from interviews with her about her reading, but I had not invited her to allow those articles to mentor her research process or her writing. Instead, I had sent her to the library, where Jaycee had read encyclopedias and other reference materials about sponges. She had taken out several books about sponges, the writing in which was not much different from that in the encyclopedia. Because that's what she'd read when she was getting information, she quite intelligently and predictably acquired the "ways with words" she found there. In fact, because she knew she could not sound as authoritative as the encyclopedia, she borrowed sections of it and attempted the school strategy of "putting it in her own words." Here are some excerpts from one encyclopedia article she used:

> Sponges, as one finds them on the beach, are brown, yellowish, reddish, or grayish, rather formless masses of soft, or dry and harsh tissue. Sometimes they are branched, sometimes in rounded or irregular clumps. In the water, and when alive, they are soft, and of various colors: bright red, brown, yellow, but never green. Often they are gelatinous to the touch. . . . Sponges may reproduce by sexual means. . . .

Sound familiar? I don't believe, however, that busting Jaycee for plagiarism is the most reasonable or helpful response I can give to her work. Because she didn't know that she could bring to her writing the genre schemas she already knew from reading magazines and the newspaper, because I did not contribute to her genre schemas by sharing texts I admired with her and her class, and because I didn't succeed in creating an environment that assisted her in a process akin to that of writers who make what I wanted her to make, she resorted to survival tactics: *This is not fiction, it's in the library, so it must work. We were supposed to take down some of what they said in there, and then make a paper about it. So I'll string some of it together and here it is.* As a matter of fact, Jaycee's research process had not been a failure. Beginning by noticing something close to her in her life, household sponges, she had collected different kinds of sponges she could find in stores and homes. She had arranged them on a shelf in the classroom, and next to them she placed photocopied sections of texts about sponges. She had drawn the different patterns of pores in the sponges and labeled them. She had interviewed her science teacher about sponges, and then taken his advice to interview another teacher whose specialty in school had been marine biology. As she researched, new questions arose, and she pursued the answers to these in the encyclopedia. In all that work was the material for a fine article about sponges, very much like the nonfiction writing I had hoped for.

But when it came time to *write,* Jaycee's mind's being full of sponges did not help. What she needed was a sense of the kind of text she was trying to write, and that she most obviously did not have. That lack was not the result of laziness or an absence of skill but came about because our community had not developed a clear understanding of the kind of writing we were exploring. Though some of the kids writing nonfiction in my classes that year managed to pull off decent pieces of nonfiction, I'd left that up to chance, to someone's accidental realization that he might have seen something like this before. Leaving to chance the principle most central to what I'm trying to accomplish with my class is not teaching, it's what Janet Emig (1983) calls "magical thinking," a tacit assumption that students will somehow pick up values and abilities to which I have failed to attend. That's why Jaycee's piece about sponges was my failure, not hers.

In saying that I failed in teaching nonfiction to that class, I don't wither under bitter guilt. I try to view teaching as a craft, and so I have to keep my ego somewhat detached from my practice. Just as I hope my students will come to view their writing and reading as crafts, assessing where they have succeeded and where they haven't, I reflect on my own teaching almost as an object outside me. I have to look at my practice as a kin of text (writing a book helps, but I don't recommend it) and not as *me practicing,* in order not to be defensive against my own growth. If my teaching is a craft, it's something I have to be getting better at, for craft never stands still in time, and I therefore have to see myself as unfinished. And with Jaycee's class, I have no difficulty seeing my practice as unfinished.

Since then, I have approached nonfiction with students more carefully and deliberately, and I've participated in a study group on nonfiction with a group of colleagues at the Teachers College Writing Project.[1] Through that work, I've outgrown my older practice, in ways that can better support the work Jaycee needed to do. Not surprising, it all has to do with getting clearer about nonfiction as a genre. It has seemed to me most helpful to proceed not from the assumptions already in place in school, but rather from the questions, *What is nonfiction like in the world of literacy outside school? When can we say it's well written? Under what conditions do people write it?*

These questions are difficult if not impossible to address if we are mixed up in various other school purposes that do not address the craft of writing nonfiction. From what I've seen, literacy educators often fall into the same trap I did with Jaycee's class, attending almost exclusively to the processes of research and inquiry, minimally or not at all to the process of writing well, apart from a few

---

1   Some of those friends, from whom I've learned much, include Kathy Bearden, Isoke Nia, Shirley McPhillips, Edie Ziegler, Lydia Bellino, Laurie Pessah, and Katie Wood, among others. As is often the case with the Writing Project community, it's hard to say where my thinking stops and theirs begins, so I owe them a lot of credit for the ideas in this chapter.

exhortations about transitions, organization, or voice. Then we ask why after all that work the writing is so boring, so deadly, so ruinous to our reading lives as teachers with more than a hundred of these monstrosities to read. The main reason we get into such a frustrating mess is that we buy, once again, into a pedagogy of preparation. We think, *Kids have to write research papers in school, so I'd better teach them how to do it so they'll be ready. They need to learn how to use the library and other resources, take notes, organize information, and write from those notes and outlines.* Never mind that I have no instructional purpose of my own in having them write the very texts they will make, not to mention that they have no purpose in writing them. As I have said throughout this book, I would prefer to block at the door anything that does not contribute directly to my main objective in literacy teaching—supporting students in making meaning of the lives they live and crafting those meanings for authentic purposes. If I had them all day every day for ten years, I might have more diverse purposes; but my time is short, so I need to stay focused. Therefore, I cannot, on behalf of the whole educational community, take the entire enterprise of research on my shoulders and, by the way, expect the kids to write well.

As Peter Elbow (1991) has pointed out, a myth is afoot, and has been for most of this century, that there is a single kind of writing for all academic disciplines, which might be called "academic writing." Presumably, this is the language of the research paper. But browse through the periodicals section of a university library. Are the papers in the physics journals really similar to those in psychology journals? Is there any way in which those texts belong to the same genre as the articles in *New Literary History?* If you knew how to write for one of those publications, would you also know how to write for *The New Advocate?* Each discipline, and in many cases each subdivision of a discipline, represents a community with its own ways with words, its own generic conventions. In most of these disciplines, the twentieth century has been so fraught with radically shifting paradigms that in many cases, the texts scholars make to convey their ideas have had to change repeatedly. What's more, the papers in any academic journal reveal little resemblance to what students do in high school research papers. When we think that by requiring a research paper in English class we are preparing our students for all the academic writing they will need, we are deluding ourselves. What we are preparing them for is more research papers in English class. But it is the mission of this book (and the community of texts to which it belongs) to suggest that English class might be different. What if we let go of the idea of preparation in nonfiction writing? How might we engage students authentically, that is, with real interests, purposes, and readers, in crafting the kinds of texts that clearly make up the majority of the literate world?

What *do* we mean by nonfiction? First of all, it's not one genre: there's no such thing as "the nonfiction genre." Just because a text seems to refer to actual events in the world does not say anything about the form it takes. There can be "true" poems, stories, and cartoons. Obviously, a memoir is nonfiction, as is an article on how to paint a house, as is an encyclopedia entry on sponges. If we are going to do a genre study on nonfiction, since the whole point is to focus our attention on the ways one kind of text is crafted, we need to select from the world of diverse possibilities what's in and what's out of the realm of our inquiry. I think we can assume that we do not include poems, novels, and stories—*not* because they do not contain information and cannot instruct the reader, but because their *form* is not what we mean to be on about here. Still, even if we remove poems, novels, and stories from our circumscribed field, we are left with texts as diverse as the world itself. Figure 10–1 is my attempt to separate and organize various genres within the world of "nonfiction." I have defined them in terms of the overall purpose I can perceive in nonfiction texts as I've encountered them in my reading life. The categories avoid the names of the traditional modes of discourse (persuasive, expository, narrative, and so on) because of the formal school-based assumptions (e.g., a persuasive essay has a certain kind of opening paragraph) readers may bring to them.

What's outside our attention—the bottom row in the chart

As the previous two chapters make clear, narratives have their own craft, and it's not the same as expository writing. Remember that in this genre study, our purpose is to be able to focus on the craft of certain kinds of nonfiction writing. Biography, autobiography, and historical narrative are, of course, nonfiction. But in

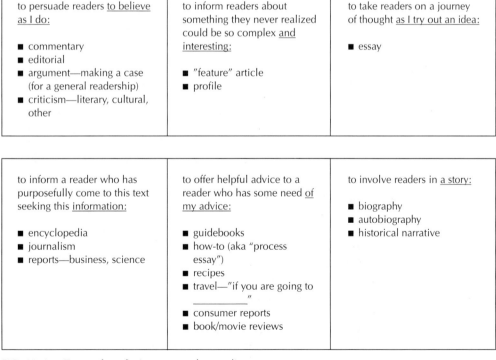

FIG. 10–1: *Types of nonfiction arranged according to purpose.*

form, they resemble short stories more than feature articles or essays. This is primarily because narratives are, by definition, organized in time, first one thing happens and then something else, and by the way this other thing happened before either of them. Expository nonfiction, on the other hand, through its language, makes a claim for being outside time. Expository nonfiction ultimately says, *This is true, not just on the day I saw it, but every day.* In writing exposition, we are trying to make statements about what is stable in the world, not what happened once. So it's not an insult to the importance of narrative to say it's outside our realm of study here, it's just that it has a different form and thus in crafting it, a writer's attention is on different things. And the whole idea of a genre study is that in order to teach craft, we focus on how one particular kind of text is made.

Nor do I have any desire to have my students write pieces that sound like encyclopedia articles. Those, along with journalism and various kinds of reports, are written in order to inform a reader who has come seeking this information. No one was going to consult Jaycee's piece for information about sponges, and if they did, it would be a dysfunctional research strategy indeed. Therefore, Jaycee couldn't have an authentic, sensible relationship to her audience while writing in that genre. She needed to draw them in, to make them interested, to explain sponges in terms of the things they already knew in their ordinary lives. An encyclopedia writer doesn't have to do that, since the reader is only reading the entry after having chosen to look up sponges. With the reader's interest a given, the writer needs only to provide information as efficiently as possible. Jaycee's writing in such a way might be appropriate if I had asked the kids to report how their research was going. I would then have a reason for wanting to know, and she wouldn't need to draw me in with a good lead, a personable voice, and the like. The readers of her sponges piece published in the class magazine, however, had not asked to be informed about sponges and so Jaycee needed to engage them, to interest them. It's those purposes that give rise to what we think of as "good writing" in nonfiction.

Similarly, readers in need of advice go to specially chosen texts seeking that advice. I would suggest that, although students may go to each other for advice, the contexts for that advice are outside the purview of a nonfiction genre study. Yes, students should be writing advice to each other about which book to read and posting it on a bulletin board, either concrete or electronic. They might, similarly, share suggestions about places and ways to publish their writing. In some contexts, they might write consumer reports for products many of them are interested in buying. In the appropriate context, people will read them, just as we all do in the magazines we read, in the postings on the grocery store bulletin board, and in electronic on-line services. But advice for a general readership just doesn't work in a nonfiction genre study, for the same reasons encyclopedia articles don't. The people who read that advice are inherently interested in it. They want to know what the writer has to say, so that they know what to spend their money on. Advice, therefore, doesn't necessarily have to be as "well written" as an article trying to interest everyone. There are contexts in which writing to advise is a good thing for students to do, but texts that belong to this category don't have to be all that "well crafted," and so they aren't appropriate for our study of nonfiction.

What's in—the upper row in the chart

There are some pieces of writing that are explicitly concerned with changing the reader's beliefs, with *persuading readers to believe as the author does.* Such pieces grab the reader by the lapel and say, *Listen to this; look at the evidence; you can't deny I'm right!* It's true that all writing is rhetorical, trying to convince the reader of something, but in texts that are explicitly argumentative, the voice is more urgently assertive and the structure of the piece is tightly controlled by the shape of the argument. Writers make decisions about what to say next based on the reader's possible objections, and they corral the reader's attention like a border collie chases sheep. Examples of this kind of writing include editorials, articles that try to get readers to purchase, vote, or behave in a particular way, most commentaries, all criticism, and, to be honest, this book.

The kind of nonfiction I'm calling feature articles, whose purpose is to *inform readers about something they never realized could be so complex and interesting,* is probably the one that springs most immediately to mind when we say nonfiction. We encounter them in magazines and some sections of the newspaper, as well as in books by authors such as John McPhee, Patricia Lauber, Gay Talese, Joan Didion, Sue Hubbell, Thomas Wolffe, Richard Rhodes, David Owen, and Tracy Kidder. Some people call this kind of writing literary journalism, because like journalists, the writers do a lot of footwork, finding the story and the characters behind the topic, going to the scene, interviewing and poking around, and pursuing some library research. In the texts, the writer seems fairly gregarious and social, thoroughly engaged with a world that is somewhat alien to both writer and reader. This world springs up behind ordinary things most of us live around every day, such as houses (as in Tracy Kidder's *House* and David Owen's pieces in *The Walls Around Us*), food (as in John McPhee's *Oranges* and in articles in magazine food sections on topics from popcorn to chocolate, coffee to beer), photocopying, toys, rocks, bugs, doors, taxis, cats, computers, and well, pretty much anything. As we read, we realize that behind such ordinary stuff there are whole worlds, interesting people with dreams and disappointments, controversies and factions, buildings and expanses of land, research and philosophy, history and ethics, changing technologies, political and economic interests. After reading one of these articles, I feel less able to take things for granted. *Everything* seems more complicated, rich, interesting, difficult, and so, so precious. The world becomes both more strange and more familiar. In order to create this response in me, authors of feature articles have to see the world as an almost infinitely rich and generous place. When writers are living like nonfiction writers, they may examine the corners of their worlds for what has been invisible, trust that what they find there will prove interesting, and then go after it, get behind it, discover the world that lived there all along.

In spite of school's misappropriation of the term, essays, historically, are texts that *take a reader on a journey of thought* and are not arguments that seek through evidence to prove their point. Montaigne, Shakespeare's French contemporary, made up the term *essay,* which is a French verb roughly translating into English as "to try," as in to consider or test out in order to discover. Contemporary writers of essays include people like Annie Dillard, Stanley Elkin, Wendell Berry, Dianne Ackerman, and Edward Hoagland. In essays, the conclusion isn't fixed in advance, so the phrase, *In this essay, I will show that . . .* is a contradiction in terms. I am not out to quibble about terms here, but rather to differentiate a meditative form from an argumentative one. An essay writer may use information as food for thought, but it's the reflection that is the focus, the careful consideration, an almost navel-gazing self-absorption. In this way, essays are not all that different from poems in the quality of their thought. Most notebook entries are like little fragments of essays, meandering, unaggressive, turning a thought this way and that. Think of the difference between an essay on abortion and an argument on abortion, between a feature article on fire safety, an argument on fire safety, and an essay on fire safety. Such discrimination should make clear how fuzzy and unrigorous our school work on nonfiction writing has been. The topics of real essays often have a different ring to them, such as Montaigne's "On Smells" or "On the Love of Fathers for Their Children," Hoagland's "City Walking" or "The Lapping, Itchy Edge of Love," Dillard's "Seeing" or "Teaching a Stone to Talk." As in poetry, the writing in many of these pieces is often crafted to a sonorous beauty that may make the meaning opaque. It doesn't matter. Such essays aren't really out to inform anybody or to persuade anyone of anything; sometimes you almost get the feeling the writers don't even much care if anyone reads them or not. We read them because we are interested in and pleased by the way these people think, regardless of what they are thinking about.

In any given piece of writing, the purposes and textual features I've described will overlap. Any good editorial will contain sections where objective information seems to be provided and often will also include narrative sections. The overall gesture of the piece, however, is one of persuasion. Feature articles cannot avoid being slanted toward some rhetorical stance toward their subject, even if it's "this thing is great and its value should not be questioned." But the overall stance in the writing, it's tone and organization, is one of making the subject interesting to the reader and touring the reader through the worlds behind what seemed like a simple subject. Meditations will also make their subject interesting, but the hard facts are only stimuli for the essayist's personal and artistic thinking, rather than a gregarious explanation of the subject to the reader. Flip through a group of magazines, trying to categorize each piece, and there will be some that are particularly difficult to classify. They seem to fall somewhere between essay and feature article or argument and essay; putting them in one pile or the other is a judgment call. That's okay. I am not trying to create absolute categories, only to clarify our thinking about nonfiction genres so that we can better teach the craft of each. If we insist on saying that everything is the same as everything else, how can we know when to teach our students techniques of interviewing or strategies for arguing in anticipation of a reader's objections?

That brings me to the question, *Should I do a study of all these genres together or of just one?* As always, it depends on my purpose in relation to what's happening with the students. Obviously, I can focus more on specific elements of craft if I and the students choose only one. On the other hand, I may want the kids to discover these differences, to collect and sort by genre examples of nonfiction they find in magazines and newspapers, to collaborate with them on the decision of what's in and what's out of our scope of attention. Then, after an initial investigation of non-fiction, I may want to do a follow-up study of argument or essay, and I can begin our more narrow study by using the examples we've already found during our general study. However I organize texts, the most important principles I follow are those that guide inquiry into the process behind the craft of nonfiction.

Principles for planning genre studies in nonfiction

1. Teacher knowledge

As the teacher, I need to *inform my own vision of the genre.* Anytime I find a piece of nonfiction I really like, whether it's in a magazine, the Sunday paper, or an anthology like *Best Essays of [Whatever Year],* I copy it and put it in a file labeled "arguments," "feature articles," or "essays." Also, I always keep in mind that I need these examples, so when I find books that might suit my purposes, I buy them and keep them in a special place on my shelves at home. Naturally, I'm especially on the lookout for topics of interest to kids, and pieces written in easy-enough language for younger students to read. When I read one of these books, I jot on a piece of paper a few notes about particular chapters, telling myself how they might be useful in teaching. I write things like "chapter 6—bees—interlacing personal life with information—easy to read for eighth graders" or "too hard for most students, but a good example of essay." Then, I put that piece of paper in the appropriate file. By doing all this, I'm creating my preferences and standards for "good" nonfiction.

When the time comes to select the few pieces I'll actually read with classes, I then can comb through these texts to choose which are appropriate for different groups I work with. Some pieces are fine for students to read on their own outside class. These may have been written for adults or for kids, sometimes even coming from the text of picture books. Other pieces that are slightly more difficult I can read with them or have them read in small groups. Some pieces are outside the acceptable range of difficulty for the kids to read but do a great job of showing something about craft I want students to know. From these texts, I plan to read aloud some sections to the whole group. In other words, choosing examples for the class is not an all-or-nothing decision but can be refined by considering exactly how the kids will work with the text. I keep in mind Margaret Mooney's distinction that texts can be read for students, with students, or by students. Each mode, reading aloud, supported reading, and independent reading, is important in different ways.

At the beginning of a nonfiction genre study, I keep my notebook going in just the ways I'm urging students to keep theirs. I use it to choose a topic, to take notes, and to reflect on my information. I find an expert to interview. I do as many of these things as possible in front of the students. I take notes on overheads, bring in the books I've found and tell how I found them, videotape my interview, make copies of the notebook entries in which I reflect on data. It's just not possible to provide adequate demonstrations of the work I want them to do without doing this stuff myself. Usually, I do not end up writing the piece. This is too bad, but it's true. Obviously, I could better demonstrate some important things in the writing process if I did write the whole thing and bring it to completion, but usually, I don't find the time. I hope and assume that the later crafting can be informed almost as well by their reading. What's most important to me is for kids to see someone doing the early stages of the work, which they cannot get from finished texts.

2. Materials

In a nonfiction study, as in any genre study, the only materials we need are *a few texts, our writers notebooks, paper, and some vehicle of publication.* The texts that matter in a nonfiction genre study are not so much the sources of information upon which the students draw, but the examples of the genre. Some teachers with whom I have spoken worry that they don't have enough texts at hand to do nonfiction and say they will have to wait until they have a file bursting with just the perfect examples. Though the desire to feel prepared is understandable, even laudable, the teacher shouldn't be the only person searching for and bringing in examples. As I discuss in Chapter 7, students can also bring in texts and do the rigorous work of classifying them, deciding whether they are the kind of thing we are trying to write, and sorting the essays from the feature articles from the arguments. The teacher can then be a colearner in evaluating the materials, deciding how close they are to what we want to write—in kind, in length, and in voice—rather than being the sole font of all knowledge.

The writers notebook is an essential tool for selecting a topic, collecting information, experimenting, and reflecting throughout the writing process. Personal investment and firsthand experience make nonfiction more interesting to read, and these qualities are easiest for students to achieve if their topics arise from their daily lives. The notebook allows such topics to emerge naturally. In fact, there will usually be dozens of possible nonfiction topics in most students' notebooks already, just waiting to be noticed. Nonfiction genre studies begin with our reviewing our notebooks in search of these topics, while we simultaneously move forward in the notebooks, learning to use them like nonfiction writers. We talk about walking through the world with a nonfiction writer's eyes, looking in the corners of our lives for items previously unnoticed, fragments behind which universes might open up. After a short while, we reread to find a topic, and then use the notebook to collect information about the topic from a variety of sources, including (possibly) memory, firsthand observation or experiences, interviews, books, videotapes, and on-line databases. Students also use the notebook to reflect on the information they have gathered, bringing their lives to the facts, connecting data to other things they know about, comparing their topic to other things in life which might be more familiar to their readers. Throughout the writing process, the notebook is a tool for experimentation and revision, as I describe in Chapter 4.

3. Topics of inquiry

Since their topics emerge from their own notebooks, students pursue *their own interests and theories about the world.* As with poetry, fiction, memoir, or other genre studies, the topic ownership is the kids'. Studies that focus a whole class on inquiry into a topic or theme are not genre studies and should be dealt with separately. (Figure 10–2 clarifies the difference in purpose and practice between a genre study and a thematic, topical, or other content-based inquiry. Thinking through this distinction might prove especially helpful for secondary school teachers working with interdisciplinary teams.) The purpose in a genre study of nonfiction is crafting the writing, not learning about the topic. Inquiry is into the form and the process of the form, not the content. In fact, in my view, the information per se is so unimportant that a genre study, even of feature articles, could be done without any research or facts at all. The inquiry into the form of writing would not be harmed if students just made up the facts. Doing so, moreover, might provide the surprising bonus of letting kids in on the trade secret that just because something is written *as if* it's true, in an authoritative style, doesn't mean the author has accurately represented the reality. That experience might even make them more critical readers of nonfiction.

4. Purpose and audience for writing

If we want them to have a reason to write well, we have to make sure that students have a *real audience for writing, whom they have to interest.* If I am sitting in a

A GENRE STUDY	A THEMATIC OR TOPICAL STUDY
■ inquiry into a kind of text, such as poetry, memoir, or essay	■ inquiry into a thing or idea, such as "sharks," "discovery," or "working"
■ the class shares a collection of pieces of writing in the genre, especially a fairly small number of touchstone texts to which frequent reference is made	■ the class shares a collection of information: experts, articles, poems and stories, trips and other firsthand experiences, videotapes, photographs, posters
■ focus is on the processes of thinking and the qualities of good writing unique to this genre	■ focus is on strategies for finding out and for interpreting what is found out about the shared topic
■ one genre for class	■ one topic for class
■ students choose their own topics, usually individually	■ students choose whatever genres they want for written projects, if they are even going to make written projects, which is not a given

FIG. 10–2: *The difference between shared inquiry in forms of writing and content of study.*

dentist's waiting room, flipping through the pages of a magazine, I read a few sentences of an article and decide whether to read on. The author has to capture my attention, draw me in, and make me care about the topic. If she fails, I don't have to read what she wrote. That's the nonfiction writer's job, and it's her main motivation to write appealingly for a general public. To have a reason to write well, students need to be under the same pressure to please. A teacher as the reader won't provide such pressure, since teachers have to read whatever crap is turned in, and the kids know it. They think we like reading that stuff and enjoy catching their mistakes. That's a very odd audience to write for. From the beginning of their writing process, students need to know that their nonfiction pieces are going to enter the marketplace of information and ideas to compete for a reader's time and attention. I usually accomplish this with a class magazine, as I discuss in Chapter 4, but there are other ways to achieve the same goal, such as school newspapers and magazines, local papers, or other venues, depending on the school environment and the collaborative imaginations of teacher and students. The eyes of an audience outside the classroom allow our roles as teachers to shift from authoritarian evaluators to coaches or directors who insist on giving our audience the best we possibly can and who have the knowledge and experience to help that happen.

5. Fitting the study into the whole curriculum

Satisfying courses of study in nonfiction writing tend to take a long time. I could imagine them being shorter, if students really did write with no research, but in my experience, it never works out that way. They get ready to do interviews, and you realize they don't know how, so you have to teach interviewing. They go to books and start copying out whole passages rather than taking notes. So you end up teaching note taking. Just bringing in texts, categorizing them, reading them, and developing a shared vocabulary for describing writers' craft can take several weeks. Most nonfiction involves such an extensive engagement with the world that students have to wait for a slot in the schedules of interviewees, wait for the arrival of requested pamphlets; and there is no point in hurrying them, since it will force them to compromise on valuable experiences. I and my colleagues have found that it is best to plan a long time, possibly as long as ten weeks, for a thorough study of this important genre.

Tempting though it may be to teach them to write this genre well early in the year, it seems ill advised for nonfiction to be the very first genre study. The feeling of keeping a notebook with objective *information* in it is significantly different from the more emotional notebook work toward poetry, memoir, or fiction. To move students right into this somewhat less personal kind of collecting just when they are getting the hang of keeping a notebook may make it more difficult to get the notebooks going again in preparation for another genre. I never do nonfiction until after Christmas. But of course, these are just guesses, and we all make our teaching decisions according to our particular purposes.

Supporting the qualities of well-crafted nonfiction

For any of the subgenres of nonfiction, we can support students' immersion in the ways of thinking peculiar to the form by creating environments in the classroom that support that thought. Since the words *classroom environment* include so much and can consequently become foggy and diffuse for planning, I try to consider each of the following areas: the use of notebooks; the physical environment of the room; conversations among students; peculiarities of the writing process in this genre; the teacher's role; and textual features that need vigilance. If we're doing all the subgenres of nonfiction at once, I may need to have several concurrent environments, something like early childhood teachers who have work/play centers with blocks, toys for dramatic play, and sand. In other words, I may have a group of desks in one area for those people working on essays, and another cluster elsewhere for those working on feature articles, and so on, with the materials peculiar to each nearby. But for the purpose of clarity here, I will give a few suggestions for each subgenre separately.

When students are preparing to write *feature articles,* I:

- Make sure the topics rise from the notebooks, so that they will experience the topic directly.

- Help them compile a list of "experts" in the community whom they might interview and who can become interesting characters in the articles.

- Give them structured opportunities to reflect personally on the information they collect.

- Encourage them to consult books only to answer questions that arise from interviews and direct experience with the topic.

- Limit the time they spend gathering information, since nothing leads to flat writing more easily than too much data in a short piece.

- Give them opportunities to teach each other about their topics and encourage listeners to insist that they be given a sensible understanding of what the writer is trying to explain.

- Show them that good articles compare what is strange and hard to understand in the topic to experiences that are common and familiar in readers' lives.

- Have them write weekly memos to me on their learning about their topic, and encourage them to use this unfolding story of discovery in the actual text of their piece.

- Push them to draft before they feel like they "have enough," so that they focus on the charm of their writing rather than on heaps of data. Blanks left for useful missing facts can be filled in later.

For *essays,* I encourage students to:

- Write many entries before looking for the few facts they might want to include.

- Use actual notebook entries as first drafts, since the essay is the closest formal genre to notebook writing.

- Allow themselves to wander from the topic quite a bit.

- Spend no time at all in the library.

- Talk about the topic as little as possible, spending their thoughts only in writing.

- Write about the topic at different times and in different places—inside and out, when things are quiet and in front of TV, morning and before bed.

- Jot down, like a poet, groups of words that come to mind just because they sound good, without worrying about where they'll go in the piece.

- See how many different emotions they can feel about the topic.

- Take as many angles on the topic as possible: what is the science of this topic? the psychology? the history? the politics? They don't have to *know;* they can speculate.

- Write the draft in as few sittings as possible.

When students are working on *arguments,* including literary criticism, I make sure they do some of the following:

- Choose a position with which someone could disagree.

- Get a partner and debate it, the partner to play an antagonistic role (i.e., force the writer to "prove it").

- Stage some fishbowl debates where we can all brainstorm rhetorical strategies.

- Learn the opposing position, so that they can caricature it, making it sound absurd, and can anticipate the objections of the other side, giving fuel to their own position.

- Write some notebook entries in two voices, to internalize the structure of their case against other perspectives.

- Pretend, when they need to, to have evidence they do not yet have, which they can then go and find.

- Develop a lead, an initial common ground on which to meet the reader, with which no one could argue, and then develop their position from there.

- Generate their own evidence, through experiments, surveys, and tests.

- Read arguments on the same topic from opposing viewpoints.

- Pay attention to the particular words of passion and reason that might inflame or inspire their readers.

- Remember that they are just learning to make a case, that they don't necessarily have to believe it with all their heart.

Writing nonfiction well

These nonfiction genres, in which students engage with the world outside themselves, in which they claim knowledge and the power to communicate it, are the forms of writing in which our society entertains its most important conversations. If they are to be empowered as serious participants in a democracy, kids have to learn to explain what they think, to argue their perspective, to inform others about subjects in which they can claim their own knowledge and authority. And if they are to be heeded by real readers, young writers have to learn to write well, engagingly and clearly, in these crucial genres. Writing poorly deprives them of the voice they deserve in conversations about important things. Therefore, they are best served if we revise the English curriculum toward opportunities for them to write with real purpose and passion, for actual audiences of readers. They need opportunities in which they can write well.

It is almost impossible to make sweeping claims about what "good" nonfiction writing is like. However, within the scope of the genres I have been discussing, it seems to have to do with what some writers and teachers have called "voice." *Voice* is a slippery word, and recently has become contentious in the field of literacy. I do not mean by it that each individual has some original personal sound that springs from their DNA. Rather, I see it as a conventional feature of nonfiction when it is persuasive to a general audience. When a piece of nonfiction has voice, we feel that the writer presenting us with information has learned it within a particular life history. The writer shows us how he understands this information within the framework of his own experience and values.

"Good" nonfiction, then, rejects the voice from nowhere that characterizes encyclopedias and text books, a stance that acts as if reality were undisputed and God-given, in favor of a particular person's situated understanding of the topic. We trust this kind of writing, because it feels like our own learning. We understand it because reading the writer's reflective explanation helps us connect what we are reading with other things we know about. In good nonfiction, somebody is home in the piece, some person is claiming this knowledge and making it mean and taking responsibility for having a perspective that comes from her own experience. The writer is a particular someone who unmasks the world behind the world we usually take for granted and thus is making our world a more interesting place in which to live. What we see around us becomes more precious, complex, intricate, and challenging. We are wiser—and grateful for the wisdom.

TIME AND TRUTH

As we accumulate experience, we come to see the difference between truth and fact. The main difference is their relationship to time. A fact is true once, but truth is true at all times. Statements of truth can, like this essay, be written in the present tense. I'm writing in the present tense because I believe that what I'm saying is true now as I write and will continue to be true later when you read. Of course, this is a linguistic trick, since what I'm saying now may just as easily be false. However, it either *is* true, or it *is* false. It's hard to imagine that what I'm writing now could suddenly *become* untrue, since I am writing about *ideas* in a way that removes them from time.

Expository writing like this is offered in the present tense and organized by category rather than chronology. Many people would rather read narrative writing because it more closely resembles the feeling of real life. But many teachers want their students to learn to write expository prose, mostly because it is the language of political discourse and other important forms in our culture. But none of the things we can say about expository writing should make us believe that it is more true or authoritative than any other kind of writing. We just tend to believe this kind of writing more, which is often a big mistake.

I once heard Donald Murray say that all writing is autobiographical, regardless of its genre. What that means about truth is that a writer has always learned the things she believes to be true from some life experience that can be told in a story. We should always read expository prose by adding to the beginning of each sentence, "I have become persuaded from my particular life experience that. . . ." We could add to the end of each sentence, ". . . and I'm trying now to persuade you that this is so, too." Though it would be tiresome, we could then begin to imagine the restoration of time and location to what is masked as objective truth.

This present tense is a trick of rhetoric. I came to believe what I'm writing right now by particular life experiences, some of them mundane and probably not powerful enough to convince you to see the world the way I do. Which is why I'm not going to tell those life experiences to you as stories, why I instead continue in the universally true present tense. But I might change my mind.

11

More than Magic
Elements of Craft in the Teaching of Literacy

y last few years as a teacher, my room was at the end of a hall. Any-time I'd walk to the office, I would pass about ten other classrooms, and I would sometimes be so bold as to listen to what was happening in them. Here was Antoinette, across the hall from me, calling out *en francaise,* exhorting the students to *répétez,* which they did in mindless monotone. Robert, a few doors down, was droning on about World War I while the kids glared stupefied. Joan was going down rows with vocabulary words, one kid at a time spelling and defining the word she called out, while the rest of the class basically went nuts. I would shake my head sadly, inside congratulating myself that though I might sometimes have felt confused about what to do next in class or about which way to go on a split-second decision, at least I didn't do that.

Then I'd come to Lesley's room. As I passed, I could tell how alive the kids were, talking together about something interesting. And Lesley was part of the discussion too. The people in the room seemed to like one another and to be engaged in an easy combination of work and play. Admiration rang like a bell in my chest. Having gotten too far past, I'd pivot, snapping my fingers as if I'd forgotten something, in case anyone was watching. (You have to be careful not to get caught admiring anyone else's teaching, don't you? It would be seen as voyeurism or espionage, certainly an invasion of Lesley's privacy.) I'd walk more slowly and furtively past again.

I took to making frequent fugitive trips to my mailbox, then would lurk guiltily outside her door, listening to this happy class while I pretended to read memos, trying desperately to learn what the hell she was doing. What made her teaching so good? She didn't seem to be saying anything I couldn't imagine myself saying, didn't seem to be teaching a superior curriculum or using gilt-edged materials, but there was something in the atmosphere of her class that was missing in my own. I had no need to compete with her, but in my desire to grow as a teacher, I wanted to be that good. My mind whipped around for an explanation. None of the things we usually say to distance the teaching we admire worked. I couldn't say it was the kids, since she taught the same grade level I did, right down the hall from me. I couldn't say she had a different teaching situation because, well, she didn't. Oh, how I wished she were teaching younger kids or older kids or richer kids or poorer kids or darker kids or lighter kids or at least in another building so that the variable wouldn't come down to ME! Finally, in frustrated admiration, I shrugged and did what people have always done with what they couldn't understand: I called it magic. While still in her mother's womb, she had been touched by angels with a special gift for teaching, a mysterious knack that cannot be explained. I said it to myself: *Well, don't worry about it, she's a magician.* I said it to others: *Oh, that Lesley, she's such a magician.* I said it to her: *Well, that's fine for you; you're a magician.*

When I started to consult, I got to be in hundreds of classrooms all over the country, and, to my astonishment, I began to notice that there were hundreds of these magicians around, enchantresses and wizards of all descriptions. They were everywhere. Those angels had been busy, because there were "gifted" teachers all over the place.

Gradually, I began to see some characteristics many of these wonder-teachers shared, and I saw that they had worked hard for years, and were still striving, to cultivate these qualities. The isolation of my own teaching had blinded me to some things I did in class, acts I'd always taken for granted because I had nothing to compare them with except the traces in the hallways. I realized that to have called Lesley a magician was an insult to the intelligence of her craft. We should leave the myth of the magical pedagogue to Hollywood, where Robin Williams can put his hand over a student's eyes, turn him around three times, and—poof!—out pops a brilliant poem. But it's an insult to good teachers in real life to call them magicians or "born" teachers, when what they have is a craft, the result of careful work and disciplined attention—sometimes conscious, sometimes only half-conscious—to the qualities in themselves that foster the most literate environment possible for their students.

Viewing teaching as a craft

We teachers are uncomfortable with discussions of skill or craft. Partly, as I've mentioned, it seems to be a natural by-product of our solitude in our work; we rarely if ever have the chance to admire anyone's teaching. Also, the idea that we might want to grow in the craft of teaching might have dire economic consequences when expressed in an administrative evaluation. Then too, most of us were "trained" in the craft before we were actually doing it. Can you imagine a stone-cutter at New York's Cathedral of St. John the Divine being trained in stonecutting with no stone anywhere in sight? And once we're in the classroom, in our forays into continuing professional education, we almost always leave the stone behind. So we may get better (or at least newer) ideas for things to do or curricular plans, but the essential character of our teaching is never a topic for discussion. When the

Teachers College Writing Project called one of its staff development courses Improving Our Teaching, many people around the city considered it insulting, as if the idea of focusing directly on getting better at the craft, rather than picking up a new curricular song and dance, were anathema.

This attitude seems less common when we consider other crafts. We commonly talk about the qualities of good writing, habits of mind writers develop and use regardless of genre or topic. An artist may use different materials but always stays aware of elements of design like line, texture, and composition. I was an actor before I became a teacher, and I spent all of my time and most of my money working on my craft—my voice, my body, ways of relating to other actors, script analysis. I worked on a lot of different scripts, but my craft, my values, my general way of working, stayed consistent regardless of the particular play I was rehearsing or performing.

Similarly, when I talk about the craft of teaching, I mean the control of certain things we do, which are similar whether we are conferring with a student about research strategies, leading a discussion about the first five chapters of *The Woman Warrior,* or explaining to the class the routine for moving from the minilesson into silent writing. What's more, these elements of craft are similar whether we are teaching kindergarten or graduate students, which means that inquiry into the teaching craft can be shared among teachers across the whole range of grade levels.

In his book about the craft of writing, which he titled *The Art of Fiction,* John Gardner, in typically curmudgeonly fashion, bemoans a general lack of craft in the world. "Most grown-up behavior," he writes, "when you come right down to it, is decidedly second-class. People don't drive their cars as well, or wash their ears as well, or eat as well, or even play the harmonica as well as they would if they had sense" (p. x).

When I first read that quote, it stuck in my memory, and it pops into my mind not infrequently, for example, when I'm driving around New York City. But more often, I'm struck by people doing their jobs well for no good reason. There's nothing really in it for them except just doing it well—a gratuitous sense of craft. A man at a parking garage is particularly quick and courteous and straightforward about the rates, when yesterday another guy at the same place was a slow, surly liar. I'm moved almost to tears when a checker at a grocery store knows all the prices and bags my groceries with intelligence and precision. Whenever I encounter someone who has a sense of craft about her job, it leaves a mark on me, the challenge of competence. A respect for work well accomplished seems to be contagious, transcending the particular nature of the work. The last chapter in William Zinsser's *On Writing Well,* the one hardly anyone reads, is called "Write as Well as You Can." In it he talks about the drive to write well, which he inherited from his mother's love of good writing but even more from his father, a businessman who wasn't much of a reader. Zinsser writes,

> He was a man who loved his business. When he talked about it I never felt that he regarded it as a venture for making money, but as an art, to be practiced with imagination and only the best materials. He had a passion for

quality and had no patience with the second-rate. As far as I know, he never went into a store looking for a bargain. He charged more for his product because he made it with the best ingredients, and his company prospered. . . . [My] gift from my father [was] a bone-deep belief that quality is its own reward. I, too, have never gone into a store looking for a bargain. Ironically, though my mother was the literary one in our family—the magpie collector of books, the ardent lover of the English language, the writer of dazzling letters—it was from the world of business that I absorbed my craftsman's ethic, and over the years, when I found myself endlessly rewriting what I had endlessly rewritten, determined to write better than everybody else who was competing for the same space, the inner voice that I was hearing was the voice of my father talking about shellac (pp. 231–32).

Since craft is so contagious, if we want our students to be risk takers, assertive inventors of their learning, craftsmanlike about their reading and writing, strategic in their thinking, we need to demonstrate those qualities in our own attitude toward our work. And we need to go one step further: we need to talk about all of this with the kids. They need to see us as craftspersons, need to hear us worry about it, deliberate, choose, reconsider, and evaluate. We should be proud to talk about our craft, especially since so much is at stake in our excellence: a more democratic society, a hope for a better world.

Don't let me or anyone else fool you. No one can talk about the craft of teaching without taking a political and philosophical stance about what education is supposed to do. *Anytime anyone* says this or that is good in teaching, they're speaking out of a particular tradition and a particular community's norms about teaching and learning. I have a goal in mind, and so does Madeline Hunter. Her "elements of instruction" were developed by researching which teachers' students got the highest scores on tests about content. For a variety of reasons, tests don't have much to do with what I value in education (Edelsky 1991; Madaus 1985; F. Smith 1986; Darling-Hammond 1991; Hill 1992; Medina and Neill 1989; Owen 1985). The teachers I want to discuss may or may not teach students who get high test scores; I've never checked and never will. I admire these teachers because of the environments they create in their classrooms every day, productive democratic environments where students have things to say, value their lives outside school, work together to formulate both individual and collective points of view. These are classrooms where there is a sustained conversation going on, among all the people who inhabit them, where people work for long stretches of time on projects that matter to them, where there is respect for differences because the class works together, collaborating on meaning. That's what I mean by a literate environment, and it doesn't evolve only because these teachers have writing workshops or notebooks or genre studies or thematic studies or print covering the walls or literature lining the shelves. None of that stuff, though it's important, is sufficient to create the environment I've described. And that's where the craft comes in. For me, the craft of teaching literacy has to do with finding a way to act in the classroom that contributes most to the literate environment.

So I've been noticing the craft of some of the teachers who have stopped me in my tracks with admiration. I've been trying to learn from them not only sensible and clever things to do, but ways to be, qualities or characteristics that seem to permeate all that they do: their minilessons on writing, their conferences, their classroom management, the ways they lead book talks. Some of their words echo in my head when I confer with a senior or talk to a group of seventh graders or teach graduate students or work with other teachers. I can't always obey all these words at once, but it helps to hear them buzzing like gadflies or to have them written on scraps of paper in the pockets of various coats, so that my craft nags at me, the way a writer knows that his first thought for a verb will flatten a sentence if he doesn't wake up or a painter concentrates to keep in mind the angle of the light.

Some elements of craft in teaching literacy

It seems to me that the teachers I'm describing give generous and disciplined attention to three areas. First, I'm going to describe some of the actions that reveal their *awareness of themselves among others,* as one person in a crowded place. Second, I'm going to describe their actions toward the *social environment* of the classroom. And third, I'm going to describe their actions with respect to *what is given and what is possible.* Each of these areas represents what John Keats called "a negative capability," a willingness to hold two seemingly conflicting ideas in mind at the same time. I've noticed, in other words, that the craft in great teachers' work is often the ability to act within a split awareness, a dialectic, between some of the dualisms John Dewey spent his life trying to collapse, especially those of self/other, individual/group, and present/future. I hope this rather abstract analysis will be clearer as we consider the real work of good teachers.

Awareness of self among others

EYEING YOUR OWN PROCESSES One quality I'm sure all the teachers I've admired have possessed is an *awareness of their own processes*—of reading, of writing, of learning. Here is the primary source of their teaching material. Just as a stonemason, once he has taken an apprentice, has to add a third eye, a point of view over his own shoulder that allows him not only to do the job but also to teach the job, so a good literacy teacher develops a third eye on his own reading, writing, and learning. He doesn't only read but also sees himself reading. Every experience with writing infuses his memory because he knows he's going to use that story to understand and to teach students. He recalls the conditions under which he's read powerfully or written easily so that he can try to create some of those conditions in his classroom. And it isn't only writing and reading processes that a good literacy teacher puts to use—it's all of learning.

I've seen Karen Rosner, a teacher in the Bronx, as she counseled a reading group that was having a hard time choosing a book, sharing strategies she knows from her own experience of being a member of a teacher reading circle in her school. Two days later, she taped an impressionist painting on the board, gathered her class around, and said, "You know about this course I'm taking at the Metropolitan Museum. Yesterday, we were looking at some impressionist paintings like this one by Monet, and I noticed that when you look at it up close, you can't tell what it is. You have to stand back from it to see it. You can try it in a little while. That made me think about your writers notebooks. A lot of you are reading your individual entries so closely that you can't see the bigger picture of what's in your whole notebook. You need to find a way to step back from it. It might help if you try reading through it faster and ask yourself, *What's this all really about?* See if you can see a design emerging. And those of you who do have a project in the works already need to ask yourself not just *What am I going to say next?* but *What am I trying to show in this whole piece?* You have to try sometimes to step back to see the picture of what you're doing more clearly." Later that same day, conferring with one of the boys in a response group about some trouble he was having getting along with the others, she told him a story about her son when he was on an athletic team and had to discover some things about being in a group.

Watching Karen interacting with her kids, I see her listen really carefully to what they're saying; then there comes a point where she sort of looks off, and she's remembering a time in her own learning life that might be analogous to what the kid is going through. And then she just tells them the story and explains how she thinks it applies. I'm sure everyone does this, but so many of us do it inside our heads and then speak with what we believe to be the voice of authority, a voice from nowhere, the underlying message being, This is not just something I believe or learned somewhere, but this *just is.*

In unmasking and locating her learning, Karen is teaching several things at once. First, the strategy itself—whatever she thinks the student needs to learn. Second, problem solving; she's demonstrating that whatever situation you're facing, you can look in memory for some similar experience and try doing the thing that got you through before. But maybe the most significant and lasting thing she's teaching is the texture of the learning life, the passion for learning that makes experience interesting.

ELEGANCE Having an eye always on our own processes doesn't mean, however, that the floor of the classroom is primarily a showcase for our own learnedness. Really good teachers seem always to be walking a line between the teacher's own learning and that of the students, a system of checks and balances that keeps the classroom from toppling either into a teacher-centered grandstand or a student-dominated free-for-all. They deliberately hold themselves in check with a kind of *elegance.* By that I don't mean they wear long gloves or tuxedos, speak in pear-shaped tones, or gesture ever gracefully. I mean the kind of elegance you find in a proof in geometry or in a poem—a clarity of action in a planned, coherent direction, without unnecessary clutter. Their teaching trails no waste.

Liz Dolan, another teacher in the Bronx, like so many of us, has her students only for forty-five minutes. Sure, she gives them homework, but she also knows that a lot of them either don't spend much time at home or else their homes are pretty crowded and that makes it hard to do concentrated work. So when they come into the room, they know to move directly to wherever they need to be for the day's work, either in groups or individually at desks, and Liz stands somewhere where everyone can see her. She does this not because she wants to be the center of the room, but because she does not; her intention is to eliminate as much whole-class movement from place to place as possible. As soon as it is time for class to start, she says directly and concisely what she needs the whole class to hear. Almost always, she talks for less than five minutes. Then she says, "Let's get to work." What she does next is the amazing part: she stops talking. She just stops—doesn't say anything else to the whole class. Sometimes she sits down to write, sometimes she says something to an individual kid, sometimes she leans against a desk and watches as the class settles in to work.

A few of the times I visited her class, I did the minilesson. I said my one thing, just like Liz, and then, "Oh, that reminds me of another thing," so I said that, and then I remembered a couple of announcements I thought the kids should know about and a couple of good things some people in the class had done that everyone should hear, and "that puts me in mind of a story. . . ." As my minilesson became a maxilesson, I could feel Liz inching toward me from the other side of the room until finally our shoulders touched. (I'm surprised she didn't pinch me.) She whispered, "*They* should really get to work." And in that simple, elegant statement, she expressed so much respect for them, so much clarity about what we were here for. I saw that same elegance in her conferences. She didn't try to fix everything about the kid's writing but helped the kid find one thing to work on or keep looking for—then she shut up and got up. When she led a literature discussion, if she had a question or something to add, she said it and then stopped, and if the kids didn't respond right away, then the group thought in silence until some student said something else. Her teaching reminded me of what David Bartholomae and Anthony Petrosky wrote in *Facts, Artifacts, and Counterfacts,* "A course in reading and writing whose goal is to empower students must begin with silence, a silence students must fill" (p. 7). Liz puts forth an invitation to her students and then leaves the silence lie, believing that the silence, like a blank page, is something students have to face if they are to take responsibility for their own learning.

I admire elegance not because of its inherent loveliness, but because of its regard for the learners, because it shows a real commitment to the belief that people construct their learning as active members of a conversation, not passive recipients of all the things a teacher can think of to say, many of which tend to be somewhat muddled anyway. Elegance shows the teacher to be aware of herself among others and to be willing to make space for others' voices.

THOUGHTFULNESS   If we expand this awareness a little, we could call it *thoughtfulness.* The thoughtfulness I admire in teaching isn't confined to the head; that isn't what we usually mean by thoughtfulness when we apply it to actions. If we say, *What you did was so thoughtful yesterday,* we do not really mean, *You seemed to be* *thinking while you did it,* but rather, *You were acting with sympathy toward others' perceptions of what was going on.* We cannot teach literacy well if we think our definition of what's happening in our classrooms is identical to our students'. In this small space of time we have together, we are each living a different story; what happens in that room has different meanings to everyone. We might think of our classes as parallel lives, all happening at the same time, and even if we are very successful at creating a spirit of community in the classroom, we should never make the mistake of assuming our success has resulted in mind control. Of course, good literacy teachers can't help but realize this. They've read their students' writing and so are mindful of the worlds contained behind each face in the classroom, of the membership each student has in multiple groups outside our classroom, including the other classes they pass through in one school day. Teachers hear their students respond personally to literature and discuss how differently people respond to the same story, so we shouldn't be surprised that everyone will make different meanings of the story of a class or period. But to be aware of the different meanings people make from the same experience is one thing, while to be truly mindful of that fact, to act with respect to it, is something else. Real thoughtfulness requires that we be moved, that we be touched by the different stories that our students are living, and that we modify our transactions with them in the light of *their* meanings, rather than always plowing forward with our own agendas.

Tact[1]

Tact is the root of *tactile,* and so has to do, metaphorically, with touching and being touched. Tact shows itself in a teacher when he is affected, touched, by his students, and when he is willing, in turn, to affect them, to touch them. He wants to make them laugh, but he's no clown, since he also wants them to make him laugh. He wants them to cry when he reads a sad story to them, just as he shows he is moved by the story and by those the students write and tell. And tact involves not only this emotional touching; it's also the willingness to touch a life, to make a difference. In a literacy classroom where students are working with the material of their own lives outside the classroom, issues become visible that, if our teaching treated everyone exactly the same, might remain concealed. A tactful teacher is willing, even compelled, by her own humanity to sympathize as a human being and also to press students to grow as persons.

   Imagine with me a classroom with a tactful teacher working there. Early in the period Abigail flings a piece of writing her way, saying "Go ahead and read it, but I'm sure you won't like it anyway." The teacher decides not to deal with the writing directly, but with what Abigail has said. She tells the girl, "You know, you do that a lot. I know you work hard on your writing and I think you are proud of

---

1   I owe this use of the word to a philosopher of teaching that more people should know about, Max van Manen. His books, *The Tone of Teaching* and *The Tact of Teaching: The Meaning of Pedagogical Thoughtfulness,* contain discussions of both tact and thoughtfulness much more elaborate than I can attempt here.

your work, because it is good, but whenever you talk to me about it, you always say I'm not going to like it, or you know I don't like it, or it's not very good, or something to put yourself down. And I'm beginning to think that you do know your work is good, but you're afraid I'm going to say it isn't or say something that will hurt your feelings, and so you say something negative to try to get me to praise you. My daughter used to do that, too. She used to come to me in the morning and say, 'My hair looks terrible, doesn't it,' just to get me to say, 'No, honey, it looks great.' It was crazy. You don't have to do that. Try just to accept that I think you are a good writer, and then let's get to work about it."

Some other students are working in response groups. The group is in turmoil because Scott has criticized another boy, whose feelings ended up hurt. Scott's teacher pulls him aside. Scott is going on and on about how the other kid is a baby who doesn't understand anything about being in a response group. The teacher says she understands but that she knows some things about Scott, too. She tells him that he often comes on too strong when he works in groups, thinking that he's the only one with any understanding, when in reality he's often wrong. He needs, she says, to listen to people more, to try to understand their position and take it into account, even if they can't make a good-enough argument for it. Furthermore, he has to learn to watch people closely. If they start to get hurt by what he's saying, he needs to back off. She's not sure whether this talk will do any good, but she's hopeful, since he was obviously uncomfortable about the social consequences of his most recent arrogance.

As the kids leave for their next class, she sees Jeremy and remembers reading as she reviewed his notebook last night about his grandmother's dying over the weekend. She wants to acknowledge that to him, and considers doing so now, but then, remembering that he has three more classes and lunch ahead of him, she just asks him to come by after school for a chat. She assures him he's not in trouble, it's just that she wants to say something to him. Tact in teaching manifests itself not only as being willing to touch, intending to make a difference, but also knowing when to hold back and wait.

Now let's imagine a different teacher. She's not tactless, in the sense of being cruel or thoughtless, but I wouldn't describe her as a tactful teacher. When a colleague tells her about writers notebooks, she says, "Oh, I used to do journals, but these kids will tell you anything in those things. I couldn't stand knowing all that stuff about the kids. I'm not their therapist; I didn't know what to do for them." I withhold the description of tactful not because of her decision about the particular tool of journals or writers notebooks, but because of her reasons for her decision and what they say about her relationship to students. A tactful teacher is not afraid of dealing with students as human beings, is not happier to cover up their lives than to touch them.

It's not that the tactful teacher *does* think she's the students' therapist. I've compressed the examples here into a single class period, leaving out the huge majority of the time when the teacher was dealing with the business of reading and writing. But in a classroom where the main objective is making meaning of lived experience, important personal issues will come up, and the tactful teacher is not afraid to touch and to teach her students as people. Teaching with tact involves a profound touching of the heart, courageous, kind, and life changing.

Environment

TRANSPARENCY   Once a teacher is aware of herself as one person in a classroom of meaning makers, her teaching takes on a *transparency,* an almost invisible presence in most striking contrast to the more common image of the teacher's face as the only vivid one in the room. It is now a commonplace among reading and writing workshop teachers that you know you're doing something right when a visitor enters looking for the teacher and they can't find him.

At its most direct, transparency in teaching is the result of placing responsibility for the running of the room into students' hands. My friend Isabel Beaton says, "I'm continually asking myself, What am I doing that someone else could be doing?" The more the kids know to do, the less the teacher has to stand in the middle of the floor and choreograph. The most transparent teaching I've ever seen is Holly Zuber's, another teacher in the Bronx. I spent weeks in Holly's classroom trying to understand what she was doing to make the classroom run so effortlessly, until I developed an almost paranoid feeling that she was hiding her actions just to make me crazy. Her students, without whole-class direction from Holly, would start out by getting their materials and beginning work. Their class meeting, which Holly likes to have with the whole class of thirty-five or so gathered close in a corner of the room (so that she can speak softly, if she's the one who's going to speak), was usually toward the end of the period. The students would be writing, Holly and I would be conferring with a kid, when again with no discernible sign from Holly, the whole class would move in a purposeful and relaxed manner into place for the meeting. In spite of Holly's demurring, I figured out a couple of things that happened. Because the meeting happened predictably by a certain time, the students always timed their work, knowing that, if at 9:50 (or whatever) she hadn't called them together, it was time to meet anyway. It was a scheduled appointment. When she did decide to meet earlier than that, she just told one student to move around the room and tell everyone to come to the meeting area. And they did, with no voice that had to carry over the entire classroom. Similarly, when the students were working, if the classroom got too noisy, any student who was finding it difficult to concentrate could flick the light switch a couple of times as a signal for the class to quiet down, and kids often went to groups who were clearly the disruptive ones and just asked them to be quiet. If no one did this on her own, Holly would ask someone to. Sometimes, of course, she would have to stop the noise and correct the whole class, but she phrased it in terms of what they owed each other, not what she demanded. Obviously, this kind of social control rather than teacher dominance requires that most of the people in the class expect to get some serious work done.

In classrooms in all kinds of settings, with all kinds of kids, I have seen that the more the environment is put into the hands of students, that is, the more democratic the classroom, the less the teacher has to have central control. This is the paradox of democratic classroom management: the less explicitly the teacher manages every move, the more effective the social control of the whole class. "Social control" is the phrase John Dewey used in *Experience and Education* to describe the order that is present when a group is doing meaningful things together. Everyone is involved in the shared project, and everyone wants it to succeed, so the actions of individuals are the interest of the group. The shared project in Holly's classroom was the environment that allowed individuals to work on their own writing and reading. When Holly or other good teachers need a student to change his behavior or need the whole class to quiet down, they may occasionally have to raise their voices above the din, but it's not a demonstration of personal power; it's a reminder, on behalf of the group, of what the environment has to be to achieve what they all expect.

AN ALTERNATING WIDE-ANGLE/TELEPHOTO LENS   These excellent literacy teachers are always concerned about the social and physical environment of the whole class, and during any given period, this larger environment needs some attention. They evaluate frequently: *Does the class as a whole seem engaged with work? Do my kids know how to use the physical environment to get what they need (paper, books, dictionaries, possibly bathroom passes) so that they aren't dependent on me? Are they using each other to collaborate on solving problems? How is the machinery of the classroom running?* But they spend most of their time conferring with individual students or small groups, assessing what kids need to learn and teaching those things directly. Effectively leading a good literacy classroom seems to involve establishing a *mental tick-tock that alternates between a wide-angle view of the whole classroom environment and telephoto close-ups of individual students.*

Often I have seen good teachers set themselves on a predictable pattern of getting up from a conference with a student and then, perhaps while making notes about that conference on a clipboard, walking to another part of the room, making a pass of the class, which allows them to take in the bigger picture and adjust whatever is necessary before settling down with another student. To be able to concentrate on individuals, the entire environment has to be running fluidly, and for the whole class to operate smoothly and *mean* anything, the teacher has to engage with individual students. This alternating valuation of the micro and the macro is one of those splits, one of the necessary tensions between side-by-side awarenesses that characterize effective teaching.

OBSERVANCY   Though careful attention to the whole classroom has intrinsic virtues in establishing the necessarily social environment for literacy learning, some of my favorite teachers were motivated to set up good workshops in the first place just because it gave them the opportunity to stand back and watch individual students. There is a longing to understand what reading and writing mean for individual students that produces in good teachers of literacy a quality of *observancy*. In order to understand writing and reading as processes, we have to look at writers and readers—literally *look* at them—while they are reading and writing. "Kid-watching," as Yetta Goodman has termed observation, may occur informally, in those passes of the room I mentioned, for example; or observations may be more formal, even scheduled. Some teachers build five minutes or so in their workshops each day during which they observe one or two students. They find that the data and insights they glean from those few minutes informs their intuition not only about those particular students, but about all learners; however small and seemingly insignificant the kid's behavior, these determined teachers find what's interesting there. Other teachers conduct such formal observations of kids writing, reading, or working in groups only when a particular student is hard to understand or seems to be an anomaly. Even when they can't always do it, passionate literacy teachers hunger for opportunities to watch particular children for several minutes and record what they see, because they know that nothing else, not staff development workshops, not books about teaching, not conversations with colleagues, can do as much as watching a reader or writer at work to provide the most essential information about how to teach.

What is—and what is possible

A HABIT OF REFLECTION   The attitude that it would be interesting to watch a student, write down what he does, and reflect on it later while making plans for him also reveals the good literacy teacher's way of acting with respect to what is given right in front of her right now and what is possible, what it can become in its future. The purpose of establishing an environment that allows me to watch a kid is not simply to watch kids, per se. The purpose is to watch a kid and make a plan; to watch a kid and then imagine what I can do to help that kid become.

Good reading and writing teachers, then, establish *some habit where they get to spend time reflecting* on what they have observed. Clearly, one excellent tool for recording and reflecting is essentially the same one we encourage students to use for their writing and their response to literature—a notebook. Many teachers I envy keep a teaching journal.

Kathy Doyle writes constantly while she is teaching, and then she writes off of it at home, as if it were a piece of literature or the left side of a double-entry journal. She writes in order to think about what her kids are doing. First, she interprets what the students did or said: *What does this mean about this student? What does it mean about the whole class? How does it reflect back to me the values I've introduced into the class? How is the student constructing his understanding of what we're about in reading and writing? How can I understand this student better, based on this thing I saw him do or heard him say?* And then, she reflects again on how she should plan to teach this student in the future: *What does this kid need to grow, based on what I can understand about him?*

I know a lot of people who do this kind of thinking in the car, using technologies other than literacy. They live a long way from where they teach, and this seems to be a good use of the car time. They may tape a reading group's conversations or their writing conferences or a whole-class meeting, and then they listen to the tape in the car and reflect on a plan for those students.

In order to consider ourselves planful, deliberate, crafting teachers, then, it is essential to find some way to step out of the rush of classroom events, pulling back to ask, *What is happening in my class and what am I trying to do with that?* Too often, our questions about planning are limited to *What am I going to say next?* or *What am I going to do tomorrow?* or *What's my activity for Monday morning?* Basic writers, the writers who struggle the most, are characterized mostly by the constant worry, *What am I going to say next? And now what? Next word, next word, next word.* They can never really think in larger chunks. They never think in terms of what they are going to *do* next, what the next part of the process should be to help them accomplish their larger purpose with respect to their audience. We all have moments, when we are not at our best as literacy educators, of basic teaching: *What am I going to do next?* What we need to learn from good teachers is the habit of pulling back and asking, *Where are we? What are we trying to do?* and then to plan a new future.

BUILDING MEANING   A writer's habit of mind involves the trust that anything can lead to meaning. If she is sitting at her desk and sees an ashtray, she can begin to write about the ashtray, knowing that it can lead, by process of association or metaphor, to significance. The teachers I admire possess that same trust in meaning and make *a habit of building meaning out of the small and ordinary.* The littlest, seemingly most insignificant thing becomes the opportunity to make something big. When they confer, good teachers know that the littlest thing a kid notices and jots in a writers notebook can develop into something of importance to the learner. The teacher usually believes in the potential for meaning long before the student has any inkling of what that meaning might be, and it's the teacher's vision of "there's something there" that gives the writer the confidence to start building. The littlest thing the teacher sees a student do as a reader can become an entire course for learning for the student and the teacher. The littlest squabble between two kids in the classroom might become an opportunity for a discussion of the meaning of collaboration or even the necessary difficulty of living in a democracy.

OBSESSIVENESS   A psychologist might say there was a little bit of *obsessiveness* about great literacy teachers, in the way they follow through on initial impulses. In this radical extension of what is called the "teachable moment," what would have been insignificant, fleeting little things become permanent classroom structures that stretch across time so they can change kids' lives. Nancie Atwell illustrates this obsessiveness in *In the Middle,* telling about seeing a couple of girls passing notes in the back of the room. When she realized they were about literature, she changed her classroom structure of dialogue journals to include students writing to other students. Lesser teachers would have said, *All right, just stop it,* without understanding what the students were doing. Somewhat better teachers would have said, *Well, if you're writing about literature, I guess it's okay.* Great literacy teachers see student impulses, understand the intelligence behind them, and extend them across time.

In one tenth-grade classroom I am visiting, a student mentions in a whole-group discussion that she reads aloud to her visually impaired younger brother. Another says he reads to his grandmother. A conversation develops about the value of reading aloud to someone, how it strengthens that inner voice that is so important to reading, how it forces you to read longer chunks, to pick up more text at once off the page. Someone mentions that sometimes you get to the end of a sentence and it says "she whispered," and you've been reading really loudly through the whole thing—so you have to kind of see the whole sentence at once when you're reading dialogue. After this visit, I don't return to the classroom for a week, and when I do, no one is there. Each student has adopted a kindergartner at the school down the road to read to, and they go there once a week for this couple of months. The teacher is also investigating making tapes for the blind and reading in a retirement home. The kids are in groups now during other days of the week, working on readers theatre performances of some of their favorite authors' work, which they will perform and record on both audio- and videotape. Each student has a read-aloud log, in which he or she notes the trouble encountered reading aloud and records when it feels good. One writes he tried different voices while reading to a child, and the kid laughed. Another writes that the sentences in one story he's trying to read well always seem to change direction right in the middle, and he can't get the phrasing right. Another writes that she's reading a story in dialect and hasn't the faintest idea what this is supposed to sound like, so she's going to the library downtown this weekend to see if they have some dialect recordings. Around the classroom are various signs and bulletin boards that support this inquiry into reading aloud. One bulletin board has three divisions separated by strands of yarn: good picture books to read alouds, good short stories to read aloud, good poems to read aloud. Index cards in each section offer student suggestions in their own handwriting. The teacher has wheedled and cajoled almost all the tape recorders in the building into the room, so that kids can practice their readings and listen to others'. There is a tape library of student readings and readings by actors and writers, and these tapes can be signed out overnight. See what I mean by obsessiveness?

This drive to follow through, moreover, is the cornerstone of curriculum grounded in student interests. If many students are experimenting with poetry in their notebook, the teacher extends that flirtation into a sustained genre study. If she sees some thematic pattern in the poems the kids write in that poetry inquiry, she extends that shared issue into a thematic study.

Sometimes, the classroom structures teachers build on student interests are less formal, almost incidental. They are, however, no less important, since in many ways the environment is the curriculum. One day, a group of students pass around pictures from someone's vacation. A few days later, the teacher has enfranchised those same students to design a bulletin board for people to post photos they'd like to share with others, along with written explanations. The students are worried that the pictures will be damaged, so the teacher finds and cuts to size a piece of clear plastic. She spends her own money on this, but it is less than four dollars, so she can spare it. This is hardly a curricular unit, but it nevertheless teaches students that their experiences are what we're about here, and that others' experiences are worth paying attention to.

When teachers indulge their obsessiveness in this way, they facilitate the essential move in inquiry. We all tend to float through life, fleetingly and vaguely interested in this and that. None of this interest results in our learning, though, until we choose something, anchor ourselves to some intention, some project, that pulls us through time and allows us as we go to scoop up the world in our hands. The obsessiveness of good teachers, then, is not arbitrary or psychologically sick, but rather invites students into deep and sustained inquiry.

CLARITY OF INTENT   In the classrooms of all the teachers I admire, the kids know their teacher intends for something important and life changing to happen there. There is a *clarity of intent* about what literacy is for, how these students should be learning literacy, and how we should work together in this classroom. A good teacher talks about his intent to the students, discussing why he's chosen to teach this way as opposed to other possible ways, so that the students can be partners in carrying out the teacher's vision of the classroom. Some teachers describe their purpose emotionally, telling their students that they want them to love reading, that they want them to find joy and satisfaction in writing. Others make frequent references to their political purpose in teaching, to empower the students as people who can use literacy to change their world. Our students can only get on board the ship of our vision for a shared curriculum and environment if we constantly explain to them what we are about. These classrooms are usually very different from any the students are used to, so they need to understand why that's so and what their role must be in building something new. If the teacher is the only one who knows the destination and the route, no one else can help drive.

EXPECTATION   Similarly, good teaching involves communicating unmistakably high expectations to students for their work. One of the teachers I admire most, Judy Davis, who teaches in New York City, makes it her project to make her students as famous as possible. She acts in the classroom with constant, unflagging confidence that her students are about to do incredible things that everyone in the world will want to know about. Judy admires even their initial entries in writers notebooks and talks about what a fantastic poem or picture book or short story or essay those entries might become. Often, when a piece is almost finished, Judy says "Why don't you get one of those big pieces of poster paper and write that on there, and we'll laminate it and put it on the wall. Make it look pretty, now." Then, when several students have done that, Judy pokes holes along one side of the poems, assembles them with rings to make a big book, and takes it to elementary teachers to use as a big book with their students. When the big book comes back, the poems might go outside in the hall or in the front office. Anytime I visit Judy's school, there are pieces of student writing all over the place: small slips of paper taped to the wall inside the entrance to the building, short essays illustrated with photographs lining the hall outside the office, book reviews with copies of the books' covers posted on a bulletin board in the library, open letters photocopied and stuffed in all the faculty mailboxes, transparencies of notebook entries and drafts in other teachers' rooms for them to use as models of the writing process. Judy makes her room available to lots of visitors from all over the city and the country and always arranges for the students to be the ones who show the visitors around, explain their writers notebooks, discuss the way the class works, explain how the year has gone so far. As a result, Judy's students are the most articulate I've ever known in describing their own reading and writing processes.

The famousness of Judy's kids isn't limited to publication. Judy also makes them famous to themselves. Often, whether they are learning new strategies for discussing books or new kinds of notebook entries or the qualities of good conversation about writing, Judy says to them, "The things you guys are doing are so smart, and I just want you all to know about them. What are some of the strategies you're using to get started in your discussions?" Then she takes dictation from them on chart paper as they describe their work. She tells them that the purpose of having a list like that is to outgrow it, to make it longer, and she invites them to add new strategies whenever they come up with them.

Like Kathy Doyle, Judy takes notes on just about everything her students say or do; she's constantly writing as she teaches. It must be a transforming experience as a student to have your teacher write down your words, as if they were really interesting and smart. It makes you say smarter things or at least what you understand to be considered smarter things. If someone is paying very close attention to what you say in order to make you famous, you start acting smarter.

This is not false praise but a cycle of expectation and affirmation. Judy lets them know that she knows they're brilliant. They act brilliantly to rise to her expectation. Then she tells them they sure enough are brilliant, but she'd never realized *how* brilliant, which makes them act even more brilliantly.

The meaning of craft

No list of the elements of craft in literacy teaching could ever be considered complete—it's too contingent, diverse, complex, and intricate a skill. This can only be a list of *some* elements of craft in teaching literacy—not *the* elements of craft in teaching literacy. But this list would be totally meaningless as a description of teachers I have admired if I neglected to say this: love permeates their craft. Love first for the kids—not, of course, the same love they have for their own children, but an active concern for the best for each student, a hope for her growth, a trust in his intelligence, a determination to believe the best about her. Second, these teachers love reading and writing, and though most of them don't write all that often and quite some time may go by between putting one book down and picking up another, they make sure they give themselves frequent, powerful experiences that reignite their passions for literacy. And either their love for the kids or their love of reading and writing has led them to find their students' learning immensely interesting. Even problems, exhausting and frustrating though they may be, are interesting. And the kids *become* more interesting, partly to keep their teacher interested.

Naturally, the point of all this discussion of craft in teaching is the mark we make on our students. We are shaping them, in a sense, and the shape we give them is determined by the tools we use in our craft—not so much the words we say or even the curriculum we plan, but rather the environments of our classrooms. We craft that environment by our presence and work, and so in the language of our teaching actions, we write our hopes for our students.

TIME AND TEACHERS' LIVES

Often I feel like my life, my being, is chopped up by my schedule. Because I have to restart my attention every forty minutes or so, I more or less leave my identity at the door in the morning and just get through all those transitions. Sometimes, when a kid is surprised to see me at the grocery store, I'm surprised to see me there, too. But sometimes in a school day, something takes me by surprise, a boy's reminding me of my own son or a kid being suddenly hilarious or suddenly heartbroken; I look down and realize, Hey! I'm still here! I'm not really chopped up by the bells; I also have a lifeline. If I give my attention to time structures other than the class period, then I can realize myself as a person growing through time.

In a school day, I tend to develop some theme—or a small group of themes—in my conversations with students. Almost everything I say will be about, for example, just focusing on what's important and omitting everything else. Or each conference and minilesson will grow out of the one before it, and all of them will be about the careful crafting of phrases; those interactions then become the footprints of my own inquiry project across the day.

In any chunk of the school year, I have several lines along which I'm learning. First of all, I'm inquiring alongside the kids in whatever the explicit curriculum is. Second, I am always doing some kind of research, whether formally or informally, on a particular kid or group of kids, and this research never fails to inform my planning for them and for my other students as well. Third, I always have topics within literacy and teaching that I've chosen to pursue, and I put myself into learning situations relative to those topics, reading books and articles, forming study groups with other educators, attending conferences, and conducting workshops (yes, even before I'm completely sure what I'm talking about). I'm usually also looking into things that *don't* have to do with teaching, such as parenting or Spanish or carpentry or computers or Russian literature or insects, and that learning feeds my teaching almost as much as my explicitly educational inquiry.

I write about my teaching sometimes, though not as often as I should. In that writing, I assess where I am in my own growth. I force myself to be explicit about what's bugging me in my teaching, and I try to come up with concrete ways of working on those areas. I have an image of good teaching, and I hold that image in mind while I try to mold myself toward that goal. The aspects of teaching on which I'm working become lines of growth for me, projects, anchors in the future, and they carry me across oceans of bells.

I am working on these long-term projects in teaching while my students work on their long-term projects of constructing their literate lives. We all transcend the schedule because even though we are working in forty-minute bursts, we are with that time following our life's work.

12

The Extracurricular Life of an English Teacher

> When a member of a bureaucracy embarks on a course of reflective practice, allowing himself to experience confusion and uncertainty, subjecting his frames and theories to conscious criticism and change, he may increase his capacity to contribute to significant organizational learning, but he also becomes, by the same token, a danger to the stable system of rules and procedures within which he is expected to deliver his technical expertise. . . .
> —Donald Schon, *The Reflective Practitioner*

> There is a lot of pressure to teach [the] traditional way, first because it is familiar and already worked out, even if it doesn't work in class. Second, by deviating from the standard syllabus you can get known as a rebel or radical or flake, and be subjected to anything from petty harassment to firing.
> —Ira Schor and Paolo Freire, *A Pedagogy for Liberation*

The week before school began, I and eight other teachers new to the school district were given a tour, a picnic, and a talking to. We met in the high school parking lot and were immediately herded onto a school bus where, like the first kids on the bus route, we all took separate seats. How would we have decided whom to sit next to? We spent the better part of the morning bouncing violently along the rural district's dirt roads. The superintendent and high school principal sat up front by the driver, giving him directions even though he drove these roads every day of his life. We didn't really see much on the ride, peering out dusty institutional windows and dealing with the added obstruction of the dark-green seat backs, taller than my head. Districts could install these extra high seat backs in lieu of seat belts; in case of an accident the high seat backs would supposedly prevent kids from flying all over the bus. This safety measure probably seemed like a good idea, but its effect was that it was impossible to see or talk with anyone not sitting right beside you, as if you were sitting in a green rectangular box. Isolated, thinking *This is ridiculous,* feeling like children dragged to visit relatives, we got little sense of our students' lives.

We disembarked at the elementary school, where a picnic lunch had been laid out under horse chestnut trees. It was beautiful. I felt so well treated. I sat down beside the elementary school principal and we chatted. She'd heard that I knew something about writing process, that I'd done some staff development. While we ate, we talked about the importance of writing, about ways of teaching, about ways teachers might feel safe enough to try something new. I was ecstatic, sitting in a beautiful setting, having a conversation about educational ideas with someone in my own district. I wanted to spend my life here.

I got up to throw my plate away and joined a knot of high school teachers near the garbage can. They were laughing. Someone was trying to build a deck off his trailer and had funny stories to tell. We talked about where we lived, whether we had children and how old they were, where the youngest teachers had gone to college, where we had grown up, when we would get our first paycheck. It would never have occurred to me to talk about writing or learning or teaching in that conversation, though I have since seen at least two of those people present at whole language conferences. If one of us had brought up educational ideas, it would have been a faux pas, he would have seemed to be grandstanding, showing off, toadying to the administration. He would have looked ambitious—zealous. Not that I think there is anything wrong with just chatting as people, rather than as school people; I hope it's clear by now that I think it's pretty important to be a human being. But it strikes me that a conversation about education was almost unavoidable with the principal and almost impossible with the other teachers.

For some reason, we went back to the high school for the part of the day where we got the talking to. Apparently, there was a shortage of big-enough chairs at the elementary school. We sat in the choir room, as if we were going to sing, with the superintendent in the conductor's swivel stool, a music stand in front of him. One of the people whom he recognized to speak was the union president, who said it was important that we join, though she wouldn't say why since the administrators were present. I knew I would sign up, since as a member of Actors' Equity and a liberal, it seemed my duty.

The superintendent delivered the usual administrators' bad advice about avoiding discipline problems by really laying into kids with clear behavioral expectations on the first day of school, and he apparently thought it was necessary to give some pointers for ways of doing so. "One way would be, if let's say a kid is talking to his neighbor, the first time, you write his name on the board, as a warning. Then, each time he repeats the behavior, you erase one letter of his name. Some kids," he said with relish, "especially younger ones, find this particularly disconcerting, since they identify with their names and they see it as you erasing *them*."

I thought he was joking, so I laughed. No one else did. I don't think I should have.

On the surface that day was not much of an orientation to the district, but if I'd paid attention to the underlying structures at all, if I'd made meaning, I would have learned some fundamental things about what working there would be like. I should, if nothing else, have predicted it was going to be a bumpy ride. I might have seen that someone else was going to be in the driver's seat and that even that person wouldn't be choosing the route but would have someone shouting *Turn here* in his ear. I could have expected to be isolated from other teachers for reasons that from the inside of a box would seem necessary even as they were absurd. I would have known that I'd only catch glimpses of my students' real lives and then only through a glass, darkly. I could have anticipated that I would too rarely be able to have professional talks with fellow teachers and that though its tone would change drastically, my conversation with bosses would force me to clarify my beliefs about teaching. I might have seen that joining the union would be more an act of political obligation than a protection of my own interests. I should have guessed that we'd all be lined up to sing but that no music would play. Certainly, if I'd been thinking, I would have realized that erasing children's names is not a suggestion one makes lightly or hollowly, that the administration's response to unsanctioned conversations would ultimately be erasure.

In most of this book, I've been describing some of what went on inside the door of my classroom and goes on in the work of teachers I know and admire. Much of the point of these descriptions has been that our students' literacy learning cannot stop at that threshold but must be a net for catching the rest of life. Being an English teacher does not stop at the door either. Teaching literacy may be described as midwifery, cultural engineering, empowerment of the oppressed, or dozens of other fine things, but it is also a job. So now, because I hope to end this book with a discussion of how necessary it is that our teaching grow from deep roots in a hopeful vision of learning in communities, I need to address the context in which we live out that vision, schools as workplaces, as the sites of teacher learning and struggle. For me only to describe my interactions with particular students would not be a completely honest portrayal of of my days of work, since I saw any one student less than one-tenth of any day. Those of us who work within secondary school schedules have our lives with students so chopped up that when we reflect after a day's work, our conversations with kids over books or pieces of writing may sometimes feel fleeting and wispy compared with the hard and real day-long entanglement with the jobness of our jobs, dealing with bosses, worrying about paychecks. Few of us believe that teaching is only a job or even primarily one. We didn't go into this line of work for the paychecks or the bosses, and that's not what gets us up in the morning. But we too rarely discuss that other aspect of our professional lives in our professional literature, even though it must affect our work with students and certainly our own growth as learners. I do not plan to offer a master plan for school restructuring, since even if I believed in such a thing or knew of one to offer, most readers of this book would be powerless to implement it. I do want to remember some critical incidents from the last school where I worked, the place where I did all of the teaching I've written about here (when I've written about my own classroom), and to reflect on those incidents in ways I hope will help others make meaning of their own struggles, so that we all don't have to feel quite so powerless, hopeless, and alone.

My school, like all schools, was a place where a lot of conversations went on at the same time. There were the conversations between students and students, which I was often trying to control. There were the conversations among me and the other teachers, conversations between us and our administrators, me and parents, the administrators and the school board, me and the community, me and my students, of course, both inside and outside the classroom. Some of the conversations were casual exchanges in the hallways, some were more sustained during a class or a free period or a lunch, some lasted for a school year, some lasted the entire time I worked there. I was also still involved in conversations about schooling outside the building. I belonged to NCTE, did workshops and institutes at Teachers College, attended conferences where I made friends with other teachers who were trying to learn, and read a lot about teaching, reading, literature, and writing: all of these, though they never occurred inside the school walls, penetrated the building by dint of their echo in my mind.

These conversations all overlapped. When I spoke with a parent, I also continued, remembered, rehearsed, the ongoing conversations with my principal about this parent or parents in general, as well as the conversations with the other parents I'd spoken to the day before, and the conversation with this parent's son, who told me today his mother wanted to talk to me, and so on. Even though they overlapped this way, the conversations felt almost as if they were in different languages; certainly they were in different discourses. Administrator discourse is different from parent discourse is different from student discourse is different from colleague discourse; and they all, as school discourse, are different from other discourses outside the educational community. When I talked with a friend from Teachers College or a friend who taught somewhere else, she would know when I was imitating my principal's words, because they sounded different from the way we usually talked to each other. But they didn't (usually) sound (as) strange in the conversation with the principal, where I expected that language and often used it myself when it suited my purpose. If I had used that language in the faculty room, I would probably have been much despised among my colleagues. Trying to coordinate all the different discourses was like trying to organize work on the Tower of Babel.

The possibility that different people, even within one conversation, could actually be making absurdly mismatched meanings crystallized in the early fall, with my visit to the Greens. The conversation on that visit was not one conversation at all. There were roughly as many different conversations occurring as there were participants, just as there are as many different Hamlets as there are actors playing the parts and audience members listening. A teacher, an administrator, two parents, three students, each a separate line that seemed, when viewed from the top, to converge at one point and go on from there, but when viewed three-dimensionally from the side, were never in the same plane and never touched. We know it is possible to have seven readers read the same poem and come away with different meanings because they each brought something different to the reading event. Even more, especially in large communities where people do not share a coherent ongoing set of meanings or values, do our glancing encounters with each other mean differently.

Every day in fourth period, Bobby Green would put his notebook away and pack up his things fifteen minutes before the end of the period. Every day, I'd tell him to get back to work, and every day, he'd refuse. It took me a long time to figure out that locking horns with him and shoving was not that effective, so every day I got angry. Finally, I spoke to his resource room teacher, who said that Bobby got sent out or written up so often, he was obviously taking it as a sign of weakness that I wasn't ejecting him from the room. Foolishly accepting this rather simplistic interpretation as reality, I wrote up a pretty searing disciplinary referral, allowing my frustration to drive the voice of my writing to a fevered pitch.

The next day, Peter, the assistant principal, came by after lunch to tell me that after school, he and I were going on a home visit to talk with Bobby's parents.

"Can't we just call them?" I said cravenly, feeling my ears getting hot at the prospect of facing Bobby and his parents on their home turf.

Peter shook his head, then met my eyes with great seriousness. "No phone."

In the car, on the way over, Peter described the Greens' home, as if he thought I would pass out if I wasn't fully prepared for what was coming. Dogs and chickens, he said, would have made a mess in the living room, I would encounter squalor like I'd never seen. He said both parents would be home, since neither had a job. He described them, the rail thin white mother with almost a full beard, the huge African American father who mostly stared off inattentively and then responded unintelligibly. He was trying to make me laugh, and I did, lamely, glad to feel somehow superior to these people with whose son I had probably dealt incompetently.

The house was small, with green siding, broken every few feet, shattered windows, holes in the roof. If Peter hadn't stopped there, I'd have guessed it was abandoned. All was as Peter had described it, only it wasn't that funny from inside the house. Fortunately, Mrs. Green suggested we talk outside under the huge oak tree in the yard. I was relieved it was early fall, that the arctic winds and lake-effect snow of western New York wouldn't force us indoors. We sat on what appeared to be apple crates, while Bobby's siblings, Billy and Sue Ellen, sat on the grass within earshot. Bobby wasn't around, for which I was glad and ashamed to be glad.

Peter asked me to explain what was going on in my class. "The way I teach," I began, "I think Bobby can get better at writing by writing and get better at reading by reading, so I give the class lots of time to write. They can choose what to write about and how to write it, but they have to write when it's writing time, or else they won't learn. Lots of times, Bobby gets tired of writing a long time before the bell rings, he refuses to get back to work when I ask him to, and then he causes a disruption and keeps other kids from working. And what starts out as a really little thing becomes a big deal."

Mrs. Green nodded gravely; Mr. Green looked off absently. Both looked like they were the adolescents called into the principal's office. This seemed wrong to me: I wanted us to collaborate to make things better, for Bobby, for me, for the class, but they seemed to see the conversation as something they had to sit and take. I couldn't help seeing in this moment their own histories with schools, their experiences of reprimands, rushing into the present and defining it. I wanted to find a way to talk to them about their son, rather than confront them about their problem. It occurred to me that I might stop talking and start asking them questions about their interactions with Bobby, let them contribute to the conversation rather than passively receive what I was telling them. But Peter was there, and I knew he would have no patience with what he'd see as a divergence from the straight pursuit of our objective, and anyway, while all this was going through my mind, he leapt in.

"What Mr. Bomer's saying is that Bobby has to be more respectful, more cooperative, and less disruptive in class. It's really as simple as that. Now, I've spoken to him about this, and not just in Mr. Bomer's class, but in several classes, in fact *most* of his classes over the past few years. He's going to be going into the high school next year, he's already fourteen years old, and it's time he got his temper under control, or else it's just going to keep causing him problems."

The Greens looked almost relieved at Peter's imperative clarity. He was fulfilling their expectations, so they figured this would be over soon. Peter turned his thick glasses back to me, clearly expecting me to pick up the ball and run with it. But I had no idea what to say now, Peter had so reduced the matter to *Bobby has to stop being bad*. For me to make it more complicated again would probably seem dense not only to Peter but also to the Greens, whose expectations for how this conversation would go had now been perfectly fulfilled. The whole thing was seeming pointless to me anyway. What could they do about what this fourteen-year-old, angry, defiant kid did in a building they never liked or understood? My own son wasn't even two yet, and I hadn't any idea how to keep him from pitching temper tantrums at day-care. I was deflated. It was at just this moment that the still-inflated Peter, in a sudden seizure of creativity, said to me, "Mr. Bomer, why don't we role-play a little bit, so that Mr. and Mrs. Green can understand the situation."

I gazed at him, unable to grasp his meaning.

"You be you, and I'll be Bobby. Okay, it's fifteen minutes before the end of fourth period." Here, he bent down to pick up a pen and notepad he had brought with him for what reason I didn't know, "and I'm putting my things away." He plopped the pen on the notepad and folded his hands on top.

Why was he doing this? Did he always do this with parents, or was it because I had been an actor and he thought I'd be good in the scene? People always assume actors love to do these little improvs, when in fact more people become actors because they like scripts, like knowing exactly what to say next. I could tell I was supposed to be a team player here, Peter and I against the Greens, but I had no idea what Peter was up to. I had to play along though, since I couldn't very well refuse the AP in front of parents.

"Okay," I sighed. "Bobby, get back to work."

"No! I'm finished!" Peter was way overacting. At this point, Mrs. Green, Mr. Green, Sue Ellen, and Billy all became hysterical, belly-laughing, slapping each other's arms and legs, the girls rolling on the grass, holding their stomachs.

"Bobby," I nobly, numbly, went on with the improv, "there are still fifteen minutes left in the period. Get back to work, now."

"No! You're just picking on me. Look at Steve, he's not working, and you're not yelling at him. You're just picking on me." Peter was so loud, I expected neighbors for miles around to join us for the *commedia*. Mrs. Green shrieked through her laughter, "That's Bobby! That's Bobby! Yeah!" Billy and Sue Ellen chimed in, "Yep, that's him!" Mr. Green was shouting too, but I couldn't understand what he said.

I went on, because Peter's face was so earnest. "Bobby, if you don't think I'm being fair, we can talk about that after school. Right now, I just need you to get writing." I tried to turn to the Greens, to break the theatrical spell, to tell them that this was the kind of thing that happened most days in class. But Peter, caught up in the improv, would not let it go.

"No!" he shouted. "You're just picking on me because I'm black!"

What? This had never happened in my class, and neither I nor Bobby had never said anything about race at all. Maybe it had been somehow at the heart of the issue, but it was not something I could have anticipated coming out in *this* way, out of *Peter's* mouth, with Bobby's black father still giggling.

I tried to stop again, but Peter was still churning. "Everybody always picks on me, and that's what you're doing now. What about Steve, what about Bev, what about Sue Ellen?"

Sue Ellen screamed at the mention of her name, right here on the stage.

"I'm going to have my father come up here and beat you up!"

Mr. Green screamed.

It went on for a while like this, me trying to stop but Peter forcing me to continue our little performance. The comment about race seemed to have gone right by the Greens, because they laughed louder and louder every time Peter spoke as Bobby. Here was the high school assistant principal, one of the most powerful people in the community, and he was *doing Bobby!*

When we got back to the car, Peter said, "I don't know. *Maybe* we got through to them."

I rather doubted it. It seemed to me that each participant in the conversation defined it so differently from the others that we might as well have been on different continents. Nothing "got through." People don't "get through" to each other. Over time, in conversation, people collaboratively construct some shared assumptions. We had no time and no conversation, either with each other or the Greens. I was assuming, from conversations I'd had in other places and at other times, that I was there to share some information with Bobby's parents and to get some information from them that might help both of us in our later conversations with Bobby. Peter was perhaps there to get right to the bottom line: he wanted Bobby fixed, so he wouldn't take up so much of Peter's time, and he wanted to use my class as an example while bringing in his own issues about Bobby, perhaps gleaned from conversations with other teachers. Maybe the Greens were remembering their own experiences of being in trouble, of conversations in which they were blamed for events beyond their control. Apparently, their definition of the conversation changed, though, leaving them in the position of an audience watching a television comedy. Same sphere of air, same sound waves, several simultaneous but very different conversations.

Looking back on it, I think the conversation among Peter, the parents Green, the Green kids, and me was not only meaningfully different for each of us, but systematically, almost calculatedly different, doomed from the outset by the resolution of each of us not to be like the others. Most certainly, Peter was trying to be unlike the Greens; they were different from him, and that's what all that rehearsal in the car was about. (Peter may have thought I was "like" him, by fiat, if nothing else.) The Greens certainly had no aspirations to be like Peter or me. I was resistant to everyone else's sense of what was going on and in despair over ever changing their predefinitions. What I mean is, not only were we understanding the same conversation differently, we were pushing against each other in order to make the conversation mean something to us each on terms we could recognize as ours. Why else would I be writing about the visit here but to reclaim its meaning against those of Peter and the Greens?

Most people in the school community, it seemed, expended a lot of energy keeping such difficult, disorienting, absurd nonconversations to a minimum. Teachers colluded in keeping at arm's length any areas where they might not easily understand each other. Most of us had no idea about what went on in the classroom next door, except when that class watched a film or got really noisy, since no one really talked about her teaching. Usually, if someone told a story around the lunch table about his classroom, it was one with a lot of human interest rather than professional interest: dramas of flagrant disrespect, fights, love affairs, that sort of thing, the type of incident that might be in a movie about teaching made for a general audience. Sure, people would say *what* they were "teaching"—*Twelfth Night,* sine and cosine, Reconstruction—but no one ever discussed the real interactions with kids where the teacher was trying to help the students learn. I didn't either, except when someone asked.

As time went on, however, people asked more and more. Student writing in our class magazines and the display cases, as well as the student-teacher grapevine, advertised to people that something strange was going on in 211. Coaches, math teachers, and counselors asked me, "Is all students do in your class write about their lives? Don't you teach anything?" Not that they didn't like the kids' work; they did. But they couldn't imagine a class in school where that work was produced. I couldn't answer their questions without explaining why we were doing "that" in my classes, which meant I had to explain some of my philosophy of learning. These explanations usually met with just "hmm," inflected in ways that revealed everything from impressed interest to skepticism to bald contempt. When I invited people to stop by during class, they seemed embarrassed, almost frightened, as if I'd asked them to watch me have sex.

The other English teachers took to referring to my teaching as "your program," a way of objectifying or commodifying my whole approach to student learning, a way of saying, *Keep that thing you do over there while we stay right here and teach real English.* They too liked what my students were writing, but they did not want, at least at first, to see my teaching as being in the same conversation as theirs. They would watch it with interest, but from a distance; they would not become engaged with it.

During that first year, it was the English department's turn to write a new curriculum. In order to avoid conflicts (and to eliminate the possibility that we would ever discuss what we were trying to *do* in English), the department chair simply asked everyone to write down what they were already doing, so that the "new" curriculum would allow everyone to keep doing it. I didn't fight it, of course, since if it came down to a vote, I'd be the one who would have to get rid of "my program." I thought that getting writing and reading workshop into an official document would protect me from people insisting I teach from vocabulary builders, Warriner's, or a list of novels.

What I did not realize was that whatever the curriculum document said, the school community had, through its sustained conversation over the years, defined English class with an *assumed* curriculum more real than the one written down. When Dr. Peck, the superintendent, asked me about my class, I described the reading-writing workshops, and he said "That's fine, as long as you're still covering the district's curriculum." I replied that that *was* the curriculum, to which he responded, "Well, surely we have an *English* curriculum in this district." He made himself a note, and I knew trouble lurked.

Another English teacher moved her son to our school from the one in the town where they lived, because she said, she wanted him to have the benefit of "my program." In December, after we'd gotten notebooks started, done two genre studies, and responded frequently to short texts, she came to me concerned that her son was still reading science fiction, just as avidly as before. I told her I didn't see the problem. "But," she said, "I really think . . . what I really want to know is . . . when you're going to get to *reading*." My answer, that the work he was doing—frequently rereading his notebook; critically reading his own drafts and those of his peers; reading poetry and memoir as a maker of poems and memoir; and maintaining his own independent reading life—was all reading and really important in his growth as a reader, did not satisfy her. To her, if I wasn't assigning books, telling them what the books meant, and giving tests, I wasn't doing reading. This from one of the few people who had actually read the curriculum.

Especially the first year, before the word was out about my class, it was also hard for my students to accept that we were doing the right kind of English in our classes. I would read other teachers' accounts of their students' unbridled joy at being given the freedom to think for themselves, and I'd wonder, What the hell is wrong with these kids? Then, remembering it does no good to blame the students, I would fail to reframe the question entirely but would substitute one term, What the hell is wrong with *me*? Many of my students would drag their feet into my class and ask in exhausted voices what we were going to do today. I'd say, "Same thing as yesterday, and the day before, and October first, and September fifteenth, and almost every other day. I'm going to talk to you for a minute, and then you're going to work on your projects."

"Oh, gaaaaaaawd," they'd say. "All we ever do is write, write, write, read, read, read. Aren't we ever going to do any *English?*"

"Do you write in some other language?" I'd ask, with some bite after a few months of this ungrateful whining.

"No—you know what I mean—like verbs and stuff," they'd say.

"I think you learn that stuff best by writing," I'd say. "If you want to confer today about your verbs, let's do it."

By then they would have stopped listening.

I had to give a final exam at the end of the year, for the simple and simpleminded reason that if I didn't, there would be nowhere else for the kids to go during the two hours scheduled for the test. I decided to have the kids review their folders and answer two or three questions about what they saw there, like, Which piece do you think you could still work on? What would you do and why? or From which piece did you learn the most about writing? What is it you learned? or In which piece of your own writing can you see the greatest influence of literature you've read? Explain. Toward the middle of June, one of my sophomores, Pam, who had entered the class at the beginning of the year showing no understanding of the idea that one sentence should share some shred of common topic with the sentence before but who had grown probably more than any other student in the class, entered the room shouting, "We're not going to have a final in here, are we? I don't see how we could; we didn't *learn* anything!"

Unlike the young children I've seen when I've consulted in elementary schools, adolescents are full participants in the discourse community that shares "commonsense" assumptions about learning and literacy, and as they become empowered, they will sometimes use that power to hammer the very teacher who empowers them. They've been in school long enough to know what to expect, and they don't always love to have their expectations thwarted, especially since if they don't know exactly what is expected of them, they run the risk of messing up and looking stupid in front of their friends, developmentally their vision of hell. As they try on adult roles, moreover, they will test out political theories, including some that oppose our own. They may, as some adults do, desire a powerful ruler to tell the group what to do and eliminate the necessity for messy and difficult negotiations. My students often gave me advice about teaching, using the most dictatorial teachers in the building as models. All of these conversations were basically friendly chats, with the kids usually gently exasperated over their incorrigible teacher. When I was researching in a suburban district two years later, however, Nathan, a junior William F. Buckley, Jr., developed in a letter what a lot of my students just didn't have the nerve to say, as long as I was grading them:

> First, I feel you have a tendency to dig too deeply into many things. You often ask not only what our reactions are, but why we have those reactions. You see the journal, in particular, as a way of exploring ourselves, you believe it should be the key to unlocking our deepest inner characteristics. What you forget, I think, is that this is ENGLISH class, not Psychology 101. The purpose of English class is to give us instruction, practise, experience, etc. in reading and writing insofar as that instruction, etc. serves to improve either the intellectual base from which we operate, or our method and skill used in expressing ourselves. I don't think that our feelings, as such, are relevant. I don't

think that (in English class) where our reactions come from is as important as how they are expressed and how persuasive and sophisticated they are. Your method is a very radical approach, it is a very sensitive approach, but I would argue, too sensitive.

So, in short, I think that English is a practical class. It should expand our basic knowledge of literature; we should read a lot of books everyone else reads, so as to broaden the common experience of Americans. We should work on our grammar and vocabulary, etc. to improve our eloquence and our persuasiveness. The basic point of English class is to allow us to communicate and relate to others, not to ourselves. Reflection is fine, but it has no place in an English class.

In addition, speaking only for myself, I think our personalities are quite different. For whatever reasons, our experiences, etc. seem to have created two very different people. I think you seem to be a very liberal, open-minded person, while I am a very conservative, stubborn, and old-fashioned person. I think you are much more daring in making your personality obvious. Most teachers dress conservatively, act conservatively, etc. simply because a personality can get in the way of teaching. Many teachers just try to be, or perhaps they are, very "typical Americans."

We are very used to having our teacher reign over us and tell us what to do. This system, though much maligned, is ingrained in us to such an extent that we are bound to see any change as an intrusion.

These were the days I got speeding tickets. The other struggles, the ones with teachers, administrators, parents, those I had expected and could understand as power negotiations or fear of change. Sure, they all gave me headaches like I'd never had before, but it was the headstrong resistance of students that sent my spirits spiraling like a burning plane. Teaching is so void of meaningful feedback that it's almost impossible to know how you're doing. Colleagues never saw me teach, and if they had, it would have been so different from the way they did that it would only have reinforced the "your program" syndrome. Administrators were similarly stymied about what to say, usually reporting to me that a couple of students were whispering in the back and I didn't catch them or saying that they'd like to observe sometime when I was really *teaching*. Their scant suggestions were not exactly life changing: "That minilesson would have been really fantastic if you had used colored chalk." Or, "When you read aloud, it's a good idea to dipstick every once in a while to make sure the kids are getting it." Most clearly, the comments about my teaching from the other adults in the building were inextricable from the ideological battlegrounds outside my classroom door. For all the talk about evaluation in schools, of teachers and students, there is rarely anything like good-faith reflection on the quality of what's happening in the moment-to-moment transactions of teaching and learning. I depended on my students to be a kind of mirror, reflecting my teaching back to me, so that I could evaluate myself. If my students were using writing to think, to construct projects they cared about, to affect the people in their world, then I was teaching writing well. If they cared about reading something, if they knew how to enlist the support of other readers, if they read in ways that allowed them to reflect critically on their own lives, then I was teaching reading well. In this way, my evaluation of students was all I needed to evaluate my teaching. They were my mirror, but sometimes I'd check myself there, neatly dressed and looking fine, and my reflection would open its mouth and say into my face, You've put on all the wrong clothes, and your hair is the wrong color. I felt like a failure.

I can see now that I only felt like a failure because of how I was defining success. Taking my cue from the very same professional literature and conference presentations that had helped me form my vision of my classroom in the first place, I had decided that if I was doing the "right" thing as a teacher, my students would always be smiling. Really, though, I had been pushing my kids to think critically, which unfortunately meant they were also free to think critically about *me,* a bonus I hadn't counted on. The very nature of teaching, moreover, makes us forever vulnerable to feelings of failure, even to real failure, because as we are trying to change people's minds, we have to hope. We don't get everything we hope for because the people we teach are free moral agents and they can choose to reject what we offer them. If it weren't so, we would be nothing but thought police. None of that makes the struggle less worthwhile. We experience failure sometimes, however much we don't like to talk about it; we continually work to change people's minds, both our students' and others'; and still, against our cynical culture's grain as it may be, we hope. That's what we do; we're teachers.

Another layer of the conversation, another layer of struggle: I wasn't the only educator in my district who hoped to change people's minds. The superintendent also had a reform mission, and since he had control of the money, he had the power to provide workshops and to require teachers to attend them. At first, most of us thought we were saying the same things, since educational reforms hadn't often visited that district in the last few decades. He didn't see the difference between our visions of learning either, since to him writing process was a subset of mastery learning, as were assertive discipline, elements of instruction, effective schools, strategic planning, and whole language. (He formed a committee of interested elementary school teachers to "look into" whole language, all of whom left the district as soon as they could get other jobs.) He demurred for a long time about even telling anyone what mastery learning was, except to murmur the axiom that "all children can learn, and learn well," which was hard to argue with. Finally, at the end of my first year in the district, he distributed copies of two articles with accompanying instructions that everyone come to the next faculty meeting ready to discuss them.

Believing that we were being invited to behave professionally, I and a few of my English teacher friends met in my classroom to discuss the articles and what they might have to say about our discipline. I wasn't even the first to criticize. Someone said that they couldn't imagine, as the articles suggested, insisting that students master the first act of *Macbeth* before moving on to Act 2. Then I said that since language was a whole system, you couldn't break it into subunits and require mastery of them, one at a time, in a carefully planned sequence, and still use language authentically. People agreed, in certain ways and with certain reservations, and we proceeded to discuss whole language, without ever really naming it, and for the first time, we had a good conversation about literacy education, leaving the articles far behind. We left that meeting feeling like colleagues, rejuvenated and glad to be educators.

The next day, we entered the chorus room together for the faculty meeting, feeling prepared and professional. None of the other departments had met about the articles, so all day we'd been teasing everyone about how much more responsible we were. When the principal finally finished all the announcements, which should have been put into a memo, and asked for responses to the article, most of the faculty swiveled in their seats on the risers toward us. The choir was not going to sing; it was time for a solo. Tina, the department chair, nudged me, but I ignored her, this being my first year in the district and all. Seeing that I would not be moved, she finally spoke, a little apologetically.

"I guess the reason everyone's looking at us is because we met as a department yesterday and talked about this, and it seems to us that what he's talking about in these articles is chopping things up and teaching it one bit at a time and then testing to see if the kids got it, and then reteaching the ones who didn't, and then testing again, and on and on until everyone gets it. And first of all, it seems like it would be very time-consuming, and second of all, we just don't think you can teach English this way. You can't say this comes first and you have to get that before you learn the next thing. We really already reteach the same things every year, and with every book or whatever. So we don't think it works with our discipline. That's all." She shrank back into her seat.

Then the math department chair spoke up and said that the same was true for math. He wanted to do more of what the state was requiring with creative thinking and problem solving, and it seemed to him that mastery learning would force him to stay with the old-fashioned mathematics instruction he'd always done. He was confused, he said, about these mixed signals.

Then a science teacher asked whatever happened to the scientific method of discovery, which he couldn't reconcile with this concept of mastery, and pretty soon most of the departments had spoken up to say that learning in their disciplines didn't fit with this administrative management plan. I had never realized that many people on this faculty knew about the constructivist, holistic views of their disciplines. The atmosphere was heady with the excitement of so many conversations about ideas, which had always before taken place at meetings or conferences away from school, coming together into what might have been the beginnings of a shared district philosophy of education. Of course, many people's motivation must have been simply to resist change, but I was still hopeful that they might begin to listen to their own rhetoric and thankful for the opening to discuss something of substance in education.

Apparently, this was not the discussion about the articles the principal had been charged to lead. This was an unacceptable conversation. He stopped recognizing teachers to speak and said, uncomfortably (he would be gone from the district within weeks), "The superintendent believes in this program, and this is the direction the district is going. People who teach in this district will teach this way."

At this point a significant number of the heads on the risers turned my way. I suppose it was because I had engaged in so many arguments with so many of them, had, with "my program," staked a philosophical ground, had made my professional conversation public. I decided, for better or worse, tenure or no tenure, to speak.

"Don't you think," I said, "that this is a little undemocratic? If we're going to have a district philosophy of instruction, shouldn't the people who instruct be included in the conversation about what that philosophy is?"

The principal looked at me incredulous. "It's very democratic. The people of the district elect a school board. The school board hires the superintendent. The superintendent directs instructional policy. The teachers carry out that policy if they're going to teach in this district. That's democracy."

I had no argument for this. It was clear that we had participated in very different conversations about democratic education and that our respective adherence to those other conversations had made this one impossible. I did say, more to the other teachers there than to the principal, that the teaching described in these articles was, to my way of thinking, inharmonious with learning—and so wasn't really teaching at all. I said I would never teach that way, because it was too important to me to be thinking and learning, in and out of my classroom, to let someone else tell me what to believe and how to carry it out.

The next morning, the superintendent called me to his office during my free period. He puzzled me with the statement that though he could tolerate dissent, he couldn't tolerate my trying to incite trouble among the faculty. I assured him that I wasn't interested in inciting trouble, although I *was* interested in education and in being able to speak my mind now and then. He was unsatisfied, as I expected.

Over the next year, new battles waited for me, it seemed like every day. Though they never criticized my teaching directly in observation reports, Peter, now the acting principal, Jean, the new department chair after Tina abandoned ship, and the superintendent always managed to find out from a student or a parent something to call me in about. Toni Morrison's *The Bluest Eye* had two pages that were too sexual for a junior honors class. The language in Amiri Baraka's "School" was too foul for seniors. A student's poem about shooting the finger being a too-common expression of hatred around the school was an inappropriate topic for the discussion that ensued when she shared it with the class. Parents were worried that the writers notebooks were an invasion of their privacy if their kids wrote about things that were going on at home. My personnel file was getting fatter. I didn't need to be J. Edgar Hoover to figure out what was happening. By December, Peter had enough ammunition to write me a "counseling letter," seven single-spaced pages long, listing my infractions and ending with the recommendation that I seek professional help for my problem with hostility toward authority. Just to prove his point, I went to him in his office and asked if the person who had written this very helpful letter was the same person who, in 1970, had used *Rules for Radicals* as required reading in his senior government class, saying as he distributed the books that the word *motherfucker* was optional reading.

I was far from the only person hounded in those months, and, compared to some, my troubles were mild. I at least did not have to hire a lawyer, and I was not fired. Systematically, in the name of district cohesion, teachers were stripped of autonomy and thus of purpose in their work with students. In the name of curriculum, the administration attempted to make every classroom look like every other. Every teacher's desk was piled high with binders articulating objectives, units, formative and summative examinations, and other papers no one read, leaving formerly strong-willed educators dazed and baffled. Eventually many of my colleagues took to staying as much as possible behind their desks, the piles a wall between them and their students. Students' faces were erased. Teachers' names were erased. Students' names, if they ever had been written, were erased. This was not why I went into teaching. I left to avoid erasure.

During the two years that followed, the teachers from this district who used to attend conferences and workshops in the area seemed to vanish. They certainly never came to any of my workshops. I heard that the superintendent, having thoroughly appropriated and controlled their professional conversations, was not allowing any teacher to attend any staff development outside the district.

When I arrived at my job in western New York, I did not really have beliefs about teaching. I had ideas, with which I had experimented in my previous teaching jobs. I had theories, which I had learned in graduate school and from my own reading. But I had no beliefs. Because I had never had to choose. If I had never met with resistance, if the trouble had been any less intense, I would never have believed as I do now in the principles I've tried to illustrate and express in this book. I wasn't free to choose until I was faced with an unresolvable tension. Maxine Greene calls this tension the dialectic of freedom, saying, "It's the tension between the desire to be and the reality. The tension cannot be resolved; there is no nirvana resolution. I have to be awake to the unresolved. . . . It is in the unease that we find freedom because it causes us to make choices." It was the struggle that felt like oppression that gave me the freedom and the courage to choose and to act.

Teaching is action, and beliefs about teaching carry with them a vision of what that action should look like. Whenever we have a vision, there are bound to be times when reality falls short of our hopes. When those failed visions are of ourselves doing our work in a certain way, a way we have chosen, we are bound to have feelings of failure. When I was teaching in western New York, I felt like a failure often, and when I think back on those years, I still get twinges of regret, along with the anger. Driving home from school, now as then, I reflect on my teaching and think, It could have been better. If only I had . . . . Similarly, thinking back on the political work of being a school employee, I say, If only I had . . . . Too often, I push back those thoughts, afraid of the damage they might do to my ego. We Americans don't like regrets. But I really believe that meditating into the feeling of failure is what keeps me growing and learning, keeps me reformulating my past so that I can now outgrow myself as I move toward the future. After all, my perception of failure is only the distance between what I was able to do at a given time and my vision of how my world might be. I'm not going to let my vision go just to ease the occasional pain of disappointment.

That vision emerged out of a conversation, a social journey of learning. For me, that conversation was with friends at the Teachers College Writing Project, with people I met at conferences, in my reading of professional literature, and in my talking about my classroom in workshops. It helped to be engaged with the profession, with ideas about literacy learning that were free of the political strait-jacket my school imposed on itself. We all need long-term associations with people to whom we feel somehow accountable for our learning and our teaching. We need those people's voices echoing in our heads as we teach. It's the continuing conversation we have across years, across jobs, across administrative regimes, that defines us as teachers, that makes us a single solid person across time rather than a liquid one that takes the shape of its current container. Allegiance to the conversations that matter most to us is the essence of faith, the spine of dignity, the only definition we can give our selves.

It is the durability of some conversation or other, the continuance of a particular dialogue or inquiry across time, that allows us to say we "stand" for something while not standing still, to believe in something without hardening our ideologies. How permanent are our conversations? How much is our commitment only to this moment's conversation?

What we do as literacy educators is too important for us not to have a point of view about it, some vision we learn from each other and help each other sustain. Think of what we might do, if we only have a vision. We might help the students we teach make meaning of the disjointed fragments of experience, to question the givens they are handed by society, to imagine how their lives might be otherwise, and to use language to form their thoughts and to take action in the world. Why would we settle for a lesser vision than that? Why would we let that vision go?

TIME FOR MEANING

Like most people, I guess, I have lived a life with many disruptions. I've moved a lot, been married and divorced, had my kids with me and away from me, changed careers, watched my family of origin change its structure. As a teacher, I've worked in urban and rural districts, taught in my own classroom and alongside other teachers in theirs. I've tried to ride out changes in district philosophies and new scheduling plans and assigned staff development and shifts in my own thinking. And through all that, I've had these bells going off every few minutes of my workday. It has not always been easy for me, as a teacher or as a person, to rock with all those changes and still maintain my sense of who I am. When the world changes over and over again, it's easiest just to mold myself with each new world.

But a few things in my mind stay my course, and keep me feeling like me. There are these words: justice, freedom, authenticity. There is the value I learned (and continue to try to understand) from the Iroquois—to make decisions based on what will benefit the seventh generation to come. There is Dewey's idea that we create schools that reflect the kind of society we want for our children's children. There are William James's words: "The greatest use of life is to spend it for something that will outlast it." And there is the concept of integrity.

I use the word *integrity* in the sense it derives from having the same root as *integer* or *integral*, meaning a unified whole, of one piece. I do not mean that I just *possess* integrity, like I possess my stereo, but rather that it's a concept I strive for. I want always to recognize the guy I accidentally catch a glimpse of in the mirror as myself. Robert Grudin writes, in *Time and the Art of Living*, that

> integrity is an affirmation of self in a world where the defining outline of the individual often seems to be no more than a transparent and absorbent membrane between impersonal inner and outer forces. . . . The person of integrity is a continuous person, for whom the present is a point on a line drawn out of memory and into the willed future, rather

223

than an unpredicted and unwieldy configuration which seems to operate under its own laws. (pp. 48, 51)

But integrity is rooted not so much in individual character as in our stable membership in some communities' conversations. We each know who we are because of the depth and tenure of our dialogue with those who are most important to us. Our learning communities center us in times when we would otherwise lose ourselves.

If we hold on to our personal sense of self, we are less likely patsies for every publisher's or consultant's gimmick. We know who we are. We know who we have been. We know who we want to become. Our present moments are precious but unintimidating, because we can connect them with many moments from our past and imagine how they will lead to other moments in the future. We have to give generously our concentration to this continuum of ourselves through time, for that's what makes our lives meaningful. We've spent enough time with a diminished sense of our work, funneling unimportant trivia into disinterested ears. Now it's time for authenticity, time for memory, time for craft, time for democracy, time for meaning.

REFERENCES

AMMONS, A. R. A Poem Is a Walk. In *Claims for Poetry*, edited by Donald Hall. Ann Arbor: University of Michigan Press, 1982.

ANGELOU, MAYA. *I Know Why the Caged Bird Sings*. New York: Random House, 1969.

APPLEBEE, ARTHUR. *Tradition and Reform in the Teaching of English*. Urbana, IL: National Council of Teachers of English, 1974.

————. Rethinking the Teaching of Literature. Presentation at the Annual Convention of the National Council of Teachers of English, November 1989, Baltimore, Maryland.

ATWELL, NANCIE. *In the Middle: Writing, Reading, and Learning with Adolescents*. Portsmouth NH: Boynton/Cook, 1987.

BAKHTIN, M. M. *Speech Genres and Other Late Essays*. Edited by Caryl Emerson and Michael Holquist. Translated by Vern McGee. Austin: University of Texas Press, 1986.

BARTHOLOMAE, DAVID, and ANTHONY PETROSKY. *Facts, Artifacts, and Counterfacts: Theory and Method for a Reading and Writing Course*. Portsmouth, NH: Boynton/Cook, 1986.

BATESON, MARY CATHERINE. *Composing a Life*. New York: Atlantic Monthly Press, 1989.

BELANOFF, PAT, and MARCIA DICKSON, eds. *Portfolios: Process and Product*. Portsmouth, NH: Boynton/Cook, 1991.

BERG, STEPHEN, ed. *In Praise of What Persists*. New York: Harper and Row, 1983.

BLEICH, DAVID. *The Double Perspective: Language, Literacy, and Social Relations*. New York: Oxford University Press, 1988.

————. *Readings and Feelings*. Urbana, IL: National Council of Teachers of English, 1975.

————. *Subjective Criticism*. Baltimore, MD: Johns Hopkins University Press, 1978.

BLOOM, BENJAMIN, et al. *The Taxonomy of Educational Objectives: The Cognitive Domain*. London: Longman, 1956.

BROOKE, ROBERT E. *Writing and Sense of Self: Identity Negotiation in Writing Workshops.* Urbana, IL: National Council of Teachers of English, 1991.

BRUNER, JEROME. *Actual Minds, Possible Worlds.* Cambridge, MA: Harvard University Press, 1986.

CALKINS, LUCY. *The Art of Teaching Writing.* New ed. Portsmouth, NH: Heinemann, 1994.

CALKINS, LUCY, with SHELLEY HARWAYNE. *Living Between the Lines.* Portsmouth, NH: Heinemann, 1990.

CLIFTON, LUCILLE. Homage to My Hips. In *Contemporary American Poetry*, 4th ed., edited by A. Poulin, 81. Boston: Houghton Mifflin, 1985.

COLES, ROBERT. *The Call of Stories: Teaching and the Moral Imagination.* Boston: Houghton Mifflin, 1989.

COPE, BILL, and MARY KALANTZIS, eds. *The Powers of Literacy: A Genre Approach to Teaching Writing.* Pittsburgh, PA: University of Pittsburgh Press, 1993.

CORMIER, ROBERT. Guess What: I Almost Kissed My Father Goodnight. In *8+1.* New York: Bantam, 1982.

CREMIN, LAWRENCE. *The Transformation of the School: Progressivism in American Education, 1876–1957.* New York: Knopf, 1961.

DARLING-HAMMOND, LINDA. The Implications of Testing Policy for Quality and Education. *Phi Delta Kappan* (November 1991): 220–24.

DEWEY, JOHN. *Democracy and Education: An Introduction to the Philosophy of Education.* New York: Free Press (Macmillan): 1966.

DILLARD, ANNIE. *The Writing Life.* New York: HarperCollins, 1989.

EDELSKY, CAROL. *With Literacy and Justice for All.* London: Falmer Press, 1991.

ELBOW, PETER. *Writing with Power.* New York: Oxford University Press, 1981.

————. Reflections on Academic Discourse: How It Relates to Freshmen and Colleagues. *College English* 53 (1991): 135–55.

EMIG, JANET. *The Composing Processes of Twelfth Graders.* Urbana, IL: National Council of Teachers of English, 1964.

————. *The Web of Meaning: Essays on Writing, Teaching, Learning, and Thinking.* Edited by Dixie Goswami and Maureen Butler. Portsmouth, NH: Boynton/Cook, 1983.

EPSTEIN, DANIEL MARK. Miami. In *The Morrow Anthology of Younger Poets,* edited by Dave Smith. New York: William Morrow, 1985.

FULWILER, TOBY, ed. *The Journal Book.* Portsmouth, NH: Boynton/Cook, 1987.

FREIRE, PAOLO, and DONALDO MACEDO. *Literacy: Reading the Word and the World.* Granby, MA: Bergin and Garvey, 1987.

GALLO, DONALD, ed. *Sixteen: Short Stories by Outstanding Writers for Young Adults.* New York: Dell, 1984.

GARDNER, JOHN. *The Art of Fiction: Notes on Craft for Young Writers.* New York: Knopf, 1983.

GHISELIN, BREWSTER, ed. *The Creative Process.* New York: New American Library, 1952.

GLAZER, SUSAN M., and CAROL S. BROWN. *Portfolios and Beyond: Collaborative Assessment in Reading and Writing.* Norwood, MA: Christopher-Gordon, 1993.

GOLDBERG, NATALIE. *Writing Down the Bones: Freeing the Writer Within.* Boston: Shambhala, 1986.

GOODMAN, YETTA. Kidwatching: Observing Children in the Classroom. In *Observing the Language Learner,* edited by A. Jaggar and T. Smith-Burke, 9–19. Newark, DE: International Reading Association, 1985.

GRAVES, DONALD. *Writing: Teachers and Children at Work.* Portsmouth, NH: Heinemann, 1983.

GRAVES, DONALD, and BONNIE S. SUNSTEIN, eds. *Portfolio Portraits.* Portsmouth, NH: Heinemann, 1992.

GREENE, MAXINE. *The Dialectic of Freedom.* New York: Teachers College Press, 1990.

GRUDIN, ROBERT. *Time and the Art of Living.* New York: Ticknor and Fields, 1982.

HAMPEL, ROBERT L. *The Last Little Citadel: American High Schools Since 1940.* Boston: Houghton Mifflin, 1986.

HARSTE, JEROME, KATHY G. SHORT, and CAROLYN BURKE. *Creating Classrooms for Authors.* Portsmouth, NH: Heinemann, 1989.

HEARD, GEORGIA. *For the Good of the Earth and Sun.* Portsmouth, NH: Heinemann, 1989.

———. Living Like a Poet. *The New Advocate 6* (1993)115–22.

HILL, CLIFFORD. Testing and Assessment: An Ecological Approach. Inaugural lecture as Arthur I. Gates Professor in Language and Education, April 2, 1992, Teachers College, Columbia University, New York, New York.

HIRSCH, EDWARD. A Photograph Ripped in Half. In *The Morrow Anthology of Younger Poets,* edited by Dave Smith. New York: William Morrow, 1985.

HISS, TONY. *The Experience of Place.* New York: Knopf, 1990.

ISER, WOLFGANG. *The Act of Reading: A Theory of Aesthetic Response.* Baltimore, MD: Johns Hopkins University Press, 1978.

KERMODE, FRANK. *The Genesis of Secrecy: On the Interpretation of Narrative.* Cambridge, MA: Harvard University Press, 1979.

LOFTY, JOHN S. *Time to Write: The Influence of Time and Culture on Learning to Write.* Albany: State University of New York Press, 1992.

MADAUS, GEORGE F. Test Scores as Administrative Mechanisms in Educational Policy. *Phi Delta Kappan* (May 1985): 611–17.

MAYHER, JOHN S. *Uncommon Sense: Theoretical Practice in Language Education.* Portsmouth, NH: Boynton/Cook, 1990.

MEDINA, NOE, and D. MONTY NEILL. *Fallout from the Testing Explosion: How 100 Million Standardized Exams Undermine Equity and Excellence in America's Public Schools.* Cambridge, MA: Fairtest, 1988.

MEEK, MARGARET. *How Texts Teach What Readers Learn.* Gloucester, UK: Thimble Press, 1988.

MILLER, ARTHUR. *Timebends: A Life.* New York: Harper and Row, 1987.

MOFFETT, JAMES, with PHYLLIS TASHLIK. *Active Voices II: A Writer's Reader (Grades 7–9)*. Portsmouth, NH: Boynton/Cook, 1987.

MOONEY, MARGARET. *Reading to, with, and by Children*. Katonah, NY: Richard C. Owen, 1990.

MURRAY, DONALD M. *Expecting the Unexpected: Teaching Myself—and Others—to Read and Write*. Portsmouth, NH: Boynton/Cook, 1989.

———. Presentation at Teachers College Writing Project, November 7, 1991, New York, New York.

———. *Shoptalk: Learning to Write with Writers*. Portsmouth, NH: Boynton/Cook, 1990.

———. *Write to Learn*. 3d ed. New York: Holt, Rinehart, and Winston, 1990.

NEISSER, ULRIC, and EUGENE WINOGRAD, eds. *Remembering Reconsidered: Ecological and Traditional Approaches to the Study of Memory*. Cambridge, UK: Cambridge University Press, 1988.

NEWKIRK, THOMAS. *More than Stories: The Range of Children's Writing*. Portsmouth, NH: Heinemann, 1989.

NORRIS, LESLIE. Blackberries. In *Sudden Fiction International*, edited by Robert Shapard and James Thomas. New York: Norton, 1986.

NORTH, STEPHEN M. *The Making of Knowledge in Composition: Portrait of an Emerging Field*. Portsmouth, NH: Boynton/Cook, 1987.

OLIVER, MARY. The Summer Day. In *House of Light*. Boston: Beacon Press, 1990.

OWEN, DAVID. *None of the Above*. Boston: Houghton Mifflin, 1985.

PATERSON, KATHERINE. *The Gates of Excellence*. New York: Harper and Row, 1984.

PATTISON, ROBERT. *On Literacy: The Politics of the Word from Homer to the Age of Rock*. New York: Oxford University Press, 1982.

PESSOA, FERNANDO. *Always Astonished*. New York: Ecco Press, 1987.

PINTER, HAROLD. Screenplay of *The Ploughman's Lunch*. 1986.

PLIMPTON, GEORGE, ed. *The Writer's Chapbook*. New York: Viking, 1989.

PROBST, ROBERT. *Response and Analysis: Teaching Literature in Junior and Senior High School*. Portsmouth, NH: Boynton/Cook, 1988.

RIEF, LINDA. *Seeking Diversity: Language Arts with Adolescents*. Portsmouth, NH: Heinemann, 1992.

ROMANO, TOM. *Clearing the Way: Working with Teenage Writers*. Portsmouth, NH: Heinemann, 1987.

ROSENBLATT, LOUISE. *Literature as Exploration*. 4th ed. New York: Modern Language Association, 1983.

SCHOLES, ROBERT. *Textual Power: Literary Theory and the Teaching of English*. New Haven, CT: Yale University Press, 1985.

SCHON, DONALD. *The Reflective Practitioner*. New York: Basic Books, 1983.

SCHOR, IRA, and PAOLO FREIRE. *A Pedagogy for Liberation*. Granby, MA: Bergin and Garvey, 1986.

SEBESTYEN, OUIDA. Welcome. In *Sixteen: Short Stories by Outstanding Writers for Young Adults,* edited by Donald Gallo. New York: Dell, 1984.

SELZER, RICHARD. *Down from Troy: A Doctor Comes of Age.* New York: William Morrow, 1992.

SHANNON, PATRICK. *Broken Promises: Reading Instruction in Twentieth-Century America.* Granby, MA: Bergin and Garvey, 1989.

———. *The Struggle to Continue: Progressive Reading Instruction in the United States.* Portsmouth, NH: Heinemann, 1990.

SHORT, KATHY G., and CAROLYN BURKE. *Creating Curriculum: Teachers and Students as a Community of Learners.* Portsmouth, NH: Heinemann, 1991.

SMITH, DORA V. *Instruction in English.* Bureau of Education Bulletin 1932, no. 17. National Survey of Secondary Education Monograph no. 20. Washington, DC: Government Printing Office, 1933.

SMITH, FRANK. *Insult to Intelligence: The Bureaucratic Invasion of Our Classrooms.* Portsmouth, NH: Heinemann, 1986.

———. *Joining the Literacy Club: Further Essays into Education.* Portsmouth, NH: Heinemann, 1988.

SOUTHWICK, MARCIA. A Burial, Green. In *The Night Won't Save Anyone.* Athens: University of Georgia Press, 1980.

SPENDER, STEPHEN. The Making of a Poem. In *The Creative Process,* edited by Brewster Ghiselin. New York: New American Library, 1952.

SPOLIN, VIOLA. *Improvisations for the Theatre.* Evanston, IL: Northwestern University Press, 1963.

SQUIRE, JAMES R., and ROGER K. APPLEBEE. *High School English Instruction Today: The National Study of High School English Programs.* New York: Appleton-Century-Crofts, 1968.

STAFFORD, WILLIAM. A Way of Writing. In *Claims for Poetry,* edited by Donald Hall. Ann Arbor: University of Michigan Press, 1982.

———. *You Must Revise Your Life.* Ann Arbor: University of Michigan Press, 1988.

STATON, JANA. Writing and Counseling: Using a Dialogue Journal. *Language Arts* 57: (1980) 514–18.

———. The Power of Responding in Dialogue Journals. In *The Journal Book,* edited by Toby Fulwiler. Portsmouth NH: Boynton/Cook, 1987.

THOREAU, HENRY DAVID. *The Portable Thoreau.* Edited by Carl Bode. New York: Penguin, 1947 (1854).

TIERNEY, ROBERT J., MARK CARTER, and LAURA DESAI. *Portfolio Assessment in the Reading-Writing Classroom.* Norwood, MA: Christopher-Gordon, 1991.

TYACK, DAVID B. *The One Best System: A History of American Urban Education.* Cambridge, MA: Harvard University Press, 1974.

VAN MANEN, MAX. *The Tact of Teaching: The Meaning of Pedagogical Thoughtfulness.* Albany: State University of New York Press, 1991.

———. *The Tone of Teaching.* Richmond Hill, ON: Scholastic-TAB, 1986.

VYGOTSKY, LEV. *Thought and Language.* Edited by Alex Kozulin. Cambridge, MA: MIT Press, 1986.

WEAVER, CONSTANCE. *Reading Process and Practice: From Socio-Psycholinguistics to Whole Language.* Portsmouth, NH: Heinemann, 1988.

WIESEL, ELIE. Why I Write: Making No Become Yes. *New York Times Book Review*, April 14, 1986, p. 1.

WINCH, TERRENCE. Success Story. In *Up Late: American Poetry Since 1970*, edited by A. Codrescu. New York: Four Walls Eight Windows, 1987.

WINOKUR, JOHN, ed. *Writers on Writing*. Philadelphia, PA: Running Press, 1986.

ZINSSER, WILLIAM. *Inventing the Truth: The Art and Craft of Memoir*. Boston: Houghton Mifflin, 1987.

———. *On Writing Well: An Informal Guide to Writing Nonfiction*. 3d ed. New York: Harper and Row, 1976.

INDEX